The African Continental Free Trade Area

Laura Páez

The African Continental Free Trade Area

Making the Most of Free Trade and Investment in Global Markets

palgrave
macmillan

Laura Páez
Vienna, Austria

ISBN 978-3-031-66604-9 ISBN 978-3-031-66605-6 (eBook)
https://doi.org/10.1007/978-3-031-66605-6

This Palgrave Macmillan imprint is published by the registered company Springer Nature Switzerland AG.
The registered company address is: Gewerbestrasse 11, 6330 Cham, Switzerland

In loving dedication to Marcel, who gave me the motivation and resolve to complete this work.

Preface

Laura Páez is affiliated to the United Nations Economic Commission for Africa (UNECA). The opinions expressed in this book are those of the author and do not represent the official views of the United Nations or its member States. The designations and terminology employed are also those of the author exclusively.

The author of this book has been very privileged in witnessing the AfCFTA taking shape, from its inception point. As with all major initiatives, things started with an idea. This was thanks to the financial crisis of 2008–2009 and the bursting of the bubble that followed, which impacted heavily on the continent's trade revenue and economic prospects for the years to come. Africa was in need of reinventing itself and was thirsty for alternatives.

Against this backdrop, African Ministers of Trade recognized the importance during their yearly African Union Ministerial in Kigali 2010 that there needed to be a solution driven by the continent, from the continent and for the continent. The solution needed to tackle the trade dependency and trade bias that weighed heavily on Africa. And then there was speak of a continental free trade area.

The author was part of a technical team comprising the United Nations Economic Commission for Africa and the Africa Union Commission, to advance the crystallization of the idea of the AfCFTA. And with the idea, there was thirst for knowledge on how to go about the grand project of creating a continental free trade area (and a book about it). It would appear an eternity, until in the same city 8 years later, the same ministers signed the Kigali Declaration on the AfCFTA. And so, the seed was sowed.

The AfCFTA negotiations experienced unprecedented dynamism in the years that followed, counting with political support and much public attention, which ranged from very optimistic to very sombre outlooks for the new kid on the block. With the Covid-19 pandemic, which brought much uncertainty to the world, so too did it put a question mark on the progress and direction of the AfCFTA and, naturally, this book. Nonetheless, the continent stayed on course and so did the author.

Subsequent to the experiences of the pandemic, as well as the ongoing Ukraine and Russia conflict, this book had to receive a jumpstart. It had to be substantially revised to do justice to the dynamism of negotiations and the unexpected effects and transmission shocks as well as latest regional developments, to also cover more topical issues of African regional integration. A greater focus of the research was also directed to issues affecting implementation and operationalization of the agreement which are seen to pose challenges to the African State Parties and, naturally, where the expected gains of the AfCFTA are estimated to be larger. This is particularly the case of sectors such as services, investment, intellectual property and the digital economy.

The motivations for this book have therefore been two-fold. At the initial stages of the book, and in absence of academic research on the topic, it sought to make a distinct contribution to start filling the void. Since the notion of the AfCFTA was shaped, an emerging body of literature on this grand integration project has been developed. Nonetheless, more analytical work is needed. Indeed, some aspects of negotiations both in goods and services, have still not been resolved satisfactorily and are lacking implementation, which should be the focus of future seminal work on the AfCFTA. Equally so, State Parties are in need of more knowledge generation to domesticate the body of AfCFTA instruments, which is the process of transposition into national laws, policies and regulation.

Therefore, the second motivation which this book garners relates to laying the foundation for future analysis that may also provide answers on how to unblock negotiation impasses and point to articulating implementation and operationalization strategies that can be domesticated by countries taking part in this bold integration process, in years to come. Future work should also cater for data needs, including usage of big data, since much of the underlying research gaps on Africa's economic development puzzle respond to the absence of sound coverage and paucity of data, as is the case with the informal sector. Ultimately, it should not be a question of lack of data or knowledge that blocks the successful conclusion of AfCFTA negotiations and implementation. It is clarity and feasibility of the way forward which can garner investment, business and employment opportunities that have a direct impact on poverty reduction and economic development that lasts.

Vienna, Austria

Laura Páez

Acknowledgements

The production of this book enjoyed from much moral, intellectual and practical support. I wish to thankfully acknowledge the contributions from each and every person who in one way or another, made this possible, even if I am unable to mention them all.

I would like to start by thanking the United Nations, for awarding me the UN Sabbatical Leave in 2022. Thanks to this award, I was able to finalize the manuscript which I had started in 2015. I would also like to recognize Stephen N. Karingi, Director of the Regional Integration and Trade Division of the United Nations Economic Commission for Africa for his support in my pursuit of the UN Sabbatical Leave as an avenue to bring this book about.

I am most grateful to the institutions which hosted me during my two sabbaticals: the Graduate Institute of the University of Geneva (UNIGE) and the Vienna Institute for International Economic Studies (WIIW). I would like to convey my gratefulness to Prof. Richard Baldwin and Dr Teresa Carpenter, the then Academic and Executive Directors of the Centre for Trade and Economic Integration at the Graduate Institute. Equally so, my gratitude goes to Dr Robert Stehrer, Scientific Director, and Dr Mario Holzner, Executive Director of the WIIW, who showed genuine interest in the work I conducted and provided an avenue for outreach and dissemination on the AfCFTA.

I hereby also wish to highlight the precious support from my family, who relentlessly provided inspiration and practical support for me to complete this work. This often meant sacrificing family time so that this book could see the light of day.

Last, but not least, I wish to convey my thanks to the anonymous peer reviewers of the book proposal, as well as to Wyndham Hacket Pain, Senior Editor, and the global productions team of Palgrave Macmillan and Springer Nature, for the tremendous efforts made to bring this book about.

About this Book

This book is about Africa's latest and most ambitious regional integration milestone: the African Continental Free Trade Area (AfCFTA). It is a novel contribution to the slowly emerging literature on the topic, offering evidence, policy, regulatory and institutional insights on key issues needing attention to ensure that the AfCFTA, which was launched in 2018 with the signing of the AfCFTA Protocol and operationalized with the starting of trade in January 2022, comes to a successful fruition. With an African regional economic space estimated at 1.4 billion consumers and a market valued at USD 2.5 trillion GDP, the AfCFTA going live offers unprecedented opportunities. The book examines the potential the AfCFTA can garner, building on existing experiences and best practices of major integration processes within the Regional Economic Communities (RECs) and the continent's policy and negotiations experience and track record in the global setting.

The scope of this book is on trade and investment, as these two types of flows are interlinked and, if harnessed together in a pan-African market, could help Africa overcome major developmental challenges the continent faces. It looks at the policy options whilst taking advantage of a more dynamic and advocating role that does justice to its size and development ambitions in global markets.

Contents

About the Author

Laura Páez a native of Venezuela, is an international development practitioner with more than twenty years of professional experience in Africa, the Americas and Europe. She is currently appointed to the United Nations Economic Commission for Africa (ECA) in Addis Ababa, Ethiopia. Her work focuses on creating knowledge on the regulatory and policy dimensions across investment, competition, intellectual property, services and digitalization in Africa, geared to support regional integration processes such as the African Continental Free Trade Area.

Within the UN system, Ms Páez also worked at the United Nations Conference for Trade and Development in Geneva on African economic development priorities. Prior to her UN appointments, she worked for the Latin American and Caribbean Economic System (SELA) and concurrently lectured at the Universidad Central de Venezuela and the Universidad Latinoamericana y del Caribe.

Ms Páez has conducted extensive technical and academic work on the regulatory impact of financial services liberalization, regionalism, foreign direct investment and trade liberalization, trade preference agreements and aid for trade. She is author of several peer-reviewed articles and the book *Liberalizing Financial Services and Foreign Direct Investment: Developing a Framework for Commercial Banking FDI*, also published by Palgrave Macmillan. She participates in conferences and seminars around the world and has delivered courses on international economics and trade negotiations for trade policy officials and graduate students. Ms Páez holds a Doctorate degree in Economics from the University of Zurich, as well as an LLM in International Law and Economics from the World

Trade Institute of the University of Berne, a both an MSc in International Economics and a bachelor's degree in International Relations from the Alma Mater of her country, the Universidad Central de Venezuela. Dr. Laura Páez is affiliated to the United Nations Economic Commission for Africa (UNECA). The opinions expressed in this book are those of the author and do not represent the official views of the United Nations or its member States. The designations and terminology employed are also those of the author exclusively.

Abbreviations

ABC	African Business Council
ACJ	African Court of Justice
ACM	African Common Market
ACP	African, Caribbean and Pacific Group of States
AEC	African Economic Community
AGCI	African Global Competitiveness Initiative
AGOA	African Growth and Opportunities Act
AIDA	Accelerated Industrial Development of Africa
AMU	Arab-Maghreb Union
AU	African Union
AUC	African Union Commission
AUCIL	African Union Commission on International Law
AUDA-NEPAD	African Union Development Agency
AfCFTA	Africa Continental Free Trade Area
AfDB	African Development Bank
AfT	Aid for Trade
AIIL	African Institute of International Law
ATF	African Trade Forum
ATO	African Trade Observatory
BIAT	*Boosting Intra-African Trade*
BIT	Bilateral Investment Treaty
BOP	Balance of Payments
CAADP	Comprehensive Africa Agriculture Development Programme
CEN-SAD	Community of Sahel-Saharan States
CIDO	Civil Society and Diaspora Department
CFTA	Continental Free Trade Area
CM	Common Market

COMESA	Common Market for Eastern and Southern Africa
COMESACJ	COMESA Court of Justice
CPC	United Nations Central Product Classification
CPTPP	Comprehensive and Progressive Agreement for Trans-Pacific Partnership
CTC	Customs Technical Committee
CSO	Civil Society Organization
CSR	Corporate social responsibility
CU	Customs Union
CCU	Continental Customs Union
DFQF	Duty free quota free
DSM	Dispute settlement mechanism
DSU	Dispute settlement understanding
DTIS	Diagnostic Trade and Integration Study
DTT	Double Taxation Treaty
EAC	East African Community
EBA	Everything but Arms Initiative
EC	European Commission
ECA	Economic Commission for Africa
ECCAS	Economic Community of Central African States
ECOWAS	Economic Community for West African States
EPA	Economic Partnership Agreement
ESA	Eastern and Southern Africa
EU	European Union
FDI	Foreign direct investment
FTA	Free trade area
FTAA	Free trade area of the Americas
GAFTA	Greater Arab Free Trade Area
GATT	General Agreement on Tariffs and Trade
GATS	General Agreement on Trade in Services
GDP	Gross domestic product
GNP	Gross national product
HIPC	Heavily Indebted Poor Countries
iEPA	Interim Economic Partnership Agreement
HATC	High Level African Trade Committee
HoSG	Heads of State and Government
ICJ	International Court of Justice
ICT	Information and Communication Technologies
IIA	International Investment Agreement
IFDA	Investment Facilitation Agreement for Development
IGAD	Inter-governmental Authority on Development
IMF	International Monetary Fund

ISIC	International Standard Industrial Classification of All Economic Activities
LDC	Least developed country
LLDC	Landlocked developing country
M&E	Monitoring and Evaluation
MFA	Multifibre Agreement
MFN	Most favoured nation
MGDs	Millennium Development Goals
MNE	Multinational enterprise
MTS	Multilateral Trading System
MU	Monetary Union
NAFTA	North African Free Trade Area
NEPAD	New Economic Partnership for Africa's Development
NT	National Treatment
NTB	Non-tariff barrier
NTM	Non-tariff measure
ODA	Overseas Development Assistance
OAU	Organization of African Unity
PIDA	Programme for Infrastructure Development in Africa
PRSP	Poverty Reduction Strategy Paper
RCEP	Regional Comprehensive Economic Partnership
RIA	Regional Integration Agreement
REC	Regional Economic Community
RTA	Regional Trade Agreement
SAATM	Single African Air Transport Market
SACU	Southern African Customs Union
SADC	Southern African Development Community
SADCT	Southern African Development Community Tribunal
SAP	Structural Adjustment Program
SAT	Substantially all trade
SDT	Special and Differential Treatment
SDGs	Sustainable Development Goals
SID	Small Island Developing State
SME	Small and medium sized enterprise
SPS	Sanitary and Phytosanitary Measure
SSA	Sub-Saharan Africa
SSATP	African Transport Policy Programme
TiSA	Trade in Services Agreement
TBT	Technical Barrier to Trade
TFTA	Tripartite Free Trade Area
TIFA	Trade and Investment Framework Agreement
TIDCA	Trade, Investment and Development Cooperative Agreement

TPA	Trade Promotion Authority
TPP	Trans-Pacific Partnership
TRIPS	Trade-Related Aspects of Intellectual Property Rights
TRIMs	Agreement on Trade-Related Investment Measures
TTIP	Transatlantic Trade and Investment Partnership
UN	United Nations
US	United States of America
US$	United States dollars
WAEMU	West African Economic and Monetary Union
WDI	World Development Indicators
WIPO	World Intellectual Property Organization
WTO	World Trade Organization

List of Figures

List of Tables

List of Boxes

CHAPTER 1

Introduction

A strong and unified Africa has been a long-standing ambition of African leaders since the time of independence. But much has stood in the way of the continent realizing this vision. Today, we are witnessing an important juncture of Africa's unification: the African Continental Free Trade Area (AfCFTA). It is a pan-African initiative comprising 54 countries. It is considered to be a stepping stone towards the creation of an African Economic Community, which epitomizes the African Union's (AU) vision of the ultimate stage of the continent's regional integration process.

The foundations of the AfCFTA were formally laid in 2012, when an African Union Decision and Declaration of Heads of State and Government mandated the fast-tracking of the establishment of the pan-African free trade area. Since then, tremendous work towards the creation of the AfCFTA has been underway, not without stops and jumpstarts.

The AfCFTA has attracted much attention due to its ambition, but also given that it has instilled fresh impetus into Africa's regional integration process. Indeed, amidst the poor track record of implementing regional integration initiatives and the hiatus that multilateral trade negotiations have experienced in recent years, the AfCFTA holds much promise. Above all, it is deemed to help boost intra-African trade from its traditionally low base and give rise to investment, employment, and business opportunities from within Africa. In-built in this promise are related prospects for Africa's economic development and transformation. And this is not

L. Páez, *The African Continental Free Trade Area*,
https://doi.org/10.1007/978-3-031-66605-6_1

without reason. The continent has a veritable opportunity to do away with its traditional performance in the global economy as a resource-rich and commodity dependent continent with few prospects for diversification.

But what the AfCFTA can deliver versus what it may deliver needs to be studied with care. Especially when the operative conditions and scope of the agreement are considered, there are caveats to all the potential benefits it can garner. First and foremost, the creation of a pan-African FTA is a herculean task, which will need more than just political goodwill and support at the highest level. In addition to financial and human resources, the implementation of the AfCFTA requires due consideration of its content and context, if it is to fulfill its ambition.

A point in case in this regard, is the lackluster outcome of the Tripartite negotiations between 26 African member States conforming the economic space of the Common Market for Eastern and Southern Africa (COMESA), the East African Community (EAC), and the Southern African Development Community (SADC). At least in its first phase, the lack of ambition of the Tripartite negotiations and its pending implementation remind us that a FTA cannot just seek the binding of the *status quo* of liberalization between its members. If it is to bring on increased trade benefits, then negotiating State Parties of the AfCFTA have to be willing to go beyond existing levels of liberalization and offer meaningful market access, as well as national treatment to regionally produced goods and services.

Second, if the AfCFTA is to become a veritable launchpad for Africa's economic transformation, then State Parties must breathe life into this distinct role from the beginning. This will mean that the AfCFTA needs to be contextualized and incorporated into existing national and regional development plans and programmes which are already in place and have momentum. It needs to have its own niche and gain acceptance by African constituencies and the general public at large. This will be critical to set the stage for greater engagement and support for the AfCFTA both in the national and regional context, vis-à-vis its stakeholders. This too needs to happen in the global context, in order to count with the necessary recognition, support, and agency. Without this, the AfCFTA could run the risk of dying a premature death, as other regional integration initiatives have experienced in the past.

Lastly, the AfCFTA will also need a proper implementation framework, strong institutions, and governance structure that allows for credible enforcement and redress. Implementation will require continuous monitoring and evaluation at various levels. This in turn will call for an institutional architecture which is adequately equipped and sufficiently empowered to take on this task. Equally important is the consideration of credible redress structures in case of disputes arising from the AfCFTA. If the agreement is to have any "teeth", then enforcement will be key.

A great amount of work towards the creation of the AfCFTA has been undertaken by institutions such as the African Union Commission, the UN Economic Commission for Africa, and the African Development Bank, as well as various development partners, just to name a few. Preparatory work at country and regional levels has yet to be substantially undertaken in order to move towards implementation of the AfCFTA Agreement, as well as the body of law and commitments emanating from it. An ancillary question in this regard is what role existing RECs are bound to play beyond the creation of and the coexistence with the ACFTA?

This book comes at a time when African member States have embarked in operationalizing the AfCFTA and need clarity and direction on the way forward. This book therefore seeks to provide an interdisciplinary and non-partisan contribution to the discussions and consultations on the policy, regulatory, political economy, and institutional elements which are required to ensure that the AfCFTA is consolidated so that Africa can harness the trade and investment opportunities resulting from this regional economic space in global markets.

In order to provide context, the book builds on existing experiences and best practices based on the evidence of major integration processes within and across the RECs as well as in the broader context of Africa's experience with the multilateral trading system. It also draws from trade negotiations with third parties and evaluates alternative approaches of the AfCFTA, given Africa's policy and negotiations experience in the global and regional setting.

The scope of the book is on trade and investment, as these two types of flows are intertwined and, if harnessed together in a pan-African market, could help Africa address important developmental and interrelated challenges. With the AfCFTA, the continent could achieve sustained growth, create employment and income opportunities, and thereby contribute to lasting poverty alleviation, whilst leveraging a more dynamic role in global markets.

A major feature of this book is the approach it proposes towards the establishment of the AfCFTA. A bottom-up rather than the traditional top-down approach is proposed through consultations, to ensure that the

AfCFTA process and outcome is not elusive to the general public. It discusses how various stakeholders also need to be involved and drive the process to ensure ownership and uptake of the AfCFTA.

Against this backdrop, this book aims to identify key prerequisites for the successful consolidation of the AfCFTA, so that Africa may make the most of this ambitious regional integration project. It also seeks to provide guidance and inspiration to the necessary policy processes in the continent.

The book compiles a collection of chapters presented as "think pieces" on various aspects of the AfCFTA, combining the legal, economic, social, and political dimensions which interplay in complex regional integration processes. These think pieces are self-contained, they can be read separately and not necessarily sequentially, since each piece deals with a trade or investment issue of relevance to Africa in the broader context of global trade and investment dynamics. An overarching commonality of the research presented in all the chapters is that it discusses possible pitfalls and challenges, emphasizing the importance of getting the AfCFTA right, so that it may realize its objectives. As such, this book is structured as follows.

Chapter 2 introduces the AfCFTA, its roadmap and architecture in the context of the African Union Decision and Declaration of 2012 that mandated the fast-tracking of the establishment of the pan-African free trade area by the tentative year of 2017. The chapter reviews the historical background of the AfCFTA, where it fits into Africa's regional integration process. It explains the current state of play of the process towards the creation of the AfCFTA. The chapter also introduces the reader to the key elements that would need to be in place for the CFTA to be established and functional, so that Africa may harness the opportunity of greater intra-African trade. It discusses the institutional and governance aspects of a AfCFTA, as well as the content of the governing agreement and negotiating tracks for a AfCFTA that liberalizes both trade in goods and services in its first phase. The chapter makes a strong case from a political economy perspective to initiate negotiations on services jointly and on parallel tracks with trade in goods, arguing for the importance services play in the production and trade of goods, and in maximizing the benefits and gains from trade for greater growth and development in the continent.

Chapter 3 focuses on the role national consultations play in vetting the creation of and generating acceptability for a pan-African FTA. A major imperative for the realization of a continent-wide free trade area is that Africans are able to harness greater intra-African trade and associated employment, income, and growth opportunities. In order for this to occur, the various sectors that are deemed to benefit the AfCFTA need to be involved in the process of negotiating and implementing the AfCFTA. A major critique to poorly implemented (continental) integration processes of the past has been the absence of adequate consultations with the various and diverse stakeholders and constituents that are involved and/or affected by trade integration processes, including parliamentarians, private sector operators, civil society and the academia. This chapter therefore looks at the necessary ingredients to ensure that the different stakeholders are involved in the crystallization of the AfCFTA. It proposes a framework for such participation to ensure ownership of the AfCFTA process, in an effort to provide the African people with a veritable platform to ensure they are part and parcel of a participatory process towards its creation.

Chapter 4 looks at the evolution and importance of services trade and services trade policy in Africa. It develops a theoretical framework to look at policy connectivity and identify the existing services trade policy disconnects that exist at the various policy dimensions. After developing a policy mapping framework of existing services trade policies, the chapter explores how a regional pan-African approach could help bring in greater coherence and harmonization to the existing services policy map and proposes elements that could be integrated into the AfCFTA to overcome the prevailing policy disconnects of services trade.

Subsequently, **Chap. 5** addresses the issue of international investment regulation with a bearing on Africa. It reviews the bilateral investment treaties (BITs) which have been signed by African countries and characterizes intra-African BITs. It then discusses regional investment regulation on the continent and the possibility of harmonizing the cluttered "spaghetti-bowl" of investment regimes in the context of regional economic communities. The chapter also provides empirical evidence to substantiate the effect regional integration has had on foreign direct investment (FDI) flows to Africa as a determinant of market-seeking and efficiency-seeking FDI. Given the existing regional integration agenda on investment, the chapter discusses the viability of an African Continental Investment Area as an alternative to the prevalent regimes that clutter investment regulation in Africa, in favor of a more harmonized and developmental approach that builds on institutions and processes.

Chapter 6 in turn approaches the AfCFTA from the optic of preferential trade agreements. Notably, Sub-Saharan Africa has been a beneficiary to the African Growth and Opportunity Act (AGOA), a unilateral trade preference scheme of the United States launched in 2000. A major critique to AGOA relates to the fact that few countries have been able to harness the opportunities and preferences under the act, in part due to the restrictions and conditionalities that are imposed by the United States. In relation to investment, a major hinge to greater FDI in the export sector of African countries to benefit from AGOA has been the lack of security on the returns on investment, especially when AGOA approached its expiry. Since the current US administration has indicated the resolve to extend AGOA beyond its expiry date in 2025, the present chapter seeks to provide actionable recommendations on what a post-2025 AGOA framework requires to ensure that greater FDI is channeled to promote US-African trade in the context of the AfCFTA. The chapter draws on the empirical evidence of how regional integration has been a pull factor to FDI in the context of the regional economic communities, as an argument for greater economies of scale and scope in a continental market, but also for creating regional value chains in a wider economic space and linking better to GVCs.

In turn, **Chap. 7** focuses on the issue of African Least Developed Countries (LDC) as their participation in global trade. It discusses issues relating to the special and differential treatment these countries have been receiving and does so in the context of their poor trade performance. It then looks at elements of variable geometry, allowing these countries sufficient flexibilities to integrate into the AfCFTA at their own speed, without missing out on the benefits of a "Single Undertaking", that the launch of the AfCFTA bring in terms of increased opportunities for trade. The chapter also discusses the role of the Doha Round and specific elements of preferential trade that have accrued to LDCs, and what is needed to support the consolidation of the AfCFTA in an asymmetric setting.

Chapter 8 revisits the old question of regionalism versus multilateralism and discusses some of the recent FTA initiatives that have gained traction outside the multilateral trading system. These include mega-regional FTAs negotiated by large country groupings, as well as bilateral FTAs with third parties. In particular, Economic Partnership Agreements (EPAs) which put an end to the unilateral trade preference scheme of the European Union with ACP countries under the Lomé Convention are analyzed. The basis for reciprocity of EPAs (and any other FTA) implies that any benefit negotiated under the AfCFTA will need to be extended to the EU (or any other third party). This could diffuse the expected AfCFTA gains that would accrue to Africa alone. This could possibly also spur legal arbitration due to incompatibilities or the ability of member States to comply with obligations that preceded the AfCFTA. Against this backdrop, the chapter discusses what actions are needed to curb these impacts and how fit the AfCFTA Agreement is to address these challenges. Lastly, the chapter tries to make a case for African countries to refrain from joining agreements that divide the continent or as frontload the agenda for future multilateral negotiations in the WTO, in particular on trade in services and investment.

Finally, **Chap. 9**, the closing chapter of the book, recapitulates all of the key messages and main findings of the previous chapters. It ties it all together to make a strong case for the AfCFTA as an imperative milestone in Africa's regional integration process. In particular, this chapter includes a forward-looking discussion of Africa's role in global trade and investment and what is required from an institutional, policy, and political economy perspective to ensure the continent assumes its rightful role in global markets.

Whether the stars remain aligned for the AfCFTA remains to be seen. While this is decided, a lot can be done to support the process of the AfCFTA, towards the realization of the African Economic Community, and which responds to the hopes and expectations of the African people. It is a humble aspiration of this book to support that process.

CHAPTER 2

An African Continental Free Trade Area: Imperatives for Realizing a Pan-African Market

1 Introduction

In today's globalized world, it is impossible to conceive the elimination of trade barriers between nations without an effective trade agreement in place. Both regionally and at the multilateral level under the aegis of the World Trade Organization (WTO), trade agreements set the operative principles and basis for a reliable, predictable and transparent legal framework that governs free trade flows between trading nations.

In recent years, regional trade agreements (RTAs) have been on the rise, in part due to the stalling of multilateral trade negotiations under the WTO Doha Round. In virtually all world regions RTAs have proliferated. Africa has not been an exception to that trend. Of the 262 RTAs officially notified to the WTO which are in force, 21 RTAs involve at least one

This chapter was originally published by the author of this book as an article entitled "A Continental Free Trade Area: Imperatives for Realizing a Pan-African Market" in the *Journal of World Trade*, Vol 50 (2016) no. 3: 533–562. This material has been reprinted with all rights and permissions from (c) Kluwer Law International BV, with amendments and updates since the date of publishing.

L. Páez, *The African Continental Free Trade Area*,
https://doi.org/10.1007/978-3-031-66605-6_2

African member State and another 5 RTAs are in the process of being negotiated by individual or groups of African member States.[1]

Africa's process of regional integration has been faithful to this trend with the creation of various intra-African RTAs in the context of Regional Economic Communities (RECs), which are considered to be the pillars of economic integration in Africa. Currently, a total of four free trade areas (FTAs), four customs unions, and two monetary unions operate within these RECs. In addition, negotiations are also underway for a Tripartite FTA between three of these RECs, covering 26 countries.[2]

To top it all, Africa is operationalizing one of the most ambitious regional integration projects to the date: a Continental Free Trade Area (CFTA).[3] An African Union Decision and Declaration of 2012 by African Heads of State and Government mandates the establishment of a CFTA by the tentative year of 2017. The CFTA is considered to be a stepping stone towards two of the deeper integration stages envisaged in the Abuja Treaty of 1991, namely the creation of a Continental Customs Union by 2019 and an African Economic Community by 2034.

As the continent embarks in the process of creating a CFTA, a major prerogative for the realization of this pan-African market is that 54 African member States make concessions for the common benefit of a greater trading space. These concessions have two components, namely, collective rules and individual commitments. The former implies countries have to collectively agree on the set of rules and obligations they are willing to assume, whilst the latter relates to the individual commitment each member State makes to open its domestic market (i.e. through the dismantling of trade barriers) to the exports from the rest of the membership. Reaching a common ground on both of these aspects has traditionally been

[1] See WTO Regional Trade Agreements Information System under: http://rtais.wto.org/UI/PublicMaintainRTAHome.aspx. These include completed RTAs as well as those in the process of negotiations which involve African countries which have been officially notified under the WTO.

[2] For an overview of the membership and status quo of agreements, see Chap. 8, Table 8.1.

[3] The CFTA was only officially renamed as the AfCFTA in 2018, through a Summit Decision on the name the Agreement that would govern this continental FTA (AU, 2018a, para. 5). Hence, when referring to official documents created prior the renaming of the CFTA to the AfCFTA, the term CFTA is being used interchangeably with AfCFTA in this chapter.

undertaken through trade negotiation processes in Africa,[4] and requires considerable (bilateral and multilateral) consultations and negotiations. Indeed, regional trade negotiations will be the *process* that results in the creation of CFTA. But beyond this process, *content* needs to be generated to instil life into the CFTA and ensure its operability.

The research presented discusses the various elements that need to be considered to generate content for the CFTA. As such, Sect. 2 contextualizes Africa's regional (economic) integration process and where the CFTA fits in this process. Section 3 describes the progress made towards the conceptualization of the CFTA. Subsequently, Sect. 4 discusses some of the envisaged elements of the future CFTA in terms of scope, disciplines, operability, institutional governance and coexistence in the multilateral environment, followed by Sect. 5, which lays out prerequisites for a functional CFTA that delivers on its objectives. Finally, Sect. 6 draws conclusions and issues recommendations on how African countries may harness the CFTA to deliver on greater intra-African trade opportunities for the benefit of all Africans.

2 Africa's Regional Integration in Retrospective: From the OAU to the Abuja Treaty and Beyond

Africa's regional integration process has been all but linear. Against the backdrop of various RTAs and regional cooperation agreements that have emerged and were dissolved since the 1960s, regional integration in Africa could be best described as a haphazard process with several jumpstarts. Invariably, regional integration has also been a learning process for the continent. Despite various iterations, this process may be characterized by three distinct phases reflecting shared historical, political and socio-economic motivations of the continent's leadership to push for convergence at a given point in time.

If timelines are to be defined, a first phase of regional integration took place between the 1960s and early 1980s and was tightly linked to Africa's independence history and the creation of the Organization of African Unity (OAU). Subsequently, a second phase which aligned Africa's regional integration process with a new development paradigm and vision

[4] The exception to this rule was the creation of SACU, which was created under colonial rule through the 1889 Customs Union Convention between the British Colony of Cape of Good Hope and the Orange Free State Boer Republic, and which was superseded by a new Agreement signed in 1910, between the Union of South Africa and the British High Commission Territories (including Basutoland (Lesotho), Bechuanaland (Botswana) and Swaziland (now Eswatini) and South West Africa (now Namibia)).

for the continent took place between the early 1980s and early 1990s. Lastly, a third and contemporary phase of Africa's regional integration initiated with the Abuja treaty in 1991 and the rebranding of the OAU into the Africa Union, which today leads Africa's continental integration programmes, including the CFTA. The present section briefly discusses these three phases chronologically and gives insights of where the CFTA fits in this process as the building bloc it is expected to be towards the realization of the African Economic Community (AEC).

2.1 *Initial Conditions*

A first phase of regional integration in Africa took place between the 1960s and early 1980s and was tightly linked to Africa's independence history. During its first phase, regional integration gained momentum when a growing number of African countries had achieved independence from colonial powers. These new nations sought to reaffirm their sovereign rights and were keen to obtain recognition of their legal status as independent States.[5]

As a consequence, various regional groupings came to being, such as the Equatorial Customs Union (1959), the African Common Market (1962), the former East African Community (1967), the SACU, which was revamped in 1970 to reflect recently gained independence of four of its members, and the Senegambia (1982).[6]

But beyond these regional integration undertakings, underpinning the independence process was the conceptualization of an ideological socialist movement of pan-Africanism. This movement called for Africans throughout the continent and diaspora to acknowledge their common culture and coined the belief of embracing Africa's unification as a means for the nascent African nations to assert themselves.[7] Many African leaders at the

[5] The same rationale applied to bilateral investment treaties that were celebrated at the time by African countries, with a view to secure their legal personality as nascent States. See Páez (2017) and also Chap. 5.

[6] Members to the African Common Market were Algeria, Egypt, Ghana, Guinea, Mali and Morocco. Members to the Equatorial Customs Union were Central African Republic, Chad, Congo and Gabon. Members to the former East African Community were Kenya, Tanzania and Uganda. Members of the revamped SACU of 1970 were Botswana, Lesotho, Swaziland (now Eswatini) and South Africa. Members to Senegambia were Senegal and the Gambia. For other examples of former African integration groupings, see Tulya-Muhica (1996).

[7] See Esedebe (1982) on the concept and historical development of Pan-Africanism.

time promoted this movement, notably the first presidents Leopold Sédar Senghor of Senegal, Kwame Nkrumah of Ghana and Julius Nyerere of Tanzania, who were strong advocates for regional integration.

A major political statement of pan-Africanism was the creation of the Organization of the African Unity (OAU) on 25 May 1963 in Addis Ababa, Ethiopia. This regional body, first of its kind and emboldened with a pan-African vision, grouped 32 of these nascent States.[8] The OUA sought to "Promote the unity and solidarity of the African States" and "To coordinate and intensify their cooperation and efforts to achieve a better life for the peoples of Africa", among other objectives, as was laid out in Article II of the *OAU Charter*. In order to achieve these aims, the same article mandated its member States to coordinate and harmonize their general policies in the field of economic cooperation, including transport and communication. Member States were thus empowered and encouraged to engage in all forms of regional economic cooperation and had a pan-African organization to facilitate that process through the creation of legally binding instruments for its membership.

However, and despite the generalized acceptance of pan-Africanism as a movement and a mandate for regional economic cooperation, most of the regional groupings mentioned earlier were short-lived and did not take off. They lacked the necessary political momentum and in some cases pragmatism to fulfil their ambition. Points in case were the African Common Market which disintegrated, the Equatorial Customs Union which evolved and in 1994 became the Economic and Monetary Community of Central African States (CEMAC), the EAC which was dissolved in 1977 due to political differences between its members and, lastly, the Senegambia which was abolished after unfruitful efforts to establish a customs union between its parties (Richmond, 1993).

Another example of the weak determination to seriously engage in regional economic cooperation was the poor implementation of legal instruments emanating from the OAU. For example, the *Constitution of the Association of African Trade Promotion Organizations*, (OAU, 1974) an instrument deemed to promote trade and share trade information

[8] Initial signatories of the OAU Charter were: Algeria, Burundi, Cameroon, Central African Republic, Chad, Congo (Brazzaville), Congo (Léopoldville), Dahomey, Egypt, Ethiopia, Gabon, Ghana, Guinea, Ivory Coast, Liberia, Libya, Madagascar, Mali, Mauritania, Morocco, Niger, Nigeria, Rwanda, Senegal, Sierra Leone, Somalia, The Sudan, Tanganyika, Togo, Tunisia, Uganda, Upper Volta, Zanzibar. They were represented by Heads of State and Government who subsequently became the Founding Fathers of the OUA.

within the continent was opened for signature 18 January 1974. In accordance with its article XV(3), this agreement could only come into force after ratification by at least 12 signatory States. This proved to be a herculean task which took 36 years, as it was not until 2010 when 12 member States had ratified the agreement. Unfortunately, other OAU agreements had a similar fate with slow ratification and did not render fruitful during this initial period in Africa's integration history (Maluwa, 2012).

A sobering realization of this initial regional integration experience was that unification of the Africa continent could not happen by chance, as an organic process, which was a major assumption of Pan-Africanism rooted in the Negritude philosophy.[9] A more pragmatic vision commensurate with Africa's reality was required to support this process.

Among the reasons cited for the stagnation of regional integration in this initial stage, was the evident disarticulation between Africa's regional integration process and the continent's development needs. This disarticulation resided in the fact that the continent's development agenda had relied on the modernization paradigm,[10] advocated by Africa's development partners and which had not translated into tangible development outcomes since independence. This paradigm was based on the notion that just as Western countries and developed nations had achieved development through a gradual process, passing from traditional to modern society, so too must Africa.

The modernization paradigm and its application to Africa was encapsulated in a World Bank's report known as the "Berg Report" (World Bank, 1981), which was severely scrutinized at the time. The Berg Report set emphasis on relying on the agricultural sector (exports) as a vector for the continent's development. It prescribed African countries to focus on efficiency and productivity of the tradeable sector, particularly agriculture, in order to boost agricultural production to overcome the ailing economic situation the continent had been facing since independence.[11]

[9] For a discussion on the relationship between politics and culture and its limitations in the context of pan-Africanism see Walters (1993), pp. 354–364.

[10] A contributor to modernization theory was Rostow (1960), who described modernization as a development process with five distinct stages, namely traditional society, preconditions for take-off, take-off, drive to maturity and lastly the age of high mass-consumption. For a discussion on modernization theory and its shortcomings, see (Hoogvelt, 1982)

[11] See Please and Amouako (1984) for a summary of the critique and rebuttal in favour of the Berg Report.

Indeed, at the time the Berg Report came out, Africa had been facing an ongoing economic crisis. Various analyses and reports at the time confirmed that poverty, growth stagnation and food insecurity had exacerbated during the 1960s and 1970s, materializing in “lost decades” for the continent.[12] This dire situation called for urgent and remedial action at the highest level.

2.2 *Getting Ready for Take-Off*

In recognition of the shortcomings of previous development approaches, African political leaders undertook to coin a new development paradigm which would take account of Africa’s development needs from an African perspective. A milestone reflecting this commitment was the endorsement of the *Monrovia Declaration*, during the 16th Ordinary session of the OAU held in Sierra Leone in May 1979 (OAU, 1979a).

The *Monrovia Declaration* set the stage for Africa’s regional integration process in three important ways. First, it recognized the various critical issues which were affecting development in the continent. Second, it argued that African development policies needed to reflect the continent’s socio-cultural values and envisioned regional integration as a vehicle for Africa’s development by committing member States to promote the social and economic integration of the African economies as a basis for self-reliance and self-sustainment and to further social and economic exchanges. Thirdly, it mandated the OAU and ECA Secretariats to set up programmes and measures for economic cooperation at subregional, regional and continental levels (OAU, 1979a).

Instilled with this new mandate, work was initiated to develop a blueprint for the continent’s development underpinned by regional economic cooperation and integration, which resulted in the *Lagos Plan of Action for the Economic Development of Africa 1980–2000* (OAU, 1980). Adopted in Lagos in 1980 by of Heads of State and Government, it laid out policy priorities under a new paradigm for Africa’s development for the next two decades.

Elaborating on the *Monrovia Declaration*, the Lagos Plan of Action was formulated as a sobering acknowledgment of failed development strategies and in response to the limitations and short-term prescriptions

[12] See for example (OAU, 1979b) and Meredith (2013) for a commented history on Africa’s lost decades.

of the Berg Report (Browne & Cummings, 1984). It is here where a second phase of regional integration in Africa initiates and gains considerable traction at the highest political level. More importantly, the Lagos Plan of Action couched the notion that as Africa has been successful in promoting political unity, so too must it strengthen its economic unity.

Substantively, the Lagos Plan of Action identified 13 priority areas for development and action with short, medium and long-term objectives.[13] In particular, "strengthening economic and technical cooperation" was conceived as a priority area in Chapter VIII of the plan, which acknowledged that the slow progress in regional integration to the date was the result of the various challenges African multinational institutions face, including those tied to poor implementation, limited membership and limited capacity of member States to pay their contributions.[14] Consequently, it set out guidelines to resolve this situation, and instructed the ECA and OAU Secretariats to undertake an assessment of the objectives and operations of the various exiting multinational institutions with a view to see how they may be better rationalized (OAU, 1980, para. 261–264).

But beyond the priority of economic cooperation, a fundamental pillar of the plan was regional integration. A concrete mandate for regional integration was elaborated the *Final Act of Lagos*, which conditioned implementation of the Lagos Plan to the creation of an African Economic Community. This new mandate instilled the OAU with a revitalized role and set the stage for the elaboration of a Treaty to Establish the African Economic Community (OAU, 1980, Annex I).

2.3 The Abuja Treaty and Beyond

Learning from the recent past and with a new mandate, the OAU initiated work to establish an African Economic Community (AEC). An African Common Market and AEC were first conceptualized in an OAU

[13] These priority areas are: food and agriculture; industry; natural resources; human resource development and utilization; science and technology; transport and communications; trade and finance; measures to build up and strengthen economic and technical cooperation including creation of new institutions and strengthening existing ones; environment and development; the Least Developed Countries; energy; women and development; and, lastly, development planning, statistics and population.

[14] Notably, among the institutions affected was the Association of the African Trade Promotion Organisations, discussed earlier in subsection 2.1.

Declaration of 1976 (OAU, 1976), which stipulated that an African Economic Community be created in a series of successive stages within a period of 15 to 25 years. But it was not until the Final Act of Lagos that this need was cast in a concrete mandate for the OAU to design a treaty which would be the basis for an AEC.

The result of these efforts was the *Treaty Establishing the African Economic Community* (OAU, 1991) better known as the Abuja Treaty, which became a second attempt to conceptualize the AEC with revised and more realistic timelines. The Abuja Treaty thus became the new navigation compass of African regional integration as conceived by African political leaders at the time. Indeed, the Abuja Treaty came at the time the OAU was ailing and needed to revitalized, marking the third and contemporary phase of Africa's regional integration process.

Article 6 of the Abuja Treaty lays out modalities for the creation of an African Economic Community and stipulates that regional integration in a process of 6 stages which are time bound and successive. This process is envisaged to take 34 years to consolidate the structures of the African Common Market (ACM). As illustrated in Fig. 2.1, this includes various actions and milestones ranging from the creation and strengthening of existing RECs (in Stage I), to the liberalization of tariffs and non-tariff measures and harmonization of various sectoral policies, plans and programmes (stages II to VI), and lastly to the creation of various Pan-African institutions, including the African Common Market (ACM) as a prelude to the AEC, as well as the achievement of the "four freedoms", implying that goods, services, capital and people can move freely in that economic space (stage VI).

This staged approach of Abuja Treaty corresponds with traditional process of economic integration. This process is characterized by a gradual succession of stages with increasing degrees of integration, with each additional stage progressively building on the prior integration stages.[15] As such, the stages identified by economic integration theory starts with a preferential trade agreement, followed by a free trade area, then by a customs union and subsequently by a common market. At the end of this process, ultimate integration leads to an economic and monetary union, coinciding with stage VI.

But beyond the establishment of an operative legal framework which circumscribed the process of Africa's regional integration process for the

[15] For an introduction to economic integration theory, see Balassa (1961) and Cooper and Massell (1965).

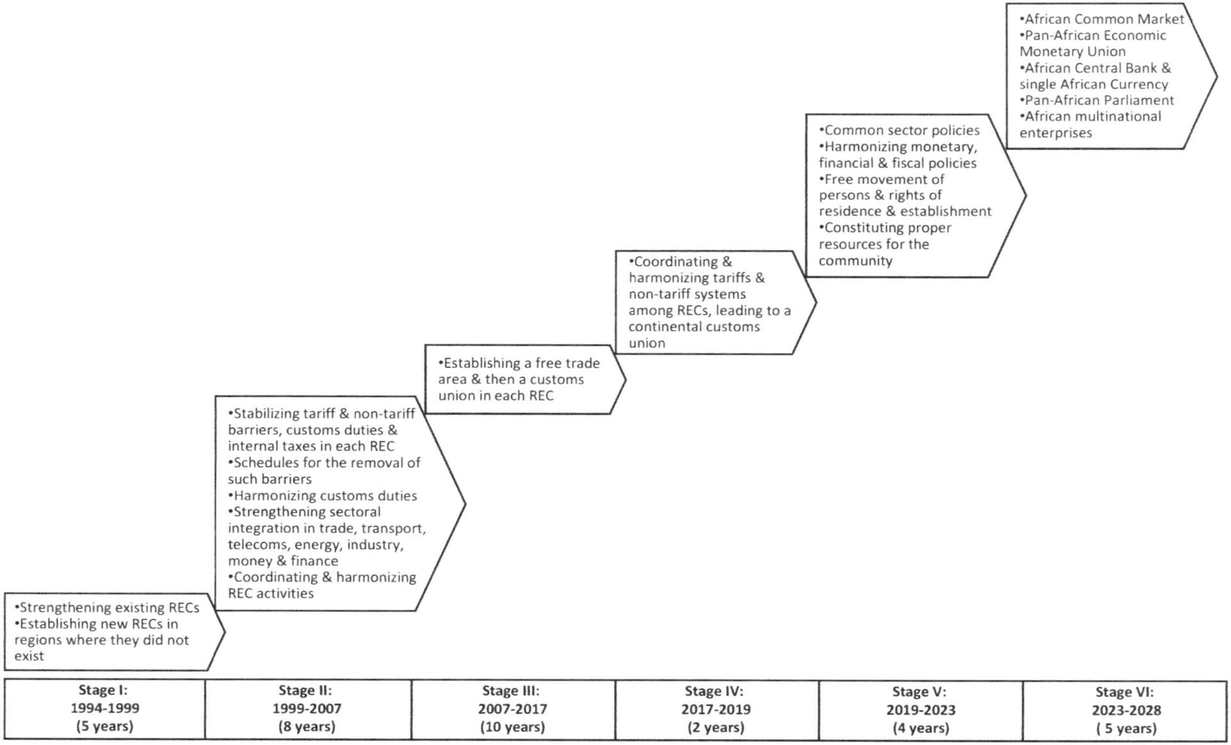

Fig. 2.1 Stages, Milestones and Timeline of Regional Integration towards the AEC. (Source: Authors' illustration based on OAU (1991), Art. 6)

next four decades to come, the third phase of Africa's integration history was also marked by a major institutional change which had long been needed, namely that of the creation of the African Union and the phase out of the OAU.

Already in the OAU Summit in Libya in 1999, the Sirte Declaration (OAU, 1999) called for the establishment of the African Union (AU), recognizing that the role of the OAU needed revitalization and that it was necessary to accelerate unification among member States. An organization which would enable its membership to address more effectively common social, political and economic problems, which reflected contemporary aspirations and realities of the African people at the time was called for. More fundamentally, this call also reflected the shift in priorities, with economic development taking the front stage over political objectives, the latter being the initial rationale behind the creation of the OAU (Senghor, 1993). This paved the way for the adoption of the *Constitutive Act of the African Union* in 2000 (AU, 2000), and leading to the eventual dissolution of the OAU, once the AU officially entered into force on 26 May 2001.

A major distinction between the OAU and AU was that the former came to being as one entity with legal personality as a result of its treaty, the *OAU Charter*, whereas the latter was derived from the Abuja Treaty (OAU, 1991). Its structures and organs are therefore drawn from the treaty itself (e.g. the Pan-African Parliament and Court of Justice and the African Central Bank). Thus, the AU became the new Pan-African organization,[16] with specific objectives, binding principles and organs that were to a great extent already encapsulated in the Abuja Treaty.

From an institutional perspective, another major milestone under this third and contemporary phase of Africa's regional integration relates to the rationalization of existing RECs. The Lagos Plan of Action, and subsequently the Abuja Treaty, as well as the Constitutive Act of the AU recognized that the regional integration landscape was too cluttered with coexisting institutions that overlapped in membership and objectives, which lead to a certain degree of paralysis in the progress of integration.

[16]The current 55 AU members are: Algeria, Angola, Benin, Botswana, Burkina Faso, Burundi, Cameroon, Cape Verde, Chad, Comoros, Congo, the Democratic Republic of Congo, Cote d'Ivoire, Djibouti, Equatorial Guinea, Eritrea, Ethiopia, Gabon, Gambia, Ghana, Guinea Conakry, Kenya, the Kingdom of Lesotho, Liberia, Libya, Malawi, Mali, Mauritania, Mauritius, Morocco, Mozambique, Namibia, Niger, Nigeria, Rwanda, Saharawi Arab Democratic Republic, Sao Tome and Principe, Senegal, Seychelles, Sierra Leone, Somalia, South Africa, South Sudan, Sudan, Eswatini, Tanzania, Togo, Tunisia, Uganda, Zambia and Zimbabwe.

It is not, however, until 2006 that the AU Commission (the Secretariat of the AU) and RECs obtain a concrete mandate to harmonize and coordinate policies and programs with a view to accelerate the integration process. At the same time, a moratorium on the recognition of new RECs was put in place, excepting eight RECs from this suspension (AU, 2006). As such, the eight RECs that were formally recognized by the AU are: the Arab-Maghreb Union (AMU), the Community of Sahel-Saharan States (CEN-SAD), the Common Market for Eastern and Southern Africa (COMESA), the East African Community (EAC), the Economic Community of Central African States (ECCAS), the Economic Community for West African States (ECOWAS), the Inter-Governmental Authority on Development (IGAD) and the Southern African Development Community (SADC).

The six regional groupings which were not considered at the time for formal recognition and which still coexist today are: the Economic Community of Great Lakes Countries (CEPGL), the Southern African Customs Union (SACU), the Mano River Union (MRU), the West African Economic and Monetary Union (WAEMU), the Economic and Monetary Community of Central Africa (CEMAC) and the Indian Ocean Commission (IOC).

It is interesting to note that though, formally, member States have set a moratorium on the RECs, this has not impeded them from deepening economic integration in both recognized and non-recognized RECs. Though quite erratically, there has been considerable activity in trade integration. Correspondingly, African member States have been quite active in terms of creating regional trade agreements (RTAs) in the context of these RECs, as well as beyond.[17] Indeed, Africa's process of regional integration has supported this trend with intra-African RTAs in the context of the aforementioned RECs, which are considered to be the pillars of economic integration in Africa. Currently, a total of four free trade areas (FTAs) and four customs unions coexist in the context of these RECs.

In addition, three of the aforementioned customs unions are also monetary unions, namely the West African Economic and Monetary Union (WAEMU), the Southern African Customs Union (SACU) and the Economic and Monetary Community of Central Africa (CEMAC). Furthermore, negotiations are well underway for a Tripartite FTA between three existing RECSs, namely the Common Market for Eastern and Southern Africa (COMESA), the East African Community (EAC) and the Southern

[17] See the discussion in Chap. 8 on existing FTAs and mega-regionals African countries are involved in.

African Development Community (SADC), and which would span over 26 African countries and comprise a population of nearly 600 million.

This flurry of RTAs, as well as their differing speeds in integration has led to an intricate and overlapping web of multiple memberships. This is a phenomenon which is observed across various world regions and which Bhagwati (1995) referred to as the "spaghetti-bowl" of RTAs. As can be appreciated in Fig. 2.2 below, most countries are members of two or even

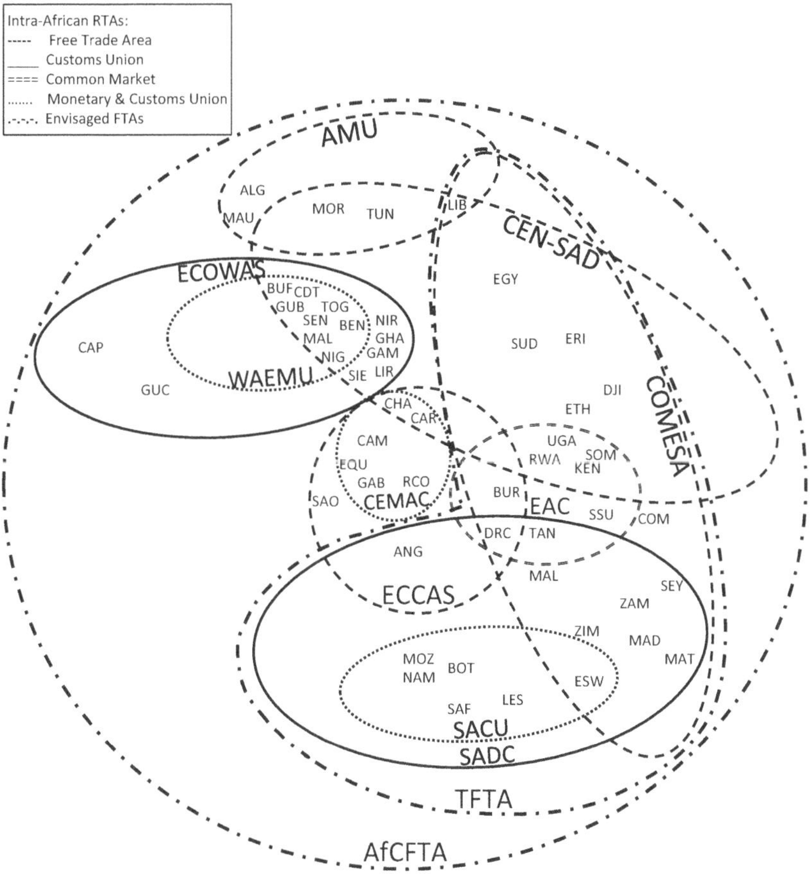

Fig. 2.2 Overview of RTAs memberships in Africa. (Source: Authors' illustration based on AU (2014b) and RECs official cites and legal instruments. (South Sudan, before independence, used to be a member of CEN-SAD. Eritrea, though depicted on the map, is the single African country that has not yet signed the AfCFTA agreement)

three RTAs. This "spaghetti bowl" of RTAs continues to burden the efforts of deepening regional integration, as it requires member States to coordinate and harmonize their tariff and non-tariff barrier systems with their various RTA partners. Since each RTA may follow a very specific approach towards harmonization, this leads to inconsistencies across RTAs as well as differing capacities of implementation across RTA partners.

Cognizant of these constraints, work towards streamlining regional integration in a more practical way for each of the recognized RECs was conducted under the haven of the AU, which lead to the design and adoption of a Minimum Integration Programme (MIP) in 2009, an operative framework for RECs to gain traction in their integration process and ultimately a mechanism for REC convergence (See AU, 2009a and 2009b). In addition, a MIP Action Plan has been developed as a major coordination effort to assist the RECs (AU, AfDB and ECA, 2012) and work has been underway to develop a mobilization strategy for the plan as well as an integration fund (AUC and ECA, 2012).

In retrospect, since the endorsement of the Abuja Treaty and despite efforts to fine-tune and streamline regional integration commitments, such as the MIP and the Decision on the moratorium of RECs, progress in implementing the envisaged timelines so far has been mixed, with some regions and sectors advancing more than others. Notably, whilst some appear to have made considerable progress in trade integration and seem to keep up with existing targets, others need to make considerable efforts to catch up.[18]

In recognition of this, a renewed effort to give regional economic integration momentum and building on the legacy of the Abuja Treaty, African Heads of State and Government recently endorsed the creation of a Continental Free Trade Area (CFTA) and an Action Plan to Boost Intra-African Trade (BIAT) in 2012. With great ambition, the CFTA was expected to be launched by the tentative date of 2017, as a prior step to the creation of the pan-African Customs Union envisaged by 2019 (which would correspond to stage IV of the Abuja Treaty, depicted in Fig. 2.1) and towards the establishment of the AEC no later than 2034.

[18] For past reports tracking the progress made by the RECs, see AU, AfDB and ECA (2010, 2012, 2016).

3 Conceptualizing the Continental Free Trade Area

3.1 The Mandate for a Continental Free Trade Area

The concept of a pan-African free trade area initially gained ground at an AU Conference of Trade Ministers in 2010 (AU, 2010) held in Kigali. The conference was particularly dedicated to the issue of intra-African trade and it was in this context that the idea of creating a larger continental economic market arose. Discussions during the Conference endorsed the idea of fast-tracking the establishment of a CFTA and analytical work was commissioned to the AUC and ECA to examine the challenges and opportunities the CFTA would represent.

The subsequent AU Conference of Trade Ministers of 2011 in Accra held a dedicated discussion on the CFTA and considered associated documentation which included an *Action Plan on Boosting Intra-African Trade* (BIAT Action Plan) and a *Framework for the Continental Free Trade Area, Road Map, Architecture* (CFTA Framework) (AU, 2011b). Following deliberations, the Conference adopted the documentation and recommended it to the Summit for endorsement (AU, 2011a, para. 30).

In the following 18th AU Ordinary Session of Heads of State and Government held in Addis on the dedicated theme of "Boosting Intra-African Trade", African leaders deliberated on the merit of creating a CFTA. During the deliberations at the Summit two important considerations arose. First, whether Africa had a disposition to trade with itself, given the notion that production structures across African countries were similar and hence the concern that there could be little incentive for African countries to trade among themselves. A second concern was related to Africa's current state of physical infrastructure, and whether the continent was in a capacity to promote the CFTA given the various infrastructure impediments often cited as a major bottleneck to intra-African trade. Because these concerns drew considerable attention during the Summit, further consultations on these two issues were requested.

The Summit had two major outcomes documents: a Decision and Declaration to fast-track the establishment of the CFTA (AU, 2012a and 2012b). Both the Decision and Declaration represent a renewed commitment to the continent's economic integration envisaged under the Abuja Treaty. The Decision endorsed the documentation submitted through the Conference of Ministers in Accra, which became the basis for the conceptualization of the CFTA. It also established that the operationalization of the CFTA must follow the established milestones in the CFTA Framework and be completed by the indicative date of 2017 and that RECs take the lead in implementing the BIAT.

In turn, the Declaration contextualized the newly established mandates on the BIAT Action Plan and CFTA Framework by recalling that the core objective of the AU is accelerating the achievement of the AEC. Hence, a formal link was established between these new regional integration initiatives and the Abuja Treaty. It also vested the AU and the RECs with the mandate to implement an Action Plan which contained short, medium and long-term milestones.

In order to address possible arising issues in the context of this new initiative, such as the ones that were discussed during the Summit, the Decision and Declaration also vested the High Level African Trade Committee (HATC), an envisaged organ in the governance structure of the future CFTA, with a concrete mandate, namely that of facilitating and unlocking any blockages arising from the CFTA establishment process (AU, 2012a, para. 3 and 2012b, para. 8). Subsequent to the Summit, two baseline studies were conducted to clarify these issues and considered by the HATC in its first session. These studies were conducted by the AUC and ECA and subsequently discussed and endorsed at a Senior Officials Meeting held in April 2012 and which informed the first HATC session and its recommendation to support the creation of the CFTA (AU, 2012e).

In the following AU Summit in June 2012 in Addis Ababa, and after considering the recommendations of the HATC, it was decided that there was indeed sufficient positive evidence on the levels and composition of intra-African trade and infrastructure density to support the creation of the CFTA and for boosting intra-African trade (AU, 2012c).

With nothing standing in the way of the CFTA, work was then initiated to give life to the BIAT through the development of a BIAT Implementation Strategy. The strategy was validated in the context of the Second African Trade Forum, jointly hosted by the ECA and AUC in September 2012 in Addis Ababa, which served as a platform for various African stakeholders to discuss their views on pan-African trade policy issues.

The 50th Anniversary of the creation of the OAU celebrated in May 2013 also marked an important milestone in the lead up to the CFTA. *Agenda 2063* (AU, 2015d) was as part of the commemoration activities of the AU. It is a vision document describing aspirational development goals of the AU for the next 50 years to come and contains an action plan with concrete timelines and milestones, among which, the resolve to fast-track the establishment of the CFTA by 2017 and double intra-African trade by 2022 is clearly reiterated.

The second meeting of the HATC was hosted back to back with Heads of State and Government Summit which followed in January 2014 in Addis Ababa. During the meeting, fundamental implementation challenges were raised, as well as concerns related to the financing of the BIAT implementation and CFTA negotiations (AU, 2014b, 2015c).

The following Summit held in Malabo in July 2014 brought another important milestone in the preparation of the CFTA. The Summit not only endorsed the recommendations of the HATC and its Terms of Reference, it also gave the mandate to the AUC to prepare relevant preparatory documentation for the CFTA, as is discussed in greater detail in the next section (AU, 2014a, para. 7).

In January 2015, and with sufficient tailwind in the preparatory process, African Heads of State and Government formulated the request for the Ministers of Trade to propose options on the levels of trade liberalization that would serve as a starting point for negotiations, as well as the AU, ECA and RECs to start preparing draft negotiating texts (AU, 2015c).

The culmination of the process described above since 2012 transpired in the Johannesburg Summit during June 2015, when Heads of State and Government adopted the documentation discussed during an extraordinary session of the AU Conference of Ministers of Trade dedicated to the CFTA in May 2015 (AU, 2015a), and officially launched the CFTA negotiations (AU, 2015b).

In conclusion, having briefly described the process through which the mandate for the CFTA was conceived and which lead up to the negotiations of the CFTA, the next subsection looks at two fundamental elements of the CFTA Framework. These are the roadmap towards the creation of the CFTA and the architecture and governance of the CFTA.

3.2 CFTA Roadmap and Architecture

The *Framework for the Continental Free Trade Area, Road Map, Architecture* (CFTA Framework). (AU, 2011b) is the departing point detailing elements of the CFTA, as initially conceived. It contains a roadmap for the establishment of the CFTA, which describes the necessary sequential steps of a process of convergence which builds on the existing efforts of market integration within and across the eight recognized RECs.

It also includes the Architecture of the CFTA, which is presented as an initial drawing board (organigram) of envisaged organs and bodies that would give life to the CFTA, as an institution.

As such, progress towards the CFTA described in the roadmap is seen as a function of regional FTAs being completed by 2014, followed by a consolidation of the regional processes into the CFTA between 2015 and 2016, and lastly the establishment of the CFTA by 2017. Further details are also fleshed out at subregional and regional levels in three distinct steps, depicted in Fig. 2.3.

Initially, at the subregional level, the COMESA-EAC-SADC Tripartite FTA is to be completed by 2014 as a first pole, and efforts should be made to ensure that those Member States which are currently outside the Tripartite FTA join this process. Concurrently, as a second pole of convergence, other RECs are sought to expedite the completion of their respective FTA by 2014 and to also ensure that those among their Member States which are currently outside any of the existing FTAs also form part of the process. Concurrently, a third pole relates to any other individual AU Member States which are left out of the prior two poles to join CFTA

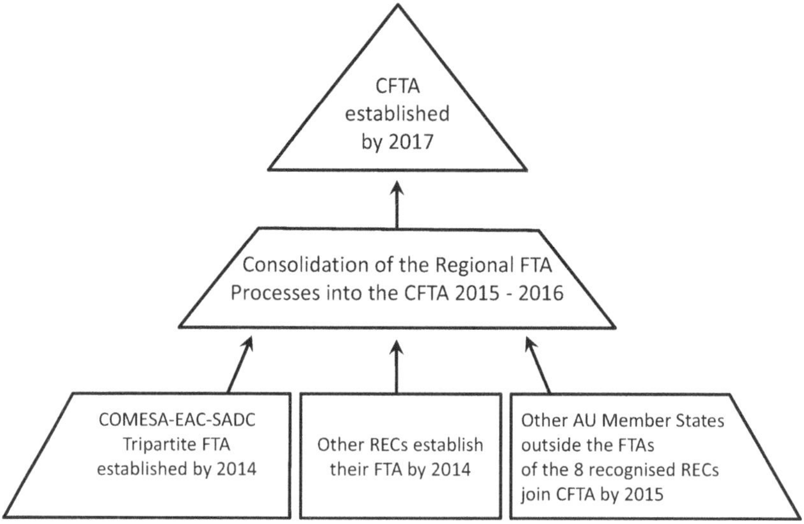

Fig. 2.3 Roadmap of the CFTA. (Source: Authors' adaptation based on AU (2011b))

process by 2015. In a second stage, the FTAs that have been created by the above-mentioned processes would be consolidated into the C-FTA between 2015 and 2016. Lastly, the third step would comprise the establishment of the CFTA 2017.

The AU summit decision on African integration (AU, 2012d, para. 7) invited the other RECs, concretely the ECOWAS, ECCAS, CEN-SAD and AMU, to draw inspiration from the Tripartite negotiations and follow suit by creating a second pole of integration so as to speed up the establishment of the AEC. This is drawn from the description of the roadmap described above, which would correspond to the box in the middle at the bottom of Fig. 2.3.

An important element of the Roadmap in order to make headway in this process is the notion of building on the *acquis* (AU, 2011b, para. 9 and 10). In legal terms, *acquis* is defined as "that which has been acquired". This term has been initially used to describe the body of law that has emanated and accumulated over time from the European Union, referred to *acquis communautaire*. In the African context, this concept has previously been used in the EAC (Thorpe, 2012). More recently, reference has been made to it in the TFTA negotiations process (COMESA-EAC-SADC Tripartite, 2011b, para. 27) in a way that was subsequently also mirrored in the *Objectives and Guiding Principles for Negotiating the CFTA*, discussed in the next section.

In these cases, however, no clear definition of what is meant by the acquis has been provided. A narrow definition of the acquis would imply that existing levels of trade (tariff) liberalization within the RECs be used. This would however, not add value to the future CFTA, as this only binds the status quo of liberalization, taking away ambition from this pan-African initiative. The expected gains from trade under this scenario would thus be significantly reduced, and the agreement would add little value for its members.[19] Fundamentally, a broader understanding of building on the

[19] It has been empirically corroborated using a Computable General Equilibrium (CGE) model, a Continental Free Trade Area was found to increase total African exports by U$25.3 billion by 2022 if all African countries were to *fully liberalize* trade in goods by 2017 (AU, AfDB and ECA, 2012). The current liberalization levels proposed by the TFTA are inferior to full liberalization, and correspond to 60–85% of the tariff lines upon entry into force of the agreement, whilst the remaining 40–15% are to be negotiated in the next 5 to 8 years. These proposed levels are lower than the existing levels of liberalizations in RECs, and has often been criticized for its low level of ambition (ICTSD, 2015). See also the discussion on the TFTA ambition in Sect. 4.1 of this chapter and Chapter 8.4 in this book.

acquis has implications on both the scope of the envisaged CFTA as well as the engagement of the member States in the construction of the CFTA is required.

A second major element of the CFTA Framework is the institutional architecture and governance structure it proposes. The point of departure is the recognition that the Abuja Treaty did not initially provide for a CFTA (nor for the possibility of greater integration across RECs), but that, indeed, the landscape has changed and it is therefore justified to think about the inadequacy of the existing institutional framework to accomplish the AEC.

The proposed architecture builds on existing bodies and organs of the AU and their already established reporting channels. This is the case of the AU Commission which regularly reports to the Conference of Ministers of Trade, as well the conference which reports to the AU Summit. The architecture however, also proposes various new bodies and organs with reporting obligations, which were envisaged as necessary for the creation and functioning of the CFTA. A major motivation for this combined approach is institutional economy, in order to avoid the setting up of parallel structures that would be difficult to manage and cost.

This proposed structure is illustrated in Fig. 2.4. It is important to note that this structure contains the envisaged architecture pre and post negotiations. All the elements of the envisaged framework agreement were not foreseen to become operative at once since there is a built-in agenda.[20] Alternatively, the negotiations architecture could also be reactivated at a later stage to continue with negotiations for the built-in agenda.

At the core of the proposed structure is the HATC, which was discussed in the previous subsection. Constituted by the Chairpersons of the recognized RECs (which are Heads of State and Government), the HATC is envisaged to expedite the CFTA by relaying continental trade policy issues, including the CFTA, to the highest level of pan-African decision-making, namely the AU Summit. It was planned to meet on the eve of each July Summit and subsequently make recommendations to the Summit.

Because the envisaged CFTA would require negotiations on various and specific trade policy issues, the organ dealing with these issues is the AU Conference of Trade Ministers and would report directly to the

[20] Indeed, the negotiations architecture which had been set up continues to coexists with the AfCFTA architecture after the AfCFTA came to existence and is now spanning over finalization of phase I, II and III of the negotiations.

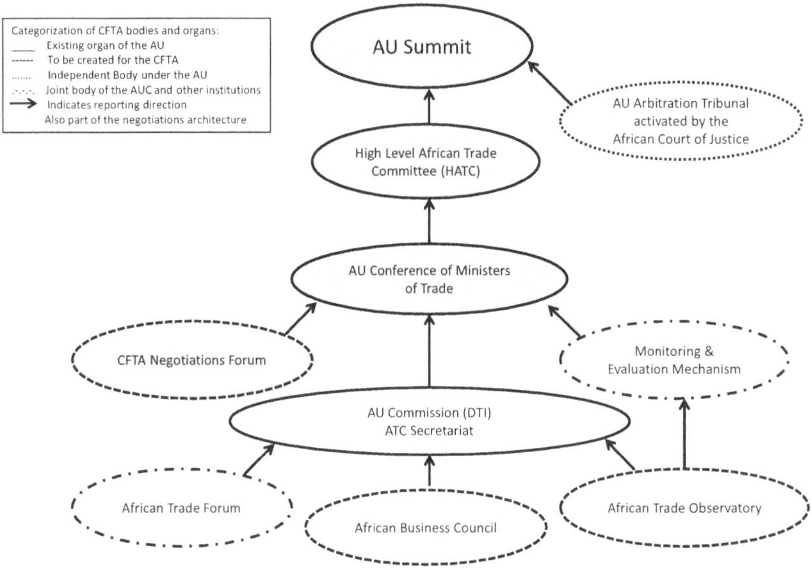

Fig. 2.4 Architecture of the CFTA. (Source: Authors' adaption based on AU (2011b) and AU (2012f))

HATC. This organ exists and meets regularly each year and is expected to receive and consider inputs from the various bodies and organs beneath it in Fig. 2.4.

The creation of the CFTA Negotiations Forum[21] was also envisaged, which would be the organ that convenes the negotiators of member States and drives the CFTA negotiations process. As will be discussed in detail in the next subsection, it is envisaged that this organ is driven by representatives of the member States which are designated as part of the negotiation delegations for the CFTA.

The AU Commission has two fundamental roles in the architecture and governance structure of the CFTA. During negotiations, it had a

[21] "CFTA" refers to the AfCFTA prior to the Thirtieth Ordinary Session of the Assembly of Heads of State and Government of the African Union, held in January 2018 in Addis Ababa, where the Assembly decided that the agreement establishing the pan-African FTA would be called the "Agreement on the African Continental Free Trade Area (AfCFTA)" (see paragraph 5 of the decision on the African Continental Free Trade Area (Assembly/AU/Dec.666(XXX)).

coordination and guidance function accompanying the process towards the establishment of the CFTA. It was also envisaged to serve as the Secretariat of the CFTA during the implementation process. The main responsible body within AUC structures is the Department of Trade and Industry (DTI), but since several dimension of the CFTA are cross-cutting in nature, other departments would also be engaged as deemed necessary. It would also serve as the Secretariat of the M&E Committee, as is further described below. Though not depicted in the figure, a Customs Technical Committee (CTC) would also provide support and report to the Conference of Ministers of Trade on rules of origin, customs regulations and transit procedures, among others.[22]

Two mechanisms are also envisaged, which are critical for the operability of the CFTA: a monitoring and evaluation mechanism and a dispute settlement mechanism. The former will deal with implementation-related processes of the CFTA, and comprise various regional institutions, including the AUC, ECA, AfDB and other major stakeholders. The latter will deal with aspects related to disputes arising from the CFTA. These functions will be vested in an AU Arbitration Tribunal operating under the African Court of Justice. It should be noted that the African Court of Justice is a standalone body already in existence. Due to the nature of its functions, it is only to be activated when disputes arise, hence following the principle of ad hoc adjudication between members due to the application or interpretation of the future CFTA agreement(s).

Lastly, the base of the architecture comprises an African Trade Forum, an African Business Council and an African Trade Observatory (ATO).[23] The ATF is already in operation and discussed the BIAT implementation plan in its second meeting in 2013. It is deemed to meet yearly and bring together various stakeholders representing civil society, the private sector and academia, and report to the Conference of Ministers of Trade through

[22] An innovation of the … TWGs rather than technical committees … See AfCFTA (2022) Annex XXX on rules of origin and also … Rules of Procedure … 2019 … AU 2019, Rules Of Procedure Of The Institutions Of The African Continental Free Trade Area,

[23] The ATO was launched at the 12th Extraordinary African Union Summit, held in July 2019, Niamey, Niger. Subsequently, it came to life together with the ABC during the 13th Extraordinary Session of the Assembly of Heads of State and Government on the AfCFTA. See https://ato.africa/en

the AU Commission. In turn, the ABC and ATO were to be created and contribute to the CFTA by providing a platform for the continent's private sector in the processes of continental trade policymaking and a repository of trade information providing inputs to the monitoring and evaluation of the CFTA implementation process, respectively. The former is deemed to report through the AU Commission, whilst the latter was expected to report to both the Conference of Ministers of Trade and the AU Commission in its initial conception.[24]

4 Instruments for Developing the CFTA

Considerable progress has been made since the mandate to establish the CFTA was officially issued in 2012. With the regular functioning of a High Level African Trade Committee and an official launch of CFTA negotiations in June 2015 in Johannesburg, work was underway. As part and parcel of this process, a series of reference documents were created to supplement and build on the existing BIAT Action Plan and CFTA Framework. This documentation would instil life into the CFTA negotiations and by extension, content into the CFTA agreement, hence it is important to give analytical consideration to the elements contained therein.

Various reference documents have been prepared to guide the creation of a CFTA since it was first conceptualized. More concretely, an important body of instruments has emanated in response to the AU Decision of the AU Summit held in June 2014 in Malabo (AU, 2014a, para. 7), which were subsequently discussed and endorsed during an extraordinary session of the AU Conference of Ministers of Trade dedicated to the CFTA in May 2015 (AU, 2015a). These documents consist of the *Objectives and Guiding Principles for Negotiating the CFTA*, an *Indicative Roadmap for the Negotiations and Establishment of the Continental Free Trade Area (CFTA)* and a *Terms of Reference for the CFTA-Negotiating Forum*. The present subsection gives careful consideration to the content of two of these instruments, in light of what the CFTA aims to achieve.

[24]With the establishment of the AfCFTA Secretariat, the ATO became one of the five recognized AfCFTA operationalization instruments of the AfCFTA and hence reports to the AfCFTA Secretariat. AU (2019).

4.1 *Objectives and Guiding Principles for Negotiating the CFTA*

The Objectives and Guiding Principles for Negotiating the CFTA is a fundamental document for the CFTA. It sets out basic modalities for negotiations that will transpire in the lead up to the creation of the CFTA, tentatively by 2017. It addresses critical aspects of negotiations, namely, its envisaged objectives, pillars of integration, scope and sequencing of negotiations and, lastly, guiding principles for negotiating the CFTA.

The document first provides for a general objective which speaks to the actual negotiations process of the CFTA and five specific objectives which the CFTA itself seeks to fulfil through its creation. The general objective enshrines the premise that the CFTA negotiations are to take place within the broader framework of the AEC and that negotiations have the ulterior motives of achieving a *comprehensive* and *mutually beneficial* trade agreement for its membership. Though what is meant by comprehensive and mutually beneficial is not explicitly defined,[25] it important to reflect on what these two notions could imply in the context of the CFTA negotiations, and their relationship with the guiding principles for negotiating the CFTA.[26]

The notion of "comprehensive" implies that the CFTA negotiations must offer members a set of preferences that go beyond the status quo of what these nations have already conferred to each other, both in terms of scope and depth of trade integration. But what is the status quo? In the African context, this may only be determined against the backdrop of what

[25] The Ministers in their report acknowledged the absence of definitions and mandate that such definitions be dealt with at an ulterior stage, by the CFTA Negotiations Forum (AU, 2015a, para. 14(ii)). This forum held its inaugural session in the Summit of December 2015, when negotiations were to be formally launched. Subsequently in 2016 in its third meeting, the Forum developed and adopted TORs for the Technical Working Groups that would then develop, consider and adopt the modalities for negotiations in goods and services, including on RoO, SPS, trade remedies and customs procedures, and lastly also trade facilitation. With the renaming of the CFTA into AfCFTA through the 30th Summit Decision in 2018 (AU, 2018a), the forum became the AfCFTA Negotiations Forum, as well as all other structures and institutions. The same approach has also been followed for the development of subsequent negotiation modalities for the phase II issues of investment, intellectual property and competition. See, for instance, AfCFTA (2022).

[26] Definitional elements of these two motives are mirrored in the principles for negotiations of the same document (AU, 2015a, Annex II, para. 10), such as reciprocity, variable geometry, special and differential treatment and substantial liberalization, which are also discussed in this section.

has been achieved in existing regional FTAs through trade negotiations. This is difficult to establish since there is considerable heterogeneity in the level of trade integration across the various RTAs to which African countries are members. As shown earlier in Fig. 2.2, trade integration ranges from FTAs (in various stages of development) to full-fledged and operating customs unions and the case of the EAC, even a common market. Thus, establishing the status quo of trade integration is not an easy task. If the CFTA is to have ambition, then FTAs that are more advanced in trade integration, notably the EAC, SADC, COMESA and ECOWAS, should be taken as the starting point to define the status quo. Consequently, comprehensiveness will imply that the set of preferences conferred under a future AfCFTA must go beyond the preferences contained in those agreements, both in terms of scope and depth of trade liberalization.

An important caveat to having an ambitious CFTA is the TFTA negotiations process. If what is being considered as a benchmark is the outcome of the TFTA negotiations, then binding minimally at the level of the TFTA negotiations and extending this level of liberalization to the remaining 28 AfCFTA countries which are not part of the TFTA would be implied. This would result in a less-than-optimum AfCFTA and would by no means fulfil the notion of a comprehensive trade agreement.

A related notion which looks at the dimension of scope of trade integration and may be considered as a measure of comprehensiveness of an FTA is the concept of substantially all trade (SAT), which is mirrored in the guiding principle of "substantial liberalization", also contained in the document. In the multilateral context, there is a big divide in what is perceived to be SAT. Though formally in the multilateral context of the WTO GATT Art. XXIV conditions the fulfilment of SAT for trade in goods in the context of RTAs between developing countries if they are to be compatible with WTO law, this definition is by no means interpreted in the same way by all the WTO membership, and remains unclear in the context of WTO case law.[27]

This consideration is key, as 43 of 54 African countries constituting the AfCFTA are members to the WTO and another eight are in the process of joining that organization. Hence, there is need to ensure that the AfCFTA

[27] For a discussion, see Trebilcock (2011), pp. 45–48, as well as Chapters 7.4, 7.5 and 8.3 in this book.

also considers the notion of comprehensiveness in light of existing WTO obligations and overall consistency and compatibility with the multilateral trading system.[28]

Equally important is the need to consider the issue of depth of trade integration as a second qualifier of comprehensiveness. Truly deep liberalization not only eliminates trade restrictions at the border between trading partners. This level of restrictions allows countries to discriminate across the universe of trading partners and is usually taken care of through MFN provisions, which generally provide for entry into a given market to foreign goods and services (hence serving the purpose of market access).

However, discrimination does not end there. A second level of trade restrictions is found behind the border, and these generally allow for discrimination in favour of domestic produce, at the detriment of foreign goods or services. This type of discrimination is more difficult to address, as it is generally contained in national regulation governing the domestic market. Such regulation may not be prima facie discriminatory (i.e. make an explicit distinction between local and foreign goods or services), but instead, may render discrimination as a result of imposing certain requirements or standards difficult for foreign providers to comply with. It is here where national treatment provisions need to deal with this second dimension of discrimination. Hence, and necessarily, comprehensiveness cannot only be a question of market access for foreign goods (Bagwell et al., 2002). Therefore, both MFN and NT are necessary to take care of both dimensions of discrimination, that ensure both de jure and de facto market access, if the CFTA agreement is to fulfil the criterion of comprehensiveness. This imperative is particularly important for trade in services, where the services provider often needs to be physically in situ in the foreign market in order to render their services to the consumer.[29] Not surprisingly, MFN and National Treatment are mirrored in the guiding principles for CFTA negotiations, as listed in paragraph 10 of the document.

In turn, the concept "mutually beneficial" implies that the complete membership has to be in a capacity to benefit from the CFTA agreement.

[28] The African countries that are in the process of acceding the WTO are Algeria, Equatorial Guinea, Ethiopia, Libya, Sao Tomé and Príncipe, South Sudan and Sudan. This notion is further elaborated in Ch. 8.3 of this book.

[29] See discussion in Chap. 4 on services delivery modes and the inseparability of services from service providers.

What is implied by mutually beneficial must also be qualified. In economic theory, an important condition for an FTA to generate benefits is that it is trade-creating, as Viner (1950) initially established. Evidence on the fulfilment of this condition in the African context at best is mixed, with some research pointing to trade creation and others to trade diversion in the context of existing FTAs.[30]

Objectively, though the CFTA may be trade-creating as a whole and interrelatedly generate higher levels of intra-African trade than currently is the case in Africa, if it does not report trade gains for each of the 54 member States that constitute it, the premise of mutually beneficial will not be fulfilled. Indeed, not all of the membership is in the same development stage nor in the same capacity to take advantage of such an agreement. Two interrelated guiding principles which cater to these differences in capacity are the principle of variable geometry and the principle of flexibility and special and differential treatment,[31] also contained in the document. There is experience in the use of the latter principle in the African context, as illustrated by the Council Decision on trade in services negotiations, which instructs that the liberalization process should take into account the different levels of development and that special and differential treatment be conferred when considering the level of liberalization commitments, and that this process should be in conformity with the principle of asymmetries (COMESA, 2009, para. 33–34). Equally, these two principles are also part of the TFTA negotiations principles (COMESA-EAC-SADC Tripartite, 2011b).[32]

Mutually beneficial also implies that the gain of one party cannot come at the loss of another party to the agreement, and, if there is such a loss, then the sum of all benefits must surpass all the losses for all parties collectively as well as individually. Alternatively, if losses outweigh the gains,

[30] See for example Carrere (2003) and Cassim (2001) for evidence on trade creation, Yeats (1998) and Schiff (1997) for trade diversion and Foroutan and Pritchett (1993) for mixed results. Evidence from the RECs is documented by Musila (2005) who finds trade integration in three RECs (COMESA, ECCAS and ECOWAS) to be trade creating, whilst Coulibaly (2004) establishes that in six of ECOWAS members exports significantly increased after joining the REC, mainly due to tariffs reductions. More recently, AU, AfDB and ECA (2010) conducted a gravity model for Western, Central, Eastern and Southern Africa and found a larger potential for trade given proximity, cultural affinity and income, particularly in Eastern and Southern African countries.

[31] See discussion on SDT and variable geometry in Chap. 7 of this book.

[32] For an elaborate discussion on variable geometry and special and differential treatment see Chap. 7 of this book.

then, they must be compensated through another mechanism of the agreement to fulfil the objective of mutually beneficial. This too has been recognized in the context of prior African trade liberalization efforts. For example, COMESA, ECOWAS and the EAC have established funds to compensate for trade losses and/or cater for achieving adequate trade capacity, which has been of benefit for the smaller and less developed countries. So too is the AfCFTA in the process of establishing a trade adjustment fund, in collaboration with and with initial seed capital from the AfDB.

An important consideration in this regard relates again to the principle of MFN. Currently, a significant number of members States of the future CFTA have FTAs (or are in the process of constituting them) with third parties.[33] Equally, 43 are also members to the WTO. The MFN treatment by definition legally requires the extension of the benefits accrued under the MFN principle to third parties, which in the two aforementioned examples, would imply an extension of the benefits conferred to 161+ countries.[34] Unless the CFTA makes provisions for exceptions to the extension of the MFN principle to third parties, the presumable benefits that would accrue to CFTA members would have to be shared with these third parties. Therefore, in order to ensure that the CFTA benefits are not diluted and diffused, the CFTA agreement needs to consider elements of legal precedence in a wider context of coexistence with other RTAs and overall compatibility with the WTO system.[35]

Turning to the five specific objectives of the CFTA, they may be summarized as: enhancing competitiveness, reducing export dependency, expand and accelerate the diversification of intra-African trade, facilitating the creation of the CCU and resolving the problem of multiple memberships within RECs in addition to accelerating continental integration processes (AU, 2015a, Annex II, para. 5). As with the general objective, these objectives respond more to economic objectives rather than political ones,

[33] These include Economic Partnership Agreements (EPAs) between the various African subregions with the EU, but also other bilateral and mega-regional FTAs. For a list of notified RTAs, see WTO Regional Trade Agreements Information System under: http://rtais.wto.org/UI/PublicMaintainRTAHome.aspx. For an overview of the various agreements, see Chap. 8, Table 8.1.

[34] For a definition and substantiated discussion on the MFN principle, see Jackson (2000, Ch. 6).

[35] See discussion on compatibility with the multilateral trading system in Chapter 8.3.

unlike integration initiatives prior to the Abuja Treaty, discussed earlier in Sect. 2.1 and Sect. 2.2.

Following the objectives, the document also touches upon what are deemed to be the pillars of integration. It states that the CFTA negotiations shall be pursued in the context of a developmental integration strategy and that it shall take into account policies that are aimed at developing the productive capacity and industrial integration of the regions, whilst leveraging existing infrastructure and industrialization programmes. It should be noted that these pillars mirror the TFTA negotiations pillars, which were developed to address industrialization and supply-side constraints with a view to enhance market integration and ensuring equity in the distribution of gains from liberalization. Further, it was envisaged that a work programme would be developed by a task force to address these two pillars (COMESA-EAC-SADC Tripartite, 2011a, para. 2 and 2011b, para. 10–12), and, more recently, work on these two pillars has been expedited (COMESA-EAC-SADC Tripartite, 2015, para. 7).

In terms of scope, the CFTA negotiations were envisaged to cover trade in goods, as well as trade in services, investment, intellectual property rights and, lastly, competition policy, as is established in the document.[36] However, negotiations would not transpire concurrently on all these issues. A first phase in which trade in goods and services are covered was foreseen, where two separate legal instruments for trade in goods and trade in services were to be negotiated in separate (but parallel) tracks. In a second phase, it was envisaged that the remaining areas be covered, namely investment, intellectual property rights and competition. Lastly, the document also enunciates a total of 11 principles which were to guide negotiations of the CFTA, as follows:

(i) it is member State/REC/Custom territory driven, with the support of the AUC and its structures;
(ii) RECs FTAs are the building blocs of the CFTA;
(iii) Reservation of Acquis;
(iv) Variable geometry;
(v) Flexibility and special and differential treatment, transparency and disclosure of information;

[36] At the time, digital trade and women and youth were not envisaged, but later integrated into the negotiations mandate as new priorities of a third phase of AfCFTA negotiations. See, for instance, AU (2020).

(vi) Substantial liberalization;
(vii) MFN treatment;
(viii) National treatment;
(ix) Reciprocity;
(x) Consensus-based decisions; and
(xi) Adoption of best practices.

As with the objectives of the CFTA, the principles are not defined or elaborated on in the document itself. There was the expectation that the CFTA Negotiations Forum would address definitional issues stemming from the principles as well as the objectives contained in the document in an ulterior stage. Despite this caveat, the principles can be categorized by their end purpose. Correspondingly, some of these principles are of substantive nature, meaning they typically add content to trade agreements and will govern (in subject matter) the trade relationships that will ensue between the member States. This will require that specific obligations or commitments be derived from the agreement itself through the inclusion of articles and/or chapters of a future CFTA agreement.[37]

By way of example, a principle of substantive nature is substantial liberalization (principle (vi) of the guiding principles). What is meant by substantial liberalization, as conceived in the context of the multilateral trading system derives from the obligation by member states to make additional commitments in successive rounds of trade negotiations that add value to what has been liberalized before.[38] A critical factor in this process of negotiations is that the rest of the membership sees the value of such an offer in that it deepens or expands market access offered earlier or, alternatively, in that it represents an initial market access offer in a sector or tariff line which was off bounds before. It is also based on the premise that trade negotiation rounds are successive and periodic and thus enshrine the notion of progressiveness of liberalization. In a sense, what cannot be offered in an initial stage is left to subsequent stages, hence there is a notion of a built-in agenda.[39]

[37] This is the case of principles: (ii) RECs FTAs are the building blocs of the CFTA, (iii) reservation of Acquis, (iv) variable geometry, (v) flexibility and SDT, (vi) substantial liberalisation, (vii) MFN treatment, (viii) national treatment, (ix) reciprocity and (xi) adoption of best practices.

[38] Also, see earlier discussion on SAT in Sect. 4.1

[39] For a discussion on the issue of progressiveness of liberalization, see (Páez, 2011, pp. 102–103).

Other principles in the document respond more to the form, structure or process that govern trade agreements, and are typically of a procedural nature. These are: (i) CFTA negotiations are member State/REC/Custom territory driven, with the support of the AUC and its structures; (x) decisions are consensus-based and (xi) adoption of best practices.

In sum, the document lays out the fundamental raison d'être of the CFTA and may be viewed as an expression of regional economic integration at the service of economic development of Africa. It clearly builds on the development strategy initially conceived under the aegis of the Lagos Plan of Action and the Abuja Treaty, based on economic fundamentals as the rationale for a CFTA that is conducive to the crystallization of the AEC. Though the document contains important elements for the CFTA negotiations in terms of objectives, scope, pillar and principles, some of these elements were left to be defined and circumscribed at a later stage. It is ultimately this which will nuance and shape the outcome of the CFTA agreement.[40]

4.2 Indicative Roadmap for the Negotiations and Establishment of the CFTA

Accompanying the Objectives and Guiding Principles is the Indicative Roadmap for the Negotiations and Establishment of the Continental Free Trade Area. Also technical in nature, the document lays out the specifics of the *process* of the CFTA negotiations in terms of draft documentation and financial and capacity needs, and lastly schedules of CFTA negotiations.

Notably, the schedules of negotiation divide the process of CFTA trade negotiations into four distinct phases, namely, an initial phase called a post launch preparatory period, followed by a negotiations period, subsequently followed by the finalization of the CFTA Agreement phase and lastly a ratification/domestication and entry into force phase of the CFTA agreement.

At the heart of this document is a time schedule with an indicative roadmap containing defined milestones, outputs, responsibilities and timelines. Even though not expressly stated, this must be read in conjunction with the initial roadmap conceived for the CFTA and contained in the

[40] A point in case were the negotiating modalities for services and goods trade, discussed in Chapter 7.4 and 7.5 of this book.

Framework for the Continental Free Trade Area, Road Map, Architecture (AU, 2011b), and contextualized in the broader time frames of the Abuja Treaty, as shown earlier in Figs. 2.1 and 2.3.

The preparatory period initiates with the launch of negotiations in July 2015 and was envisaged to the last for 6–12 months, followed by a negotiations period which will extend until the end of 2017. The finalization phase was expected to take place between October and December 2017 and be followed by the domestication phase from 2018 onwards, as depicted in Fig. 2.5. This holds some resemblance with the initial Roadmap for Establishing the TFTA launched in 2011, which had a preparatory phase of 6–12 months, a subsequent negotiations phase for 24–36 months and lastly a finalization phase which was to ensue right after negotiations (COMESA-EAC-SADC Tripartite, 2011b, Annex III).

A major difference between the CFTA and TFTA is that the CFTA in its initial phase of market integration is focusing on both goods and services, with a built-in agenda considering additional elements of

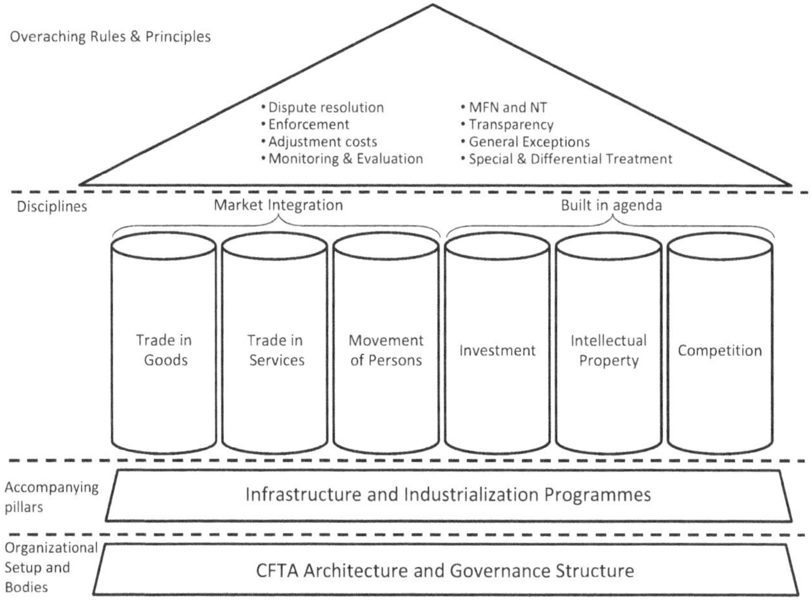

Fig. 2.5 Rules, principles and disciplines of a CFTA Framework Agreement. (Source: Authors' illustration based on AU (2011b and 2014b))

investment, intellectual property rights and competition policy in its second phase. The TFTA only focused on goods in its first phase, but also included an element of movement of persons concurrently under a parallel track to market integration (Pillar I) during Phase I led by a separate Committee (COMESA-EAC-SADC Tripartite, 2011b, para. 13).

The proposed timelines of the TFTA were partially met for Phase I. Especially since the negotiations on movement of business persons were not completed at the end of Phase I in February 2015 hence countries were instructed to continue (COMESA-EAC-SADC Tripartite, 2015, para. 8). Furthermore, since not all countries had finalized their tariff offers they were given time until June 2016 to do so.

In light of these considerations and learning from the TFTA experience, it is important to consider related challenges and the feasibility of implementing this roadmap. First, the envisaged negotiation Phase I of the CFTA is considerably reduced, compared to that of the TFTA. At most, and assuming that the preparatory period is kept at its shortest (i.e. 6 months), the negotiations phase would count with a maximum of 22 months in the proposed roadmap, well below the lead time of the TFTA.

Second, the Indicative roadmap builds on the assumption that the consolidation process of the RECs would have been finalized by 2015. Apart from the relative progress made on TFTA, other subregions have not progressed in emulating the example of the TFTA. Further, there is an implicit allusion to a timeframe through the roadmap, which locks in the commitment by members of the various RECs to implement their FTAs within the established deadlines. To underscore the point, if negotiations of the TFTA as well as those of other RECs FTA were not consolidated by 2016, as originally envisaged in the Roadmap, the CFTA establishment was bound to be delayed, as would be the case for the establishment of the Continental Customs Union and which will also require a preparatory period prior its establishment in 2019, as depicted in Table 2.1.

In this context, learning from the recent experience and given the existing links between the TFTA and CFTA negotiations, it is of utmost importance that the member States make far-reaching commitments (keeping within the established timeframes). This is especially so because the CFTA roadmap is based on a major principle, which is building on the *acquis* of existing regional integration processes. As discussed earlier in subsection 3.2 and 4.1, there is a tension in fulfilling this principle and meeting the objective of a comprehensive CFTA, in light of the outcome of the TFTA negotiations of its Pillar I.

Table 2.1 Phases of the CFTA and TFTA negotiations processes

Activity	Timeline																	
	2011		2012		2013		2014		2015		2016		2017		2018		2019	
	1	2	1	2	1	2	1	2	1	2	1	2	1	2	1	2	1	2
Tripartite FTA (FTA)																		
Preparatory Phase																		
Negotiations Phase (Pillar I)																		
Negotiations on Movement of Persons																		
Technical preparations for Pillars II & III																		
Finalisation of TFTA agreement																		
Continental Free Trade Area (CFTA)																		
Preparatory Phase																		
Negotiations Phase I																		
Finalisation of the CFTA agreement																		
Negotiations Phase II																		
Domestication of CFTA agreement																		
Continental Customs Union (CCU)																		
Establishment of the CCU																		

Source: Authors' illustration based on AU (2011b and 2015a) and COMESA-EAC-SADC Tripartite (2011a)

In order to overcome part of this tension, a broader definition of what is meant by the acquis will be required, beyond what has been common practice in existing RECs and the TFTA.[41] The limited definition of the

[41] For a discussion on the acquis in the context of the TFTA see Luke and Mabuza (2015), but also see discussion on how notions of the acquis have evolved in AfCFTA interpretation and African jurisprudence in Chapters 7.4 and 7.5 and 8.3

Tripartite negotiating principles rendered a limited result, as it was based on the consolidation of tariff liberalization levels in each REC FTA (COMESA-EAC-SADC Tripartite, 2011b, para. 27). This resulted in finding a minimum common denominator, which was binding at the tariff level the majority of countries had already reached in their respective RECs and hence did not render an additional deepening of liberalization. Only countries which had not entered into an RTA in the context of their existing REC membership were subject to this limited liberalization level. This basically comprised four SACU countries (plus Angola and Mozambique) vis-a-vis the 21 COMESA countries, as depicted earlier in Fig. 2.2.[42] In other words, no additional tariff liberalization commitments were made within existing RECs. Therefore, the principle on the reservation of the acquis, defined in the CFTA Framework (2011b, para.10) must go beyond this, and refer to a commitment to liberalization above the existing levels of liberalization both *within* and *across* RECs.

Finally, the fact that now both negotiation processes (TFTA Phase II and CFTA Phase I) are virtually transpired in parallel tracks achieving systemic coherence between both agreements once the TFTA kicks in will represent a major challenge for 26 African countries, as resources will have to be stretched to accomplish consistency both integration processes, as is further discussed in Chap. 8. However, this may also represent an opportunity for countries to avoid the pitfalls of the TFTA negotiations and to embrace more than minimal liberalization commitments and frontload negotiations, particularly in the services trade sector, as is further elaborated in Chapter 4.5.

5 Imperatives for Realizing a Pan-African Market

Having looked at what has been achieved so far in conceptualizing the CFTA, it is important to look at what is still pending. The *Objectives and Guiding Principles for Negotiating the CFTA* indeed contain a starting menu of some of the desirable elements of a CFTA agreement that are yet to be defined and be given careful consideration. They are however by no means exhaustive or sufficient to have a fully functional pan-African FTA which meets the standards of being comprehensive and mutually beneficial.

The present section therefore looks at some of these elements in terms of a functional agreement that promotes the operability of the CFTA once

[42] Also see Table 8.1 in Chap. 8 with an overview of the membership status quo.

it is established, as well as the need to ensure that the CFTA can coexist within the myriad of other regional integration priorities of various programmes and initiatives, as well as institutions in the wider African context.

5.1 Towards a Framework Agreement for Realizing the CFTA

Some of the critical definitional issues of the AfCFTA which merit consideration have already been laid out in Sect. 4.1 of this chapter. Some have to be dealt with in much more detail, notably the concept of variable geometry, special and differential treatment, and the notions of MFN and NT as they apply to trade in services and investment, all of these being the focus of subsequent chapters in this book.

As a learning experience, during the Tripartite negotiations some definitional issues were left for an ulterior stage of the process, which actually jeopardized completion timelines and also diminished the initial level of ambition of the TFTA. In particular, the absence of clarity on definitions gave way to a narrowly defined acquis. As has been argued here, a definition which considers a broader scope of what is meant by the acquis is necessary, to avoid a major TFTA pitfall. Equally important is to avoid potential conflicts between principles, as reportedly occurred in the TFTA negotiations between the principles of variable geometry and the principle of decision-making on the basis of consensus (ICTSD, 2015 and Luke & Mabuza, 2015). Here too, learning from this recent experience, defining a precedence structure for the use of these principles will be required for CFTA negotiations.[43]

But beyond definitions, which are helpful in circumscribing the scope of the CFTA, as well as the obligations deriving from the CFTA agreement, a high degree of consistency in the application of the CFTA agreement will also be required by the membership. A framework agreement can vest the members of the CFTA with a structure that allows greater consistency in the incorporation and application of the rules that emanate from the CFTA agreement, as it takes shape. This is particularly relevant as the negotiations scope of the agreement has been circumscribed to two

[43] See discussion on the precedence of the AfCFTA Agreement in Chapter 8.3 of this book, as well as the issue of superseding principles when advancing at differing speeds of liberalization in Chapter 7.5.

phases.[44] With a built-in agenda, it is important to have a legal skeleton in place that will allow the incorporation of subsequently negotiated texts of the phase II items, notably, investment, intellectual property and competition, as established in the instruments discussed in the previous subsections. Indeed, given the timelines and organization of the negotiations process, these instruments suggest that the intention of the AU members was to have a framework agreement in place by the end of 2017. This deadline was slightly overrun with the coming of age of the AfCFTA in 2018.

The need to have a framework agreement cannot be underestimated, especially given the timelines envisaged and the limited financial and human capacity of the African Union. A "Single Undertaking" would bring on the immediate creation of the CFTA and facilitate an earlier achievement of the operability and associated gains of the CFTA compared to a framework agreement. The principle of a "Single Undertaking" or single package was introduced in the context of the multilateral trading system for the first time during the Uruguay Round which was built on the premise that, unlike prior negotiation rounds, all parties had to agree on all that was on the table, and there was no room for opting out of aspects of the agreement (i.e. "à la carte" negotiations). Jackson (2000, pp. 46–47). Understandably, given the high standard for reaching an agreement, the Uruguay Round took 8 years to be accomplished, and was criticized by many the for the absence of flexibilities to accommodate developing country needs. (Trebilcock et al., 2013, p. 612).

Africa has had experiences with framework agreements. Indeed, in order to cope with their built-in agenda on services trade and movement of persons, the COMESA, the EAC and the SADC, all developed framework agreements in order to launch their respective FTAs and have an "early harvest" in disciplines which have been concluded through negotiations. More recently the TFTA itself is a framework agreement, with a built-in agenda for successive negotiations phases.[45] The continent

[44] At an ulterior stage, a third phase of negotiations was recognized by the AfCFTA negotiating parties to be able to bring in new topics, namely digital trade and women and youth. See discussion in Sect. 4.1 on the scope of the objectives and guiding principles for negotiating the AfCFTA.

[45] Trade and investment framework agreements have been conducted in the context of the African Growth and Opportunity Act (AGOA) between the US and some RECs, as is discussed in Chap. 6.

therefore had experience in dealing with trade matters under this type of operative framework.

A framework agreement for the CFTA was developed and concluded in parallel with the technical work that preceded phase I of the AfCFTA negotiations. As proposed in Fig. 2.5, a framework agreement could contain four parts dealing with: (i) the overarching rules and principles, (ii) the disciplines subdivided in market integration and a built-in agenda for trade "and" issues, (iii) the accompanying pillars on infrastructure and industrialization, and (iv) the organizational setup and bodies of the future CFTA.

The overarching rules and principles would govern all the disciplines of the agreement and cater for providing clearance on definitions and in the event of violations of the agreement or differences in its interpretation, provide legal redress. In turn, the disciplines would be the actual substance of the framework agreement, covering the scope that has been agreed for Pillar I of the CFTA. Here, a section or chapter would deal with trade in goods, a second one with trade in services, and subsequent ones with movement of persons, investment, intellectual property and competition, respectively, once negotiations on these issues have been concluded. These disciplines would also serve as entry points to connect with infrastructure- and industrialization-related programmes in the accompanying pillars. Lastly, the CFTA architecture and governance structure would be the basis for and set the context for the operational aspects of the agreement.

An important caveat on this proposed structure must be made here. The scope presented in the *Objectives and Guiding Principles for Negotiating the CFTA* says nothing about movement of persons. As noted earlier, this is unlike the TFTA process which did contain and envisage work on this discipline in the first phase of negotiations but in a parallel track. A strong case had to be made for the incorporation of disciplines on movement of persons, if the CFTA is to represent a true continental market integration platform. Especially in today's world of global value chains, where trade is no longer conceived as the flow of finished goods across borders, but rather an exchange of task and inputs embedded in intermediated goods, movement of persons today also conforms part of the reality of trade in goods and services. Hence, if the CFTA was to be a truly integrated continental space, then factor market mobility must also be facilitated, which envisages both the movement of labour and capital. This was deemed as particularly important if Africans are to enjoy the benefits of the

CFTA from the start. It is with that impetus that efforts were also channelled to include a Protocol on the Movement of Business Persons[46] at an ulterior stage and which was concurrently adopted with the AfCFTA agreement in 2018.

5.2 *Mainstreaming the CFTA into Existing African Initiatives and Programmes*

It is important to stress that the CFTA did not figure in the regional integration stages of the Abuja Treaty. While this has been duly acknowledged by the AU,[47] neither did the TFTA, nor institutions such as African Monetary Fund nor the African Investment Bank, which today figure as part of the envisaged AEC. Just as the latter two, the CFTA was conceived out of necessity. Another point in case is that milestones which were envisaged at a later stage in the integration process of the Abuja Treaty, notably the Pan-African Parliament[48] and the African Court of Justice and Human Rights, were brought forward and exist today. These are examples which portray regional integration in Africa as a dynamic learning process, which adjusts to cater for emerging and/or changing priorities of the continent. Hence, it is unconceivable that the CFTA being part of this process could operate in a vacuum, or not subject to experiencing iterations and innovations in its formation trajectory.

Because of this realization and due to the broad scope of the CFTA, it is precisely all the more important to ensure that there is consistency between the CFTA and existing regional integration initiatives and programmes. Indeed, this has been recognized through the incorporation of an infrastructure and industrialization pillar in the Objectives and Guiding Principles for Negotiating the CFTA, as discussed in the previous

[46] See AU Decision on the Protocol; on the Free Movement of Persons and Right of Residence and Right of Establishment (AU, 2018b, 2018c) and also see discussion in Sect. 4.5 on the issue of factor market mobility.

[47] AU Ministers of Trade recognized that Stage III of the Abuja Treaty only referred to the establishment of CUs in each REC by 2017 while the continental CU would be established in 2019 (AU, 2011a, para. 27 and para. 29).

[48] Recognizing the absence of involvement of Africans in the regional integration process and the need for a platform for discussing and making decision on common problems and challenges, the Pan-African Parliament was envisaged as the institution which would be the entry point for civil society and grass-root organizations to engage on regional integration issues. See discussion in Chap. 3 on multistakeholder participation.

subsection 5.1. This implies that the future CFTA agreement will need to establish and qualify its relationship with existing pan-African and subregional programmes, notably the Accelerated Industrial Development of Africa (AIDA) and the Programme for Infrastructure Development in Africa (PIDA), as well as components of the Comprehensive Africa Agriculture Development Programme (CAADP), just to name some of the existing regional integration initiatives.

More comprehensively, mainstreaming the CFTA in this respect of Agenda 2063, which is the development roadmap of the next half a decade of the African Union, will be paramount, and will imply that due reflection is given to how the CFTA may be operationalized to achieve the various milestones contained in Agenda 2063, including but not limited to the doubling of intra-African trade. Due consideration will also need to be given to more specific policies and programmes which have a bearing on market integration issues, such as the Migration Policy Framework (on interrelated issues of movement of persons) and Yamassoukro Declaration (on services trade from the perspective of commercial air transport).[49]

In addition, because mainstreaming of the CFTA involves both a pan-African and subregional dimension, as there are several programmes and initiatives that are also coordinated and run by the RECs on all of the aforementioned areas, which also need to be considered. In reflection of the spaghetti-bowl of RTAs and as part of the rationalization efforts, indeed the CFTA could represent an opportunity to consolidate these processes in a more pragmatic and results-oriented manner.

Furthermore, mainstreaming must also be conducted at the national level, as has been sufficiently acknowledged by the AU (AU and ECA, 2012). Mainstreaming the CFTA will require the domestication of the CFTA agreement in each of the member States. This process may differ from country to country and will require the formal ratification and transposition of the agreement, into national laws and policies if the CFTA agreement is to have any "teeth". This will also demand funding and resource allocations in order to build capacity and popularize the agreement, which represents a challenge for many African countries. Point in case is the services sector, where because of absence of adequate services trade policy mainstreaming, African countries are yet to harness the gains from trade liberalization they have pursued (UNCTAD, 2015).

[49] See associated discussion in Chapter 4.5 on the Yamassoukro Declaration and Decision, as well as associated Single African Air Transport Market.

Lastly, adequate monitoring and evaluation of the mainstreaming of the CFTA will also be required, and, here too, the architecture and governance structure of the CFTA needs to be vested and empowered with the mandate to do so. The M&E mechanism proposed in the structure and shown earlier in Fig. 2.4 would be the entity to undertake this evaluation and review given the role it will play in the implementation of the CFTA, but this too needs to be explicitly fleshed out in the framework agreement, as part of the reporting structures of the AfCFTA.[50]

5.3 Institutional Governance of the CFTA and Coexistence with Other Regional Bodies

A third crucial element for the operability and functionality of the CFTA will be the institutional landscape it will navigate in. As was mentioned earlier in this chapter, the CFTA cannot operate in a vacuum, since the continent already counts with some pan-African institutions that govern various aspects of intra-African trade.

The Roadmap and Architecture of the CFTA, as discussed earlier in Sect. 2 indeed embeds the CFTA in this context of existing AU bodies and structures, in order to rationalize the costs of a parallel structure, but also with a view to raise the visibility and importance of trade integration in AU processes. This is indeed a unique opportunity in the history of Africa's integration which must be harnessed. But beyond the AU, other regional structures must also be taken account of.

An important question in this regard is how the CFTA, once established and with a functioning secretariat, will relate with the various RECs across Africa, which traditionally have been the motors of trade integration. Here the Abuja Treaty give some direction in its Article 88, which stipulates the role of RECs in the broader context of regional integration and towards the creation of the AEC. It establishes that member States

[50] Indeed, in the aftermath of the creation of the AfCFTA, the African Trade Observatory (ATO) was launched as one of the five operational instruments during the 12th Extraordinary African Union Summit, held in July 2019, Niamey. See AU (2019), para 7. The other four operation instruments comprised the AfCFTA Rules of Origin; an AfCFTA Trade in Goods Password Protected Dashboard; a mechanism for monitoring, reporting and elimination of non-tariff barriers; a digital payments system known as the Pan-African Payments and Settlements System (PAPSS). In that perspective, these instruments support the reporting and governance structures that were initially envisaged at the time the CFTA was designed, as was discussed in Sect. 3.2 of this chapter and also footnotes 24 and 25.

have the responsibility of promoting coordination and harmonization activities within the context of their RECs with those of the AEC, especially as the AEC is conceived as the ultimate objective towards which the RECs must be geared.

Hence, regional integration activities in the context of the RECs operate as a function of and are subjugated to the process of establishing the AEC. Because the CFTA was conceived at a later stage, its role in this process is not clearly established in the Abuja Treaty. However, and given the precedence of the RECs and their recognized role as the "building blocs" of the CFTA and towards the creation of a CCU, RECs may be placed in a subsidiary function with respect to the CFTA. More importantly, if both RECs and the CFTA are to coexist, it is important that the governance structure of the CFTA reflects their relationship and reporting functions. This would also need to form part of the framework agreement of the CFTA.

A last point of consideration relates to the functioning of the various bodies and institutions that operate at the service of the CFTA, and ultimately the CFTA secretariat itself. In order for them to achieve their mission, these institutions will need to be fit for purpose. A high standard of institutional governance will therefore need to be in place, which vests these institutions with the capacity to enjoy a degree of autonomy, transparency and independence in their day-to-day functions. Securing adequate financing of the CFTA will be critical to achieve this and must also figure in the framework agreement to constitute the CFTA.

6 Conclusions

Africa's regional integration over the past half century has been a lengthy process distinguished by starts and stops. Inspired in a shared vision of pan-Africanism, this process has evolved from an initial stage based on political motivations of unification and independence from a colonial past, over to a secondary stage where economic and social development of the continent starts to distil as the new rationale for regional integration in the 1980s and finally to a third stage where economic development underpins and drives the integration process.

A major milestone has been the creation of the Abuja Treaty, which is the guiding blueprint of regional economic integration in Africa since the

1990s. In this gradual process of regional integration, trade liberalization in the broader context of market integration has been prioritized, as exemplified by the various and overlapping memberships in RTAs across Africa. It is on this basis that the African Union promoted the creation of a CFTA, as a building bloc towards the establishment of an African Economic Community in years to come.

This chapter critically assessed various elements of the process and content of the AfCFTA negotiations, in terms of objectives, scope, disciplines and timelines, prior to the coming of age of the AfCFTA in 2018. Based on recent integration experiences of various RECs, the chapter drew attention on various definitional issues that are critical for the AfCFTA to meet the objectives of being comprehensive and mutually beneficial, as well as time constraints related to the negotiations roadmap. From this assessment, the chapter clearly made a case for greater clarity and broader scope in definitions and principles from the outset of negotiations, in order to ensure that the ambition of the AfCFTA is maximized and retained during negotiations that were to follow its creation.

More importantly, because the AfCFTA is a critical stepping stone in the conceptualization of an African Customs Union and subsequently also the AEC, the chapter also drew caution on the need to mainstream the ACFTA in existing pan-African and regional initiatives, beyond its suggested industrialization and infrastructure pillars. An important entry point in this respect is of course Agenda 2063, which is the development roadmap of the next half a decade of the African Union, but equally so are other existing initiatives which touch upon trade-related issues, such as services trade and movement of persons.

The chapter also contemplated necessary elements of operability and functionality of the AfCFTA agreement as initially conceived, in particular with regards to the feasibility of a framework agreement in order to realize the prospective gains of the AfCFTA given the time constraints and the need to ensure that it is mainstreamed as a process in existing pan-African and regional initiatives. Lastly, this chapter also gave consideration to the institutional landscape the prospective AfCFTA would navigate in, with a view to ensure that institutional governance also contributes to the functionality and operability of the AfCFTA.

References

Literary References

AfCFTA (2022), Guidelines And Principles For Negotiating The African Continental Free Trade Area (Afcfta) Protocol On Competition Policy, March 2022.

AU. (2020). Decision On The African Continental Free Trade Area, Doc. In *Assembly/AU/4(XXXIII), 33rd Ordinary Session of the Assembly of the Union, 9–10 February 2020.* Ethiopia.

AU (2019), Decision On The Launch Of The Operational Phase Of The African Continental Free Trade Area (Afcfta), Ext/Assembly/AU/ Decl.1(XII), 12th Extraordinary Session of the Assembly, 7 July 2019, Niamey, Niger.

AU (2018a), Decision On The African Continental Free Trade Area, Doc. Assembly/AU/4(XXX), 30th Ordinary Session of the Assembly, 28–29 January, Addis Ababa, Ethiopia.

AU (2018b) Agreement Establishing the African Continental Free Trade Area. https://au.int/sites/default/files/treaties/36437-treaty-consolidated_text_on_cfta_-_en.pdf

AU (2018c), Decisions of the 31st African Union Assembly of Heads of State and Government in July 2018 (Assembly/AU/Dec.690(XXXI).

African Union (AU) (2015d), *Agenda 2063. The Africa We Want.* African Union (AU), Addis Ababa.

African Union (AU)(2015a), "Report of the Meeting of Ministers", Dedicated Session of Experts and Senior Officials followed by Ministers of Trade on the Continental Free Trade Area, at the AU on 8–15 May 2015, Addis Ababa.

African Union (AU) (2015b), *Decision on the Launch of Continental Free Trade Area Negotiations,* Assembly/AU/Dec.569(XXV), 25th Ordinary Session of the Assembly of Heads of State and Government, 14 to 15 June, Johannesburg, South Africa.

African Union (AU)(2015c), *Decision on the Report of the High Level African Trade Committee on Trade Issues,* Assembly/AU/Dec.555(XXIV), 24th Ordinary Session of the Assembly of Heads of State and Government, 30 to 31 January, Addis Ababa, Ethiopia.

African Union (AU)(2014a), *Decision on the Report of the High Level African Trade Committee on Trade Issues,* Assembly/AU/Dec.531(XXII), 23rd Ordinary Session of the Assembly of Heads of State and Government, 26 to 27 June, Malabo, Equatorial Guinea.

African Union (AU). (2014b). *African Union Handbook.* Ababa.

African Union (AU) (2012a), *Decision on Boosting Intra-African Trade and Fast Tracking the Continental Free Trade Area*, Assembly/AU/Dec.394(XVIII),

18th Ordinary Session of the Assembly of Heads of State and Government, 29 to 30 January, Addis Ababa.

African Union (AU) (2012b), *Declaration on Boosting Intra-African Trade and Fast Tracking the Continental Free Trade Area (CFTA)*, Assembly/AU/Decl.1(XVIII), 18th Ordinary Session of the Assembly of Heads of State and Government, 29 to 30 January, Addis Ababa.

African Union (AU) (2012c), *Decision on Boosting Intra-African Trade and Fast Tracking the Continental Free Trade Area*, Assembly/AU/Dec.426(XIX), 19th Ordinary Session of the Assembly of Heads of State and Government, 15 to16 July, Addis Ababa.

African Union (AU) (2012d), *Decision on African Integration*, Assembly/AU/Dec.392(XVIII), 18th Ordinary Session of the Assembly of Heads of State and Government, 29 to 30 January, Addis Ababa.

African Union (AU) (2012e), "Report to the Committee of 7 Heads of State Constituted to Review Concerns and Issues Raised at the 18th Summit Debate on Boosting intra-African Trade and the Establishment of the CFTA", TD/BIAT/cm.1/R1, Consultative Meeting of the Senior Officials of the Committee of the Assembly of Heads of State and Government on Boosting Intra-African Trade, Addis Ababa, 3–4 April.

African Union (AU) (2012f), "Draft Terms of Reference of the African Union High Level African Trade Committee", TD/BIAT/cm.1/Tor1, Consultative Meeting of the Senior Officials of the Committee of the Assembly of Heads of State and Government on Boosting Intra-African Trade, Addis Ababa, 3–4 April.

African Union (AU). (2011b). *Action Plan on Boosting Intra-African Trade and a Framework for the Continental Free Trade Area, Road Map, Architecture.* AUC and ECA.

African Union (AU) (2011a), "Report of the Meeting of Ministers", AU/MIN/TD//Rpt(VII), 7th Ordinary Session of the African Union Conference of Ministers of Trade, 29 November to 3rd December, Accra.

African Union (AU) (2010), "Report of the Conference of Ministers of Trade", 6th Ordinary Session of the African Union Conference of Ministers of Trade, 29 October to 02 November, Kigali, AU/TD/MIN/RPT.

African Union (AU), 2009b), "Follow-up Report on the Implementation of Recommendations of the Third Conference of African Ministers in charge of Integration," by Ministers in Charge of Integration at their Fourth Conference, in Yaoundé, from 7 to 8 May 2009.

African Union (AU), (2009a), "Minimum Integration Programme", Addis Ababa.

African Union (AU), (2006), *Decision on the Moratorium on the Recognition of Regional Economic Communities (RECs)*, Assembly/AU/Dec.112(Vii), Banjul, The Gambia.

African Union (AU) (2000), *Constitutive Act of the African Union*, entered into force 26 May 2001.

AU, AfDB and ECA. (2012). *Assessing Regional Integration in Africa (ARIA V): Towards an African Continental Free Trade Area*. Addis Ababa.

AU, AfDB and ECA (2010). *Assessing Regional Integration in Africa (ARIA IV): Enhancing Intra-African Trade*. Addis Ababa.

AU and ECA (2012), Meeting of the Committee of Experts of the 5th Joint Annual Meetings of the AU Conference of Ministers of Economy and Finance and ECA Conference of African Ministers of Finance, Planning and Economic Development. Addis Ababa, Ethiopia 22–25 March.

AfDB and ECA (2016), *Assessing Regional Integration in Africa (ARIA V): Innovation, Competitiveness and Regional Integration*. ECA: Addis Ababa.

Bagwell, Kyle, Petros C. Mavroidis and Robert W. Staiger (2002), "It's Question of Market Access", *The American Journal of International Law* Vol. 96, No. 1 (Jan., 2002), pp. 56–76.

Bhagwati, Jagdish (1995), '*U.S. Trade Policy: The Infatuation with Free Trade Agreements*' in Jagdish Bhagwati and Anne O. Krueger, *The Dangerous Drift to Preferential Trade Agreements*, AEI Press.

Bela Balassa. (1961). *The Theory of Economic Integration*. Homewood.

Browne, R. S., & Cummings, R. J. (1984). *The Lagos Plan of Action Vs The Berg Report: Contemporary Issues in African Economic Development*. Howard University Press.

Carrere, C. (2003) "Revisiting the effects of regional trading agreements on trade flows with proper specification of the gravity model." Working Paper 200310, Centre d'Etudes et de Recherches sur le Développement International, Clermont-Ferrand Area, France.

Cassim, R. (2001). *The Determinants of Intraregional Trade in Southern Africa with Specific Reference to Southern Africa and the Rest of the Region.*", DPRU Working paper no 01/51,. University of Cape Town, South Africa.

COMESA (2009), *Official Gazette of the Common Market for Eastern and Southern Africa*, 15(4), 9 June http://www.comesa.int/attachments/article/26/2009%20Gazette%20Vol.%2015%20No4.pdf

COMESA-EAC-SADC Tripartite. (2015). *Sharm El Sheikh Declaration Launching the COMESA-EAC-SADC Tripartite Free Trade Area*, June, Sharm El Sheikh.

_____. (2011a). *Declaration Launching the Negotiations for the Establishment of the Tripartite Free Trade Area*, 12 June, Johannesburg.

_____. (2011b). "Report of the Meeting of the COMESA-EAC-SADC Tripartite Ministerial Committee in Preparation for the Tripartite FTA Negotiations", TP/II/3, 13 May, Lusaka.

Coulibaly, S. 2004. "On the assessment of trade creation and trade diversion effects of developing RTAs." Paper Presented at the 2005 annual meeting of the Swiss Society of Economics and Statistics on Resource Economics, Technology, and Sustainable Development Zurich, March 17–18. http://www.wif.ethz.ch/resec/sgvs/078.pdf

Foroutan, F., & Pritchett, L. (1993). Intra-Sub-Saharan African Trade: Is it Too Little? *Journal of African Economies, 2*(1), 74–105.

Esedebe, P. O. (1982). *Pan-Africanism. The Idea and Movement 1776–1963.* Howard University Press.

C. A. Cooper and B. F. Massell (1965), "Toward a General Theory of Customs Unions for Developing Countries", in *Journal of Political Economy* (Chicago), 74, October, pp. 461–476.

Hoogvelt, A. M. M. (1982). *The Third World in Development.* The Macmillan Press LTD.

ICTSD (2015), "Low Ambition in Tariff Liberalisation Cited as Key Challenge in TFTA Negotiations", 6 February, Geneva.

Jackson, John H. (2000), *The World Trading System. Law and Policy of International Economic Relations.* Second Edition, Cambridge, Massachusetts and London: The MIT Press.

Luke, David and Zodwa Mabuza (2015), "The Tripartite Free Trade Area Agreement: A Milestone for Africa's Regional Integration Process?", *Bridges Africa* 4(6): 4–7, 6 July.

Maluwa, T. (2012). Ratification of African Union Treaties by Member States: Law, Policy and Practice. *Melbourne Journal of International Law, 13*, 1–49.

Meredith, M. (2013). *The State of Africa: A History of the Continent Since Independence.* Simon and Schuster.

Musila, J. W. (2005). The Intensity of Trade Creation and Trade Diversion in COMESA, ECCAS and ECOWAS: A Comparative Study. *Journal of African Economies, 14*(1), 117–141.

OAU (1999), *Sirte Declaration*, Fourth Extraordinary Session Of The Assembly Of Heads Of State And Government. 8–9 September, Sirte, Libya, Eahg/Draft/Decl. (Iv) Rev.1.

OAU (1991), *Treaty Establishing the African Economic Community.*

OAU (1980), *Lagos Plan of Action for the Economic Development of Africa 1980–2000.*

OAU (1979a), *Monrovia Declaration of Commitment of the Heads of State and Government, of the Organization of the African Unity on Guidelines and Measures for National and Collective Self-Reliance in Social and Economic Development for the Establishment of a New International Economic Order*, AHG7ST.3(XVI)Rev.1, Assembly of the Heads of State and Government, Sixteenth Ordinary Session, Monrovia, 17–20 July.

OAU (1979b), *Interim Report of the Secretary General on Development and Economic Integration of Africa*, Annex II, Doc CM/983(XXXIII).
OAU (1976), *Kinshasa Declaration*, adopted by the OAU Council of Ministers in December.
OAU (1974), *Constitution of the Association of African Trade Promotion Organizations*, OAU Doc CAB/LEG/23.2.
Páez, L. (2017). Bilateral Investment Treaties and Africa's Regional Integration: Towards and African Continental Investment Area. *Journal of World Investment and Trade, 18*(2017), 1–35.
Páez, L. (2011). *Liberalizing Financial Services and Foreign Direct Investment: Developing a Framework for Commercial Banking*. Palgrave Macmillan. http://www.palgrave.com/products/title.aspx?PID=412979
Please, S., & Amouako, K. Y. (1984). The World Bank's Report on Accelerated Development in Sub-Saharan Africa: A Critique of Some of the Criticism. *African Studies Review, 27*(4), 47–58.
Richmond, Edmun B. (1993), "Senegambia and the Confederation: History, Expectations, and Disillusions". *Journal of Third World Studies* 10 (2): 172–194 [p. 176].
Rostow, W. W. (1960). *The Stages of Economic Growth: A Non-Communist Manifesto*. Cambridge University Press.
Schiff, M. (1997). Small is beautiful: preferential trade agreements and the impact of country size, market share, and smuggling. *Journal of Economic Integration, 12*, 359–387.
Senghor, Jeggan (1993), "The Treaty Establishing the African Economic Community: An Introductory Essay", Abdulqawi. A. Yusuf (Eds.), *African Yearbook of International Law*, Vol I. pp. 183–194, Martinus Nijhoff Publishers.
Thorpe, T. (2012). The Rule of Law and the Implementation of an Economic Acquis Communautaire in Sub Saharan Africa: Legal Challenges for the East African Community. In C. Hermann & J. P. Terhechte (Eds.), *European Yearbook of International Economic Law 2012, Vol. 3*. Springer Verlag.
Tulya-Muhica, Sam (1996), "Creating and African Common Market", Tajudeen Abdul-Raheem (Eds.) *Pan-Africanism: politics, economics and social change in the Twenty-First Century*, pp.145–166, New York University Press, New York.
Trebilcock, M. J. (2011). *Understanding Trade Law*. Edward Elgar.
Trebilcock, Michael J., Robert Howse and Antonia Eliason (2013), *The Regulation of International Trade*, 4th ed., Routledge: London and New York.
UNCTAD. (2015). *Economic Development in Africa Report: Unlocking the Potential of Africa's Services Trade for Growth and Development*.
Viner, J. (1950). *The Customs Union Issue*. Carnegie Endowment for International Peace.

Yeats, A. (1998). *What can be expected from African regional trade arrangements? Some empirical evidence*. Mimeo.

Walters, R. W. (1993). *Pan Africanism in the African Diaspora*. Wayne State University Press.

World Bank. (1981). *Accelerated Development in Sub-Saharan Africa: an agenda for action*. World Bank. http://documents.worldbank.org/curated/en/1981/01/438047/accelerated-development-sub-saharan-africa-agenda-action

CHAPTER 3

An African Multistakeholder Participation Framework for the African Continental Free Trade Area

1 Introduction

The African Continental Free Trade Area (AfCFTA) is a pan-African regional integration initiative of the 54 member States of the African Union. Endorsed through the AU Summit of 2012, the AfCFTA builds on the Abuja Treaty of 1991; the navigation compass of modern African regional integration conceived by African political leaders at the time the Organization of African Unity was revitalized and rebranded as the Africa Union. With great ambition, the AfCFTA was expected to be launched by the tentative date of 2017, as a prior step to the creation of the pan-African Customs Union, as per the envisaged timelines of the Abuja Treaty. With some delay, the AfCFTA was born in 2018 (AU, 2018).

The research presented here seeks to shed light on the importance of an initial stage of negotiating regional trade agreements (RTAs), namely, national consultations involving the various stakeholders of an RTA. It further proposes a multistakeholder framework to facilitate engagement of these stakeholders. As such, the chapter is organized as follows: Section 2 provides the rationale and history of national consultations in Africa's regional integration process. Section 3 discusses some of emerging best African practices in national consultations for both regional and multilateral trade negotiations, followed by Sect. 4, which proposes a framework for multistakeholder participation for AfCFTA negotiations. Finally, Sect.

L. Páez, *The African Continental Free Trade Area*,
https://doi.org/10.1007/978-3-031-66605-6_3

5 draws conclusions and issues recommendations on how African countries may overcome the pitfalls of poor national consultations to ensure that the AfCFTA is conceived through a broad and representative participatory process, for the benefit of all Africans.

2 The Rationale and History of Trade Policy Consultations in Africa's Regional Integration Process

It is well established that international trade relations between nations are traditionally governed by trade agreements. (Jackson, 2000, pp. 25–28) These agreements are increasingly take the form of regional trade agreements (RTAs). These have arguably picked up in their numbers given the modest progress in multilateral trade negotiations under the WTO.

And though many of these RTAs make headlines when they are launched, most of them are negotiated behind closed doors. As is customary in today's world of international trade agreements, the outcome of these negotiations are generally made public once there is an agreement ready for signature.[1] This is one of the main reasons why RTAs often face stark opposition from the private sector and/or civil society organizations (CSOs), or even fail to be ratified, as was the case of the Economic Partnership Agreement (EPA) between West Africa and the EU in 2014. As will be discussed subsequently in the present chapter, adequate consultations did not prelude the EPA signature, which lead to its demise and rejection as well as a subsequent doubling of efforts for deeper consultations at national level in various ECOWAS member countries *ex post*.

A pertinent question that arises in this context is to what extent are the relevant stakeholders considered in the design of these types of agreements in Africa? What evidence exists in this regard on stakeholder participation influencing regional integration processes taking place on the continent? The present section looks at some of these issues in detail, prior

[1] Points in case are the current mega-regional agreements involving trading partners across continents, such as the Transatlantic Trade and Investment Partnership (TTIP), the Trade and Investment Agreement (TiSA) and Comprehensive and Progressive Agreement for Trans-Pacific Partnership (CPTPP), which are discussed in Chap. 8 of this book. Negotiations of these agreements are shrouded from the public eye, some of which have come under heavy scrutiny when the negotiating texts of these agreements are leaked (ICTSD, 2015).

exploring some of the experiences in the context of regional integration in Africa and prior making a case for multistakeholder consultations.

2.1 *Why Consultations Are Needed in Trade Negotiations*

In today's world of trade agreements, little attention is given to the process of consultations prior the negotiations and enactment of such agreements. Unfortunately, these agreements often only make headlines at the time they are signed and not whilst they are being negotiated. Indeed, little is known about the process which leads to their creation and which is presumed to involve a great deal of technical consultations. And yet, despite the little attention consultations receive, they are critical to trade negotiations.

From a trade negotiations perspective, where representatives of two governments may be engaged in a negotiations process, domestic consultations need to prelude actual negotiations. When governments take on the role of negotiators of trade agreements, they are doing so on behalf of their constituents. In today's evolving nature of trade diplomacy, it is impossible to ignore these constituents. Lee and Hocking (2010), argue that trade diplomacy needs rethinking given the rise in influence and role non-State actors play in the international trade arena. Therefore, trade diplomacy can no longer be viewed as a State-centric exercise involving on the State, as in earlier realist models explaining international trade relations.

Hence, multistakeholder consultations at national level need to take place even before the actual negotiation process starts. This is needed to help determine what it is that these stakeholders are willing to negotiate and eventually give up in return for something. Consultations are therefore a vital exchange process which will help establish negotiation priorities, address information asymmetries, define the potential zone of possible agreement or bargaining range, and ultimately determine the relative bargaining power of the negotiating counterparts.[2]

The idea of multistakeholder consultations in trade is not new. Notions of it were first developed by Putnam (1988), who described international economic negotiations as a two-level game where the first level entails international negotiations and the second level the domestic negotiation or bargaining between the domestic stakeholders of the negotiations outcome. Evans et al. (1993) complemented this notion by arguing that

[2] See Fisher and Ury (1983) for the various negotiation concepts.

legislators have a stake in this process and indirectly, so do their constituencies (i.e. civil society). This concept has been further expounded through contributions by Stairs (2000), and notably Hocking (2004), who coined the term by distinguishing the three levels of a trade consultation process, namely a first level or club model of trade policy making which transpires at government level, as initially suggested by Keohane and Nye (2000); a second level, under the adaptive club model which envisages a business-focused consultation, and lastly a third level which entails a mixed mode consultation under the multistakeholder model.

From a development perspective, the absence of multistakeholder consultations in trade negotiations processes is not desirable, for several reasons. First, the expected beneficiaries or "stakeholders" of trade agreements such as RTAs are deemed to be the nationals of the countries that negotiate them and not necessarily those government agents who negotiate on their behalf. These stakeholders may be grouped into producers and traders, be represented by a civil society group or apex body or simply be the average citizen or consumer of that which is being trade under the agreement. The benefits that accrue from a trade agreement are thus not exclusive of the State, and even though State actors are traditionally signatories of these agreements, they do so on behalf of these stakeholders. However, these stated benefits often remain elusive to the stakeholders and this has to do with the fact that gains and losses are often diffused across a wide constituency and are therefore difficult to capture. The State has therefore the responsibility to capture the views and aspirations of its citizens pertaining to these agreements before they are negotiated and to take account of them in their negotiating position.

Second, many RTAs also embody major development objectives in their constitutive agreement. These agreements often make explicit reference to development outcomes which target these stakeholders and which are expected from the realization of these RTAs, such as "economic growth and development", "poverty reduction" or "employment creation". Hence, stakeholders that are the potential and direct beneficiaries of these objectives need to be involved early on in the formulation stage of these agreements. In Africa, various RECs protocols establishing RTAs make allusion to one or a combination of these expected development outcomes.[3]

[3] For example, Art. 3 of the Treaty establishing the COMESA refers to the objectives of attaining "economic growth and development" through the common market and Art. 4 of the Protocol establishing the EAC Common market refers to "accelerating growth and development" in the EAC region.

Third, because the beneficiaries of these agreements are the citizens and the various sectors or groupings they embody, the success of these RTAs is dependent on the ability of its stakeholders to harness these agreements. Therefore, the absence of consultations with these stakeholders will render a suboptimal outcome and a possible disconnect between what has been agreed and what may indeed be instrumental for these stakeholders to take advantage of the preferences in these agreements.

Fourth, an important constraint to striking a deal through trade negotiations is the high transaction costs of information due to information asymmetries and distance from markets. Export markets are by definition opaque and given the distance to these markets, may bare many information asymmetries, which in themselves may also constitute non-tariff barriers to trade. Some of the transaction costs posed by information asymmetries may be eliminated through consultations and clarify information and communication gaps, which in turn may help stakeholders make better use of these agreements to know their prospective and potential markets. Consultations are a necessary instrument to collect information on what the defensive and offensive interests may be, as well as for identifying opportunities to add value to negotiations.

Fifth, because trade negotiations in the context of RTAs are increasingly cross-sectoral, and may integrate various disciplines,[4] it is more difficult to determine what the zone of possible agreement (or bargaining range) may be. For example, many RTAs being negotiated today go beyond the negotiation of trade in goods and also incorporate trade in services, as well as other disciplines, such as intellectual property, investment and competition, among others. This expansion of the trade agenda also implicitly entails and expansion of stakeholders which will need to be consulted.

But even the simplest of RTAs focusing only on trade in goods will entail negotiations on various complex issues such as tariffs, most-favored nation treatment, rules of origin, special safeguards and countervailing measures. Setting the "reservation price" or bottom threshold for tariffs alone will require consultations with at least the exporters and importers of various trading sectors, as these are not likely to agree on a tariff level *ex ante*. Take the textile sector in a given country for example. A cloth producer from country A who seeks to increase exports under an RTA being

[4] See for instance the allusions made to "trade *and*" or WTO+ agreements made in Chap. 8, Sect. 2.

negotiated will be motivated to gain access to country's B textile market at the lowest possible tariff and may have no objection in reducing the existing import tariff of their country (A) in return. An importer from the same country who supplies the local garment industry will lobby for the exact opposite, namely maintaining the highest possible import tariff in country A, so that his domestic market remains protected from foreign competitors of country B. Consumers of textile products in country A will naturally side with the exporters, if lowering the import tariff also translates into lower prices of textile products in the domestic market. Environmentalists, however, may make a case for raising the tariff of textile imports from country B, arguing that the carbon footprint of such imports is too high, especially given the transport conditions. In turn, human rights groups may lobby against the exporters suggestion as this will exacerbate the dire conditions of domestic textile workers and engender the proliferation of sweatshop industries which exploit them.

Sixth, given the complexity of negotiating RTAs, it is important to be able to explore integrative negotiations solutions. The hypothetical example of the textile sector above clearly puts in evidence the monumental task trade negotiators have in trying to bridge to the various and conflicting interests. More importantly, it also exposes the limitations to finding a negotiated solution through distributive bargaining, as opposed to integrative bargaining.[5] But integrative bargaining solutions may not be known to negotiators *ex ante*, as they are determined by the priorities and preferences of the various stakeholders described earlier. Consultations are instrumental in such cases because they are processes where information is exchanged, allowing negotiators to understand the priorities and preferences of stakeholders and where these may potentially converge or conflict.

Seven, when consultations are undertaken in a broad-based manner and considering the various stakeholders, negotiating solutions may be more easily exposed, as stakeholders will naturally set their own bargaining limits. In a sense, multistakeholder consultations are a prelude to negotiations vis-à-vis the negotiations counterpart, in that they help prioritize the various and sometimes conflicting interest that may exist at national level.[6]

[5] Distributive bargaining presupposes a zero sum-game outcome, where the loss of one party becomes the gain of the other party. This gives rise to a prisoner's dilemma and opportunistic behaviour. Integrative bargaining supposes that what is being negotiated is not finite and can be expanded (Fisher & Ury, 1983).

[6] Evans et al. (1993) argued that negotiations entail a 'double-edged diplomacy', with bargaining first taking place domestically with domestic interest groups prior undertaking negotiations at the international level.

Hence, consultations are also critical to understand what forces may be at play and what impact a certain negotiating position may have on the whole stakeholder group and whose best interest it may serve.

But consultations are often criticized for adding to the complexity of trade negotiations. (e.g. Capling & Low, 2010, p. 7) Furthermore, though consultations may serve as a platform for various stakeholders to voice their concerns, these may ultimately not garner the desired change or influence trade policy outcome. Dür and De Bièvre (2007) In order for consultations to work they need to render an *efficient* and *effective* negotiations outcome.

In the case of RTAs, because these are trade agreements which are preferential, they may garner some form of trade protection (e.g. tariffs and quotas) which distort the gains from trade. It is important therefore to ascertain what trade distortions an outcome may bring and to which stakeholder group in an RTA. Consultations that lead to choosing the least distorting trade protection outcome (and where economic gains from trade may be maximized for the largest common denominator of stakeholders) would be considered *efficient*. In turn, an *effective* outcome will be the one where the consultation process is broad-based and representative of the stakeholder sample. In most cases, it is virtually impossible to obtain both an *efficient* and *effective* outcome through negotiations. Various stakeholder groups have different lobbying setups and relative bargaining power and this has a bearing on negotiation outcomes. For example, groups which are more fragmented and where the gains from trade are generally more diffused among a larger set of beneficiaries tend to have weaker influence over the outcome, as is the case of consumers.[7]

On the other hand, sectors which tend to be more concentrated and organized are the exporters and/or importers through trade unions and other umbrella organizations and, depending on their setup these generally have access to government through more formal consultation and may even count with lobbying clout to promote their sectoral interests.

Interestingly, and perhaps because of this bias, other organized groups from civil society have become very active in recent years. Civil society organizations (CSO) have been on the rise in the trade arena and represent a plethora of interests, including environment, human rights, worker

[7] There is ample literature explaining the forces underpinning policy outcomes based on diffusion and concentration of interests in consultative processes. See for example Lohmann (1998) and Bailey (2001).

rights, religion, and gender just to name some. These have increasingly become vocal through mobilization and advocacy work in the field of trade policy, given the expansion of the trade policy agenda. (Capling & Low, 2010, p. 6) At multilateral level, this has perhaps most been felt in the context of the World Trade Organization's Third Ministerial Conference which took place in 1999 in Seattle and which almost came to a halt due to street protests and large-scale of CSOs.[8]

Lastly, a major critique that is often made in conjunction with such groups is that they often fostering demands which are too distant or difficult to bridge with what may be achievable through a trade agreement, and the related concern that consultations with them may bog down or even halt negotiations processes (e.g. Weston, 2005). Nonetheless, consultations also serve an ulterior and perhaps more important motive. They bring a sense of ownership to the negotiations process and its ultimate outcome. More often than not, trade deals tend to fall through the cracks because of the absence of ownership. Various assessments such as those by Ostry (2002) and Hocking (2004) underscore the additional benefits of consultations in terms of legitimizing the process of trade policy formulation, promoting transparency and further guaranteeing social cohesion and support to a trade agenda. This will further reduce the likelihood of a trade agreement getting stuck at an ulterior ratification or implementation stage, and/or being the target of heated critique, as was the case of the NAFTA negotiations. (Duina, 2006, pp. 39–40 and 122–123) and this agreement's subsequent demise.

2.2 *Evolution of Multistakeholder Consultations on Africa's Regional (Trade) Integration*

In the African context, there is no documentary evidence of multistakeholder consultations having taking place in Africa's first phase of regional integration, under the aegis of the OAU and later in its second phase also under the Lagos Plan of Action. Regional integration in Africa in the two decades that followed independence was an exercise conducted at the highest political level, where Heads of State and government took the front stage of consultations and negotiations. As Harsch (2002a) noted, at

[8] It should however be noted that evidence of CSO engagement since the Tokyo Round in the 1970s, which predated the Seattle Ministerial, through formal participation of trade unions (Pérez-Esteve, 2010).

the time these frameworks were negotiated, they tended to emphasize the preponderance of the State.[9]

The Abuja Treaty, which is the cornerstone of Africa's regional integration today and the basis for virtually all of the existing African RTAs discussed earlier in the previous chapter of this book, did not envisage consultations with the various stakeholders at national level. At the time the treaty was negotiated, as State-centric model prevailed, characterized by the reaffirmation and legitimization of the role of the nascent African States post-independence. The Treaty indeed gave the State a stellar role in shaping Africa's regional integration process, though a gradual shift from the political realm to more economical and developmental motivated rationales.

An initial attempt to formally integrate consultations with non-State actors in the regional integration process materialized under the aegis of the Constitutive Act of the Africa Union of 2000. Civil society at the time had become vocal, pointing to their exclusion from regional integration processes. Indeed, the rebranding of the AU also responded to the loss of political credibility of the OAU. The inclusion of two organs in the newly created AU structure was deemed to cater for consultation mechanisms in the process of designing regional integration strategies and programmes. (Harsch, 2002b) With the creation of the Pan-African Parliament (and the Economic, Social and Cultural Council, as per Art. 5 of the *Constitutive Act of the Africa Union* (AU, 2000) formal mechanisms to consult with civil society were created.

Though initially suggested as a Pan-African organ in the Abuja Treaty (OAU, 1991, Art. 7), it was not until 2004 that the Parliament came into effect, and in 2014 its Protocol was adopted. (AU, 2014) Members of Parliament are elected through the legislative bodies of member States across Africa. With a formal Committee dealing with Trade, Customs and Immigration Matters, African citizens are indirectly represented through these parliamentarians when consultations on trade policy take place.

A more direct form of consultation with civil society was envisage through the Economic, Social and Cultural Council (ECOSOCC), which is composed of over 150 CSOs representing diverse social and professional groups of African member States, as per its Statutes (AU, 2004). The first

[9] This was also a deliberate focus of the recent independence processes many nascent States had recently experienced, as a means for them to assert themselves in their new roles as State actors. See also discussion in Chap. 2, Sect. 2.1.

General Assembly of this organ, which is the principal consultation forum, took place in 2008 and gave life to formal consultations that contribute to AU policymaking processes. Of the ten Sectoral Cluster Committees which conform ECOSOCC, a dedicated Committee deals with issues of trade and industry. The ECOSOCC recently became active in 2015 on trade policy matters through its secretariat, the Civil Society and Diaspora Department (CIDO) of the AU Commission, which hosted its Fourth Annual African CSO Continental Forum on the issue of a Joint Africa EU Partnership Strategy (JAES). Though this initiative is indeed a step forward towards continental CSO mobilization on African trade policy, this mechanism also appears to face major challenges in terms of financing and capacity constraints, given the slow progress to the date in hosting the envisaged yearly Joint Annual Forum (JAF) which is deemed to inform the Africa-EU dialogue on the EPAs (AU, 2015b).

Other notable efforts to engage with civil society at pan-Africa level, have been in the context of the UN Economic Commission for Africa (ECA). For example the Third African Development Forum in 2002 hosted in Addis Ababa on the theme "Defining Priorities for Regional Integration" (Harsch, 2002a), the Highly Level Symposium on Regional Integration in 2011 focusing on the role civil society should play in Africa's regional integration, and lastly, the mobibilization of Africa's civil society and parlamentarians in the context of the African Trade Forum in 2011 and 2013 which also has served as a platform for civil society to channel their contributions to the process of Boosting of Intra African Trade and establishing the AfCFTA.[10]

In light of the above, and given the relatively recent incorporation of formal consultation processes with African stakeholders in the African Union context, it follows that the resulting treaty work instituting RECs based on the Abuja Treaty did not envisage consultation processes around the time they were negotiated. However, in recognition of this omission, newer generation RTAs resulting from some of these RECs have gradually incorporated consultation mechanisms, notably with business sector organizations, such as the COMESA Business Council and the East Africa

[10] Indeed, the Architecture for the Continental Free Trade Area adopted by the aforementioned AU Summit took due cognizance of this initiative by including the ATF and an African Business Council as part of their governance structures, as discussed earlier in Chap. 2. Their contribution has been acknowledged in the HATC report (AU, 2012) and the intention to include these sectors in the CFTA process (AU, 2015b).

Business Council and the SADC region has the Association of SADC Chambers of Commerce and Industry (ASCCI). All are very active and contribute to their regional trade policymaking processes in their respective RECs through formal consultation channels.

In contrast, ECOWAS has taken a slightly different approach, instituting formal channels for consultation with CSOs through regulation, which enables it to approve the granting of observer status to CSOs and which in 2000 accorded the African Business Roundtable with observer status (ECOWAS, 1994, 2000), providing a channel for this organization to contribute in policymaking processes of ECOWAS. Other efforts to engage with civil society have been in the context of convening CSOs through similar structures to those of the AU, namely an ECOWAS Parliament and an ECOWAS ECOSOCC (ECOWAS, 2023).

In the ECCAS region, efforts to formalize the exchanges with civil society have slowly taken shape, with the hosting of a Regional Forum of Civil Society in Central Africa in 2015. This was established mainly through a network of NGOs known as the Réseau de Plate-formes Nationales d'ONG de l'Afrique Centrale (REPONGAC) which groups 1200 NGOs in Central Africa which have engaged with the ECCAS authorities to establish a platform for dialogue on regional integration policymaking processes within ECCAS as well as the Economic and Monetary Community of Central Africa (CEMAC) (REPONGAC, 2015).

Parliamentary consultations have also gradually taken shape at the regional level. As noted earlier, the ECOWAS has a Parliament, the SADC a Parliamentary Forum, and the EAC has its East African Legislative Assembly. Though these are avenues for civil society engagement, members of these parliaments are not elected by African citizens on the basis of universal and direct elections. Rather, they assume their functions on appointment or through elections by their national parliaments. In addition, some of these organs do not officially report to REC decision-making bodies hence the level of influencing in policymaking is rather limited. Another initiative to develop a legislative body is the IGAD Inter-Parliamentary Union, initially established in 2008 to promoyr popular participation in decision making of the IGAD goals (Weldesellassie, 2011).

It should be noted that some of these consultation mechanisms within RECs have been gradually incorporated in the context of implementing already existing RTAs or built-in elements of their liberalization programmes. Hence, consultations have tended to focus on *ex post* contributions after an RTA has been launched, rather than on substantive consultations on the design, governance and purpose of these agreements prior negotiations.

This too is the case of the EAC Common Market Protocol which envisages the movement of persons and labor. In order for EAC citizens to enjoy this freedom, the protocol contains provisions committing member States to undertake the mutual recognition of academic and professional qualifications (EAC, 2010, Art. 11 and Annex VI). Work towards achieving this commitment has included regular consultations with business sector representatives of the EABC through its East African Professional Services Platform (EAPSP) and professional regulatory bodies to develop adequate benchmarks for the recognition of foreign academic and professional qualifications that would set the basis for Mutual Recognition Agreements (MRAs). This has subsequently led to signing of mutual recognition agreements (MRAs) in various professional services disciplines, such as architecture, accounting and engineering. Further consultations have also been hosted to sensitize the various stakeholders and further facilitate uptake of the benefits of these MRAs, such as the EAC Forum on Mutual Recognition Agreements for Professional Services in 2013 and the Regional Training Workshop on the Mutual Recognition Agreement for Engineering Professionals in the EAC in 2014 (EABC, 2014a, 2014b).

Another related example is the recent mobilization of the private sector to host a consultation on the Tripartite FTA, only after this FTA was launched in 2015.[11] The Inaugural Tripartite Regional Dialogue was held under the theme: "Harmonizing and developing a private sector position on TFTA Rules of Origin for Increased Market Access". Hosted in February 2016, it brought together, the various business councils of the RECs mentioned earlier. (EABC, 2015) Despite this laudable effort, an overall major critique that followed has been the absence of civil society participation in the lead-up to the Tripartite FTA (Andriamananjara, 2015).

As noted in the previous section on the increased activity of non-State actors in the field of trade policy, Africa has not been an exception to this trend. Several pan-African, regional and national groupings have risen with a focus on issues of trade integration, and are very active in African trade policymaking. However, certain interest groups have been arguably more successful than others in influencing the trade agenda. Traditionally,

[11] This is not to say that consultations with private sector representatives *within* individual RECs did not take place prior the launch of the TFTA, as is later discussed in the case of educational services in the EAC region in Sect. 3.2 of this Chapter.

these have been the various stakeholders of the private sector. Indeed, "second level" consultative processes are more established in Africa, both at national and regional level in consonance the practice in many developing countries, as described in the previous paragraphs and observed by Capling and Low (2010, p. 8).

For example, in addition to the regional business councils, other regional institutions such as the Pan-African Chamber of Commerce and the African Business Roundtable also represent the interests of the private sector and regularly take part in regional policymaking events. Regional sectoral organizations are also very engaged in such consultation processes, such as the African Shippers Council, on issues of trade and transport facilitation affecting their private operators, and the African Alliance for E-Commerce, which represents various single window operators in Africa.

Other non-State actors, notably regional CSOs representing the various interests of civil society have also been on the rise, though arguably with more limited capabilities and resources than the private sector in influencing trade policy. Various regional think tanks have emerged and contribute to the trade policy debate, notably the African Economic Research Consortium (AERC), the African Capacity Building Foundation (ACBF), the Trade Policy Training Centre in Africa (TRAPCA) and Trade Law Centre for Southern Africa (TRALAC). These are some of the institutions active in the realm of trade policy analysis, research, advocacy and capacity building which further also liaise with African academic networks as well as the government to promote further research and capacity building on trade issues.

At this point, it is important to say that various other groups have also become very vocal on trade policy issues, across Africa. However, attempting to list the major groupings would not do justice to the myriad of CSOs and other non-State actors, that also operate at country and grassroots level, and which may not be as visible as their regional counterparts.

In conclusion, it becomes apparent that Africa's regional integration process has been gradually exposed to various stakeholder consultation processes in recent years, mainly with the business sector, but also increasingly with other non-State actors. From the evidence presented in this section, the emphasis of multistakeholder consultations has been on establishing formal mechanisms and platforms for consultation, both at pan-African and REC level. Though civil society mobilization around broad issues of regional integration, the EPAs and trade liberalization is on the rise, these efforts are yet to be assessed in terms of influencing trade policymaking at the regional level. This is very critical to gain an understanding of the composite experiences and best practices, with a view to understand how they may themselves support and shape AfCFTA consultations processes in the future.

3 African Experiences and Impact of National Consultations on Trade Negotiations

A major concern in the literature on civil society participation in trade policy processes is whether non-State actors such as the private sector and CSOs have an influence in trade policy outcomes. An overall critique which prevails when discussing the impact of such groupings is the lack of clarity of whom they represent, what their ultimate purpose is and whether they may have any impact, even if formal mechanisms to voice their positions do exist. Research in this regard points to mixed results of CSOs influencing trade policy, even in instances where formal channels to lobby government do exist.

There is ample literature documenting consultation experiences of countries in the context of RTAs negotiations. Though Africa has had relatively more recent exposure to such consultation processes, there is already an accumulated set of experiences worthy of deeper analysis. Some of these experiences have been painful learning processes, whilst others have crystalized as laudable examples of consultation for trade policy and trade negotiations, which could arguably be replicated within the continent given their effectiveness in influencing trade policymaking from the bottom up. The present section reviews some of these experiences, reflecting on their process and impact.

3.1 *Impact of Multistakeholder Trade Policy Consultations in Africa: Evidence from the EPAs*

Most of the literature on trade policy consultations in Africa naturally revolves around a set of agreements which engage Africa with the European Union (EU), namely the Economic Partnership Agreements.[12] Since virtually all African countries have been engaged in the negotiations on EPAs

[12] See Chap. 8 which discusses some of the issues of EPAs affecting Africa, as well as the current status quo of EPAs across African countries and regions.

with the EU and there is cumulative experience with these negotiations, it is worthwhile assessing whether these processes have envisaged multi-stakeholder consultations and whether such consultations have had a discernible impact on the outcome of these negotiations.

Civil society participation figures as part of the negotiations mandate of the EU. With the establishment of a formal mechanism known as the Civil Society Dialogue originating in 1998, the EU engages with CSOs of its internal market on various issues, including the EPAs. Dür and De Bièvre (2007) point out that in the context of EPAs negotiations, though NGOs have been able to formally voice their positions to trade policy makers, they have not been successful in influencing policy outcomes in their favor. They argue that the lack of influence stems from the fact that these groups have diffused costs and benefits from trade policy and unlike business lobbies, the representative of these groups may not have an actual stake in such negotiations nor enjoy political backing or lobbying power. This is compounded by the fact that the formal consultation mechanisms that exist are either influenced or vetted by the EU and hence resulting in biased outcomes, as Hurt et al. (2013) and Iheduru (2015) expose. This sheds light on the conflict of interest of EU financing in the engagement of these groups.

This contrasts with Ngethe and Olomo (2010, pp. 228–233), who argue that in the particular case of Kenyan trade policy, civil society has been most successful in influencing the government into not signing the EPA in the past, albeit with the financing support of the EU.[13] Thanks to the establishment of a mechanism for formal consultation under the Ministry of Trade, known and KEPLOTRADE in 2001, Kenya develops national positions on EPAs through stakeholder consultations. Another major determinant reported in the success of non-State actors influencing trade policy processes in Kenya relates to the various mechanisms they use to voice their stance, including but not limited to participating in meetings hosted by the government, self-initiated interaction with government, publishing or broadcasting material and public campaigning. Some of these actors (notably business sector representatives) also form part of the negotiating team. This is contrasted with the less successful and fewer consultations on multilateral trade issues, which tend to receive less

[13] With the recent signing of the EU-Kenya EPA in December 2023, this argument no longer holds.

attention from the public compared to regional issues and which do not count with adequate funding.

Another example from the recent past in this regard has been the mobilization around the ECOWAS EPA, which was deemed to be signed by the 15 governments of the ECOWAS member States in 2014 and which had taken 12 years to negotiate. At the eve of the signature of the agreement during the ECOWAS 44th Heads of State summit, Nigeria and some other member States, raised technical issues[14] with the agreement and decided to officially postpone the signature. A Communiqué to that effect was issued, instructing the Chief Negotiators to establish a technical committee to undertake more exhaustive consultations with representatives of Nigeria, Ghana, Senegal and Côte d'Ivoire (ECOWAS, 2014a, para. 18) To the date, such issues have not been fully resolved and some countries have signed interim EPAs bilaterally with the EU, as is discussed in Chap. 8 of this book.

In several West African countries there has been vehement opposition by various civil society groups and business groups to the signing of this agreement (Modern Ghana, 2014; Iheduru, 2015). Nzewi (2009) argues that despite the various mobilization efforts, there has been hardly any impact of CSOs on ECOWAS's work, and notes that the efforts of ECOWAS in establishing formal channels for consultation are yet to be harnessed by these groups. Indeed, the Nigerian Federal Ministry of Trade and Industry (2014) only documents consultations with the private sector, as exemplified by a statement after the postponement of the EPA signature. Iheduru (2015) further argues that this has been the only sector effectively being able to influence the EPAs negotiations in the ECOWAS region, largely also due to an inherent fragmentation among the various CSOs which are unable to raise a unified voice against the EPAs. Indeed, once the technical issues had been resolved, the subsequent 45th ECOWAS Summit endorsed the agreement and instructed the signature and implementation the EPA, whilst encouraging the chief negotiators to "sustain

[14] The technical issues related to confluence of trade adjustment costs which the concurrent entry into force of the ECOWAS CET in January 1 2015 and the EPAs would have implied for the ECOWAS business sector. In particular for Nigeria, which has an industrial and transformation policy that is inconsistent with the CET and is facing additional pressures from informal trade from its neighbours, this would have been unmanageable. In addition, the market access offer would have eliminated the prospect of grooming certain industries as they would have had to compete with European products (Iheduru, 2015; CTA Agritrade, 2014).

their efforts" to inform and raise awareness among the national and regional actors (ECOWAS, 2014b, para. 16–18).

Hurt et al. (2013) support the notion of positive influencing by providing evidence at regional level of how African negotiators have been able to build their argumentative capacity against signing the EPAs thanks to the vocalism, mobilization and campaigning of CSOs both in Europe and Africa. This activism has translated into a deferral of signing EPAs in most subregions, as well as a more nuanced position of African negotiators vis-à-vis the EPAs.

Draper et al. (2010, pp. 277–278) note that in the context of Southern Africa EPA negotiations, civil society positions were taken seriously by government, though arguably, the space CSOs are afforded to consult and influence the government is much more limited and less transparent when compared to consultations on multilateral trade issues, with a certain preference for consulting certain established business groups on an ad-hoc basis rather than through an established process. This is further compounded by the fact that traditionally, consultations with the business sector in South Africa have been behind closed doors and often only focused on developing a defensive position around the interests of the business sector Draper (2007, pp. 260–261).

At regional level, the AU Commission has also hosted regular EPA negotiations coordination meetings to ensure trade policy coherence and developing common positions on the issues of EPAs through the RECs, as per a mandate it received from its Heads of State. (AU, 2003, para. 8) CSOs have been part and parcel of these meetings.[15] An important level of influencing may be discerned as the outcome of these meetings has fed into pan-African trade policy processes, notably through the Conference of Ministers of Trade, which have endorsed various decisions as well as a Common Position on the EPAs in 2010, which informed the Africa-EU Summit hosted in Libya later that year. (AU, 2010, para. 10) Notably, in

[15] For example, in the EPA Coordination meetings held in Gaborone in 2009 and Abuja in 2010, CSOs such as the National Association of Nigerian Traders (NANTS), Third World Network (TWN), International Lawyers and Economists Against Poverty (ILEAP), South Centre and European Centre for Development Policy Management (ECDPM) were present. Some of these CSOs are known for their trade advocacy and trade policy discourse, as exemplified by their various position papers and materials, as well as participation in various trade policy forums, notably in Geneva and Brussels, which are recognized centres of trade diplomacy.

the common position, one of the options discussed was that of not signing EPAs, which is the known stance of many CSOs vis-à-vis the EPAs.[16]

In conclusion, the discussed literature exposes mixed results in terms of non-State actors influencing trade policy processes in the context of EPA negotiations in Africa. In the instances where there has been an impact, what appears to be evident is that where some consultation mechanism is in place, and when there is a strong public opinion and sense of proximity to the subject by the African constituents they represent, CSOs and the private sector appear to be actively engaged. Furthermore, CSOs resort to various methods for influencing trade policy processes beyond consultation, ranging from campaigning and mobilization to being part of the negotiating team. Successful mobilization of CSOs together with consultation appears to translate into "uptake" of their views or positions by policymakers through the channels of established trade policymaking processes, as exemplified by the Kenyan and African Union examples discussed earlier.

3.2 Towards Emerging Best Practices for Trade Policy Consultations in Africa

Having reviewed some of the literature and evidence on the impact and capability of trade policy influencing on behalf of civil society in Africa, this chapter now looks at some of the consultation experiences which have worked and may be considered as emerging best practices in terms of influencing trade policymaking from the bottom-up.

A crucial question for multistakeholder consultation is what makes certain consultations best practice versus others? As discussed earlier in Sect. 1, an *effective* negotiations outcome will be the one where the consultation process is broad-based and representative. But effectiveness also requires exhaustiveness of action, meaning a causal effect may be established between a given action (i.e. broad-based and representative consultations) and an outcome (i.e. trade policy position). Hence, from a process perspective, multistakeholder consultations need to precede negotiations in order to be *effective* and translate into trade policy actions.[17] Some

[16] Please also see the associated discussion on AU positions in EPAs Chap. 8, Sect. 4.

[17] See associated discussion on trade policy disconnects and the importance of adequate policy mapping prior negotiations in Chap. 4, Sect. 4.

degree of influencing from the "bottom-up" prior actual negotiations needs to take place in order to ensure uptake through the channels of established trade policymaking processes. It is important to note that though a policy process may not render the outcome stakeholders expect, the fact that their input was considered and taken into account in trade policy processes is critical for validation and uptake at the broadest level once a decision has been formalized. This is necessary for the survival and implementation of any trade agreement.

An example of a poor practice is what happened with the Morocco-US FTA, which suffered from poor implementation precisely because its major stakeholders were neither involved in the consultations or subsequent negotiations phase of the agreement. The Morocco-US FTA, which came into force in 2006 has been criticized for its lackluster performance in terms of promoting Moroccan exports to the US, at the time when US exports to Morocco under this agreement boomed. Among the reasons cited for US's success has been the ability of the private sector to engage and prepare through its business networks, well before the agreement entered into force. (Hufbauer & Brunel, 2009, pp. 238–239) Hence, there was willingness for uptake of the agreement's entry into force because it was co-developed by US stakeholders, enabling them to take advantage of the existing preferences contained in this FTA, unlike Moroccan stakeholders of the agreement, who criticized the absence of business support structures and promotion of trade and investment opportunities in the context of this FTA.[18]

The preceding sections of this chapter made one thing very clear: trade policy negotiations are multi-level and multi-faceted processes where negotiators engage to exchange requests and offers on the basis of their needs and objectives. Especially when regional trade negotiations beyond trade in goods are envisaged, the level of complexity in this exchange tends to increase as a function of the number of disciplines and stakeholders within that discipline.

A noticeable experience of consultations at the national level being tailored to match the increased level of complexity is the negotiations of Ugandan educational services in the context of services trade liberalization

[18] This critique has been later corroborated when it comes to assessing the impact of the agreement on Moroccan stakeholders. The expected benefits have not fully materialized as empirical evidence discussed in Chap. 8, Sect. 4 suggests.

within the East African Community. In recent years, has become a successful exporter of higher educational services in the East African region. (Othieno & Mampewo, 2012) The EAC Common Market Protocol (EAC, 2010, Annex V), lists educational services as one of the seven priority services sectors to be liberalized. The implementation of the Protocol requires the negotiations of commitments in the services sector. In preparation for this, the Ugandan government has been actively seeking out the council and engagement of the stakeholders in this sector through its Inter Institutional Trade Committee (IITC), which is part of the Ministry of Trade Tourism and Industry (MTTI) and was established in early 2000, as a multistakeholder consultation structure. A reporting structure has been set up through the IITC which prioritizes trade policymaking at the highest level, as the outcome of IITC discussions are then passed on to the president's office and parliament for subsequent approval and adoption. (Kiuluku & Chekwoti, 2012) The IITC also sources trade information and intelligence from business organizations, such as the Uganda Services Exporters' Association, which also forms integral part of its Trade in Services Working Group. Consultations with this association on educational services have led to the formulation of a position and defining of market access commitments for the negotiations of educational services under the EAC and COMESA services negotiations (Walumbisi-Mpanga, 2006; Stephenson & Walusimbi-Mpanga, 2015).

At the regional level, a consultation process worthwhile noting is in the context of preparations for the COMESA-EAC-SADC Tripartite tariff negotiations. In Eastern Africa, the EABC conducted a study and mobilized and consulted its constituencies to develop a position reflective of the EAC private sector for these negotiations. The council also attended meetings of the EAC Tripartite Technical Working Group on Tariff Liberalization, engaging with EAC officials to define viable tariff line offers for the envisaged tariff negotiations with COMESA and SADC counterparts. This working group also communicated its position to EAC negotiators on the eve of the negotiations of the 6th COMESA-EAC-SADC Tripartite Trade Negotiations Forum, who subsequently took this information into account during negotiations (EABC, 2013a, 2013b).

Another regional experience involves the development of the ECOWAS Agricultural Policy (ECOWAP) which was adopted in 2005 and which is the regional policy to operationalize the Comprehensive Africa Agriculture

Development Programme (CAADP) in the West African region.[19] In order to implement the ECOWAP, a Regional Agricultural Investment Plan (RAIP) has been developed, which envisages an important component of national, regional and international trade, through the development of agricultural value chains, hence the relevance of this example from trade policymaking. The Process of developing and adopting the RAIP involved broad-based consultations, engaging representatives of professional agricultural organizations, as well as civil society and the private sector, who together with the ECOWAS authorities signed a compact in 2009 for this purpose.[20] In an evaluation of this process, it was determined that it had undertaken broad-based consultations as well as endorsement and validation elements at the highest political level, with the signing of the compact (AU/NEPAD, 2013, pp. 5–6).

Some of the common characteristics that are shared by the consultation examples above, which appear to lead to successful uptake of trade policy negotiations include: (1) A formal consultation mechanism is in place or is instituted for the purpose of consultation, which is hosted by a government agency or body dealing with trade negotiation issues. The mechanism or figure is composed by government officials, trade negotiators, the business sector and representatives of civil society; (2) Consultation processes are preceded and supported by underlying studies or other support material to inform the consultation sessions. A considerably amount of "trade intelligence" and information is prepared or drawn from the industry players or stakeholders themselves; (3) The consultation process itself is on the basis of consensus, stakeholders have a vote and/or validate or vet the outcome; (4) the outcome of consultations is formulated as clear priorities or objectives, negotiating positions or programme of action; (5) the outcome of the consultations are shared with the highest level of government and put forth for consideration and approval, legitimizing the content of consultation and relaying it to the relevant channels for uptake.

[19] The CAADP is a pan-African programme for the development of the agricultural sector across Africa. It is one of the pillars of the New Economic Partnership for Africa's Development (NEPAD), spearheaded by the AU as a strategic framework for Africa's socio-economic development.

[20] These organizations were: Network of Farmers and Agricultural Producers Organizations (ROPPA), the West Africa Network of Economics Journalists and West African Platform of Civil society organizations (WANEJ/POSCAO) and the Network of African Chambers of Commerce (RECAO). See (ECOWAS, 2009).

Though these are examples of some of the positive consultation experiences in Africa, it is also important to highlight the inherent and perceived weaknesses the existing mechanisms portray. A study conducted by CUTS (2009) on the inclusiveness of such consultations across five African countries established that though consultation processes in Uganda, Tanzania, Zambia and Kenya reveal above average inclusiveness in terms of participatory engagement in trade policy making, these processes still suffer from human and financial capacity constraints. Furthermore, these countries appear to encounter limitations in terms of lack of trust in the consultative process, insufficient outreach to CSOs and a good understanding of trade issues on behalf of CSOs.

In conclusion, it does not suffice to have a consultation mechanism in place. It is important to also consider how to improve and facilitate the mechanism's inclusiveness, so that it becomes a true representation of the universe of stakeholders and their abilities to advocate for themselves. This implies that such mechanisms may have to be adequately and sustainably sourced with financial and human resources in order to support consultation processes. In addition, they will need to have regular informative and outreach activities to engage with their various stakeholders. Lastly, these mechanisms must also enjoy a certain degree of independence and the outcomes be enforced so as to gain legitimacy as entry points for civil society engagement in trade policy processes.

4 Towards a Multistakeholder Framework for the AfCFTA

As Africa has embarked in one of the most ambitious regional integration projects: a continental free trade area (AfCFTA). It is important to consider what role national consultations have had in the past for the 54 member States undertaking trade negotiations, and how these experiences may have been useful in shaping national trade policy positions.

From the various examples and experiences discussed in the previous sections of this chapter, and given the emerging best practices on the continent, it becomes apparent that consultations in trade policy formulation and negotiations are a prerogative for the AfCFTA. Furthermore, the AfCFTA structures incorporate formal consultation mechanisms in its governance structure, in the form of the ATF, which was envisioned as a consultation platform with civil society, but also the African Business Council, which is the continent-wide apex of the private sector.[21]

More generally, broad-based discussions need to feed into the consultation process so that the various stakeholders and potential beneficiaries of these agreements can inform a country's position in respect of trade policy. This last section therefore reflects on perspectives for the AfCFTA to engage in multistakeholder consultations, discussing first the mandate for such consultations, prior proposing a framework for a broad-based participatory process of building the AfCFTA as an institution moving forward.

4.1 *Deriving the Mandate for a Multistakeholder Framework of the AfCFTA*

Among the various requirements for the establishment of a multistakeholder framework is determining whether in effect there is a mandate for it. As was discussed in the previous section, a mandate for third level type of consultations may be distilled from existing AU documentation on the AfCFTA. First and foremost, the AU Decision of 2015 (AU, 2015a), indeed emphasizes the importance of involving various stakeholders in the AfCFTA process, notably the private sector, parliamentarians, civil society, academia to ensure ownership by Africans.

A second element derived from these decisions is the governance structure discussed amply in Páez (2016) and Chap. 2 of this book. The governance structure alludes to two consultative mechanisms, namely the ATF and ABC. If a bottom-up approach is to have influence, then these two forums need to influence the process at the national and subregional front and the work in these setups need to prelude actual negotiations.[22] This has not been the case of the former, which was last held in 2013. The latter was recently brough to life in 2020 AU Summit.

[21] The African Business Council (ABC) was established as an institution in line with the African Union Assembly Decision (Assembly/AU/Dec. 394(XVIII)) of 2012 on Boosting Intra African trade and Fast Tracking the Establishment of the African Continental Free Trade Area. It was subsequently brought to live in 2020 during the 13th Extraordinary Session of the AU Assembly, which endorsed the establishment of the ABC as part of the AfCFTA architecture. See https://africanbusinesscouncil.org/.

[22] Instead, several regional trade forums have been held and organized in various subregions. See for example, ITUC (2019) and (ECA, 2019).

A third entry point which is vital for the process of multistakeholder negotiations is the *Terms of Reference for the CFTA-Negotiating Forum* (TOR)[23] It builds on the best practices in both the RECs and Tripartite FTA and lays out the main responsibilities of this forum, as well as parameters for its composition and the role of the AUC. Though this is a document of procedural nature, it vests the forum and the AUC with important roles and delegated authorities which will guide the negotiations process (AU, 2015c).

There are two important elements that arise from the reading of this document. First, the fact that member States are encouraged to make arrangements to receive inputs from their respective civil society, and second, that they also retain their freedom to have private sector representatives as part of the negotiations delegations, a practice which is not uncommon in international trade negotiations in Africa.[24] On the second element, the question here is whether in addition to private sector representatives, other stakeholders could be considered. Though less traditional, there are experiences of civil society representatives conforming part of the negotiating team. (See Dür & De Bièvre, 2007, p. 85) However, a major challenge in this setup is how to deal with arising differences between members of the delegation (i.e. private sector vs. civil society representatives) during negotiations when weighing out defensive and offensive interests. Given the dynamic and evolving nature of trade negotiations, negotiating implies making rapid decisions on defensive and offensive interests, which from a practical standpoint may not be feasible with negotiating team members representing often conflicting or starkly opposed interests, as illustrated earlier with the example of the textile sector negotiations stakeholders in Sect. 2.1 of this chapter.

Alternatively, other modalities to influence the trade negotiations forum could be considered. This is intricately linked with the first element of the TOR, which encourages members to make arrangements to engage with civil society on the AfCFTA. This should ideally be undertaken at national

[23] This forms part of the reference documents which were endorsed during an extra-ordinary session AU Conference of Ministers of Trade dedicated to the CFTA in May 2015, and which also included the *Objectives and Guiding Principles for Negotiating the CFTA*, and the *Indicative Roadmap for the Negotiations and Establishment of the Continental Free Trade Area (CFTA)*. See also Fig. 2.4 and footnote 23 in Chap. 2.

[24] Among the countries which include private sector representatives in their delegations are Kenya (Ngethe & Olomo, 2010, p. 229), Uganda (Walumbisi-Mpanga, 2006) and South Africa (Draper et al., 2010, p. 277).

level with the myriad of national constituencies which have a stake in the AfCFTA but is limited by financial and capacity constraints in many countries.

Hence, an alternative and complement to the existing ABC and ATF that could also be considered by those countries which face limitations in conducting such consultations could also be the Pan-African Parliament and the ECOSOCC, which were mentioned earlier in Sect. 2.2. These two consultative organs of the AU could be entrusted with a dedicated consultative role on the AfCFTA. Indeed, they currently do not figure in the envisaged AfCFTA architecture. And yet, the Pan-African Parliament has a Committee dealing with Trade, Customs and Immigration Matters. Furthermore, Art. 8 of its Protocol vests the Pan-African Parliament the adequate power and functions to engage in any matters relevant to the AU and its regional integration process. (AU, 2014) Equally so, the ECOSOCC has two committees dealing with trade policy and economic integration issues which could be activated for this purpose and is vested with the power to discuss issues pertaining to trade and regional integration (AU, 2004, Art. 11).

Thus, domestic stakeholders could exercise a secondary level of influencing the AfCFTA process through their nominated parliamentarians in the Pan-African Parliament and their nominated CSO representatives in the ECOSOCC. A suggested entry point in the existing governance structure of the AfCFTA for these two organs should be at Summit level. In other words, these two institutions should hold regular deliberations on the AfCFTA and report the outcome of its hosted deliberations in each of its ordinary sessions to the Heads of State Summit. Discussions in the Pan-African Parliament would be informed and initiated through consultations with the network of national parliaments which constitute its base and in the ECOSOCC a similar procedure would ensue with its national constituencies of CSOs.

4.2 *Setting the Basis for a Multistakeholder Framework*

As a starting point for a discussion on a multistakeholder framework, consultation platforms are already formally integrated into the governance structure of the AfCFTA, which was presented earlier in Páez (2016), as well as in the previous chapter of this book. However, for the proposed structure to work, multistakeholder consultations *processes* must be activated so as to imbibe the existing platforms with content. In other words,

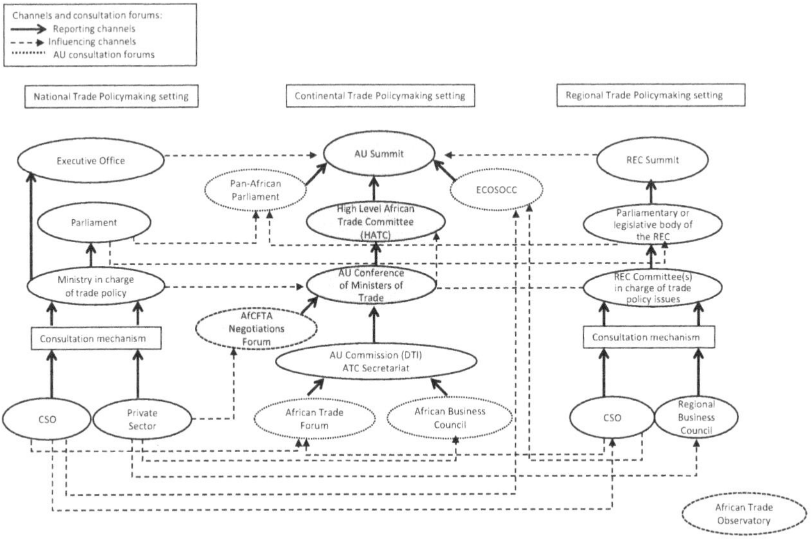

Fig. 3.1 A Multistakeholder Framework for the AfCFTA. (Source: Author's representation)

in order for the ABC to be effective consultative platform, consultations *processes* need to initiate within the member countries and networks need to be established across national and regional consultation platforms in order to influence and impact in the outcome of trade negotiations of the AfCFTA from the bottom-up. Some of this work has started with the creation of the ABC in 2021 as part of its formal remit.[25]

A proposed multistakeholder framework is depicted in Fig. 3.1. It would envisage reporting structures of trade consultation processes where civil society is engaged in national, regional and pan-African settings in order to inform and influence the discussions and trade policy making taking place in existing bodies and organs of the AfCFTA. Formal information channels are those of the reporting structures are depicted in solid arrows, whilst influencing channels are illustrated and dotted arrows.

In this regard, the proposed framework assumes that exchanges across the various settings and levels are possible. For example, CSO stakeholders

[25] As mentioned earlier, this has not been the case of the ATF, which is yet to be instilled with life and a mandate.

in the national setting will also engage with like-minded peers at the regional level and share their positions and outcome of their respective domestic consultations, with the objective of influencing consultations taking place at the (lower) regional (higher) and pan-African levels through their CSO regional bodies and the ATF, once formally established as reflected by the dotted arrows at the bottom of the Fig. 3.1. The same is true for national business constituencies, which will mobilize themselves and put forward their agenda so that at both the REC and pan-African policymaking settings, their positions and views may gain ground in the context of their regional business councils and the ABC.

Furthermore, as consultations are held with the government counterpart in the national setting through an established consultation mechanism, which tends to be coordinated by the line ministry in charge of trade and/or regional integration issues, the outcome of these consultations will be reported to a higher level of government (i.e. the executive), as well as parliament. A similar situation will transpire in the regional setup, where consultations with the regional business council and other regional non-State actors will be relayed by the relevant REC committee in charge of trade policy issues to the REC parliament or legislative body, as well as the REC council. In both these settings, the relayed outcomes will influence trade policymakers which attend the African Union Conference of Ministers of trade, as well as those who attend the HATC on issues of the AfCFTA, and which are located in the middle and upper middle upper levels of the reporting structures.

In addition, the domestic private sector can also influence AfCFTA negotiations mid-level, if they are invited to form part of their respective countries' negotiation delegation, as per the *Terms of Reference for the CFTA-Negotiating Forum*. Lastly, both domestic and regional CSO have the opportunity to influence the debate around the AfCFTA directly through the ECOSOCC and indirectly through the Pan-African Parliament. Being organs of the AU, a reporting structure could be activated at the Summit level, which could provide for an additional medium for influencing at the highest pan-African level.

In sum, through the proposed consultations framework, it is possible for CSOs and the private sector to influence and impact the AfCFTA process across the national, regional and pan-African settings from the bottom up and across the various level of trade policymaking. It is important that the various players are sensitized of these possibilities, in preparation for the various AfCFTA negotiations tracks so that they may make the best use of them.

5 Conclusions

The present chapter focused on the role of multistakeholder consultations as part of trade policymaking and trade negotiations processes in Africa. In light of the experiences and examples provided, the continent seems to be gaining rapid momentum in engaging with the private sector and civil society in trade policy making. Given the efforts towards the establishment of a CFTA, this chapter made a case for the involvement of various stakeholders that are deemed to benefit from the AfCFTA in the process of negotiating this pan-African market. This chapter therefore explored the necessary elements for broad-based participation of stakeholder through consultations in the context of the AfCFTA negotiations. It proposed a framework for such participation through a bottom-up approach rather than a traditional top-down approach through broad-based consultations so that the various stakeholders and potential beneficiaries of the AfCFTA have the opportunity to engage, in an effort to provide the African people with a veritable platform to create the AfCFTA through a consultative and participatory process.

References

African Union. (2015a). *Decision on the Report of the High Level African Trade Committee on Trade Issues.* Assembly/AU/Dec.555(XXIV), 24th Ordinary Session of the Assembly of Heads of State and Government, 30–31 January, Addis Ababa, Ethiopia.

African Union. (2015b). *Communiqué of the 4th Annual African CSO Continental Forum on the Joint–Africa EU Partnership Strategy (JAES): Towards Preparation for the Joint Annual Forum (JAF), Djibouti, 20 September 2015.* Press Release N° 243/2015, September 23. http://pages.au.int/cido/events/communiqu%C3%A9-4th-annual-african-cso-continental-forum-joint-%E2%80%93africa-eu-partnership-strateg

African Union. (2015c). *Report of the Meeting of Ministers.* Dedicated Session of Experts and Senior Officials followed by Ministers of Trade on the Continental Free Trade Area, at the AU on 8–15 May 2015, Addis Ababa.

African Union. (2018). *Decision on the African Continental Free Trade Area.* Assembly/AU/Dec.666(XXX), 30th Ordinary Session of the Assembly, 28–29 January 2018, Addis Ababa, Ethiopia.

Andriamananjara, S. (2015). *Regional integration in Africa: Can the Tripartite FTA be a stepping stone toward a Continental FTA?, Brookings Commentary, 24 August.* https://www.brookings.edu/articles/regional-integration-in-africa-can-the-tripartite-fta-be-a-stepping-stone-toward-a-continental-fta/

AU. (2000). *Constitutive Act of the Africa Union*. Adopted By The Thirty-Sixth Ordinary Session Of The Assembly Of Heads Of State And Government, 11 July, 2000–Lome, Togo.

AU. (2003). *Declaration of the Heads of State and Government of the African Union on the EPA Negotiations*. Assembly/AU/Decl.5 (II), Assembly of the African Union Second Ordinary Session 10–12 July, Maputo, Mozambique.

AU. (2004). *Statutes of the Economic, Social and Cultural Council*. Adopted by the African Union (Assembly/AU/Dec.48(III)), 3rd Ordinary Session of the Assembly of Heads of State and Government, 6 to 8 July, Addis Ababa, Ethiopia. http://pages.au.int/ECOSOCC/pages/statutes-economic-social-and-cultural-council-african-union

AU. (2010). *Kigali Declaration On The Economic Partnership Agreement Negotiations*. Au/ Exp/Td/Decln/2 (Vi), Au Conference Of Ministers Of Trade, 6th Ordinary Session, 29 October–2 November, Kigali, Rwanda.

AU. (2012). *Report to the Committee of 7 Heads of State Constituted to Review Concerns and Issues Raised at the 18th Summit Debate on Boosting intra-African Trade and the Establishment of the CFTA*. TD/BIAT/cm.1/R1, Consultative Meeting of the Senior Officials of the Committee of the Assembly of Heads of State and Government on Boosting Intra-African Trade, Addis Ababa, 3–4 April.

AU. (2014). *Protocol to the Constitutive Act of the African Union on the Pan-African Parliament*. Protocol to the Constitutive Act of the African Union on the Pan-African Parliament adopted by the African Union (Assembly/AU/Dec.529(XXIII)), 23rd Ordinary Session of the Assembly of Heads of State and Government, 26 to 27 June, Malabo, Equatorial Guinea.

AU/NEPAD. (2013). *CAADP Post Compact Review ECOWAS*. Review Report, Dakar, June 13. http://www.resakss.org/sites/default/files/pdfs//caadp-post-compact-review-ecowas-review-report-jun-45330.pdf

Bailey, M. (2001). Quiet Influence: The Representation of Diffuse Interests on Trade Policy. *Legislative Studies Quarterly, 26*(1), 45–80.

Capling, A., & Low, P. (2010). The Domestic Politics of Trade-Policy Making: State and Non-State Actor Interactions and Forum Choice. In *Governments, Non-State Actors and Trade Policy Making. Negotiating Preferentially or Multilaterally?* (pp. 4–28). Cambridge University Press.

CTA Agritrade. (2014). West Africa Heads of State Defer Final Decision on the Regional EPA Agreement.

Draper, P. (2007). Consultation Dilemmas: Transparency Versus Effectiveness in South Africa's Trade Policy. In M. Halle & R. Wolfe (Eds.), *Process Matters: Sustainable Development and Domestic Trade Transparency* (pp. 241–264). International Institute for Sustainable Development.

Draper, P., Disenyana, T., & Biacuana, G. (2010). South Africa. In *Governments, Non-State Actors and Trade Policy Making. Negotiating Preferentially or Multilaterally?* (pp. 249–283). Cambridge University Press.

Duina, F. (2006). *Social Construction of Free Trade: The European Union, NAFTA, and Mercosur*. Princeton University Press.

Dür, A., & De Bièvre, D. (2007). Inclusion Without Influence? NGOs in European Trade Policy. *International Public Policy, 27*(1), 79–101.

EABC. (2013a). Report of The EAC Tripartite Technical Working Group on Tariff Liberalisation for the COMESA, EAC, SADC. http://www.eabc.info/resources/view/report-of-the-eac-tripartite-technical-working-group-on-tariff-liberalisati

EABC. (2013b). Progress Report on the EAC COMESA EAC SADC Tripartite (TFTA) Negotiations. http://www.eabc.info/uploads/progress_report.pdf

EABC. (2014a). Mutual Recognition Agreement for Engineers. Retrieved February 12, 2016, from http://www.eabc.info/resources/view/mutual-recognition-agreements

EABC. (2014b). *Report of the Regional Training Workshop on the Mutual Recognition Agreement for Engineering Professionals in the East African Community*. Held on 2–3 September 2014, Nairobi, Kenya. http://www.eabc.info/uploads/Report_of_the_Training_on_the_MRA_for_Engineers.pdf

EABC. (2015). *Eabc Update On 1st Private Sector Dialogue on the Tripartite Free Trade Area Rules Of Origin- 5th February 2016*. East African Business Council. Retrieved February 10, 2016, from http://www.eabc.info/uploads/1st_Tripartite_Rules_of_Origin_Dialogue_-_Key_Recommendations_final.pdf

EAC. (2010). *Protocol of the Establishment of the East African Community Common Market*. Entered into force on 1 July.

ECA. (2019). *AfCFTA Regional Trade Forum – Horn of Africa*. UN.ECA AfCFTA Regional Trade Forum (2019, JUN.27–28: Addis Ababa, Ethiopia). Addis Ababa. © UN. ECA.

ECOWAS. (1994). Regulations for the Grant to Non-Governmental Organisations (NGOs) the Observer Status Within the Institutions of the Community; Decision A/DEC.9/8/94 dated 6 August. http://cidcom.cgeci.org/civ/fr/1/p/489/pdf.do

ECOWAS. (2000). Decision A/Dec.9/12/00 on the Grant of Observer Status to the African Business Round Table, XXX. http://www.ecowas.us/files/9_12_2000.pdf

ECOWAS. (2009). *Pacte régional de partenariat pour la mise en œuvre de l'ECOWAP/PDDAA [Regional Partnership Compact for the Implementation of the ECOWAP/CAADP]*. Adopté lors de la Conférence international sur le financement de la politique agricole régionale de l'Afrique de l'Ouest, Abuja, 12 novembre (French Version). http://agric.comm.ecowas.int/IMG/pdf/Pacte-fr.pdf

ECOWAS. (2014a). Final Communiqué. Forty-Fourth Ordinary Session of the Authority of ECOWAS Heads of State and Government, Yamoussoukro, 28–29 March.

ECOWAS. (2014b). Final Communiqué. Forty-Fifth Ordinary Session of the Authority of ECOWAS Heads of State and Government, Accra, 10 July.

ECOWAS. (2023). *ECOWAS Commission Pushes for the Establishment of an ECOSSOC that Responds to the Deeper Socio-Economic and Cultural Needs of West African Citizens.* 12 December. https://www.ecowas.int/ecowas-commission-pushes-for-the-establishment-of-an-ecossoc-that-responds-to-the-deeper-socio-economic-and-cultural-needs-of-west-african-citizens/

Evans, P. B., Jacobson, H. K., & Putnam, R. (Eds.). (1993). *Double-Edged Diplomacy: International Bargaining and Domestic Politics.* University of California Press.

Fisher, R., & Ury, W. (1983). *Getting to Yes.* Penguin Books.

Harsch, E. (2002a). Making African Integration a Reality. *Africa Recovery, 16*(2–3), 10–12.

Harsch, E. (2002b). Le rêve de l'Union africaine est en cours de réalisation mais se heurte à un certain scepticisme. *Afrique Relance, 16*(1), 1–5. http://www.un.org/fr/africarenewal/vol16no1/161unfr.htm

Hocking, B. (2004). Changing the Terms of Trade Policy Making: From the Club to the Multistakeholder Model. *World Trade Review, 3*(1), 3–26.

Hufbauer, G. C., & Brunel, C. (Eds.). (2009). *Capitalizing on the Morocco-US Free Trade Agreement: A Roadmap for Success.* Peterson Institute for International Economics.

Hurt, S. R., Lee, D., & Lorenz-Carl, U. (2013). The Argumentative Dimension to the EU–Africa EPAs. *International Negotiation, 18*(1), 67–87.

ICTSD. (2015). TISA Talks Continue in Geneva, Eyeing July Stocktaking Session. *Bridges, 19*(6), 13.

Iheduru, O. C. (2015). Organized Business and Regional Integration in Africa. *Review of International Political Economy, 22*(5), 910–940.

ITUC. (2019). *Regional Trade Forum for West and Central Africa: AfCFTA in Motion: Taking Africa's Integration to the Next Level for a Prosperous Continent.* African Regional Organization of the International Trade Union Confederation. https://www.ituc-africa.org/REPORT-Regional-Trade-Forum-for-West-and-Central-Africa-AfCFTA-in-motion-Taking.html

Jackson, J. H. (2000). *The World Trading System. Law and Policy of International Economic Relations* (2nd ed.). MIT Press.

Keohane, R., & Nye, J. (2000). *The Club Model of Multilateral Co-Operation and the WTO: Problems of Democratic Legitimacy.* Paper presented at a conference on 'Efficiency, Equity and Legitimacy: The Multilateral Trading System at the Millennium', Kennedy School of Government, Harvard University, 1–2 June.

Kiuluku, P., & Chekwoti, C. (2012). Trade Policy Making in East Africa. In K. Heydon & S. Woolcock (Eds.), *The Ashgate Research Companion to International Trade Policy*. Ashgate Publishing Group.

Lee, D., & Hocking, B. (2010). Economic Diplomacy. In R. A. Denemark (Ed.), *The International Studies Encyclopedia* (Vol. II, pp. 1216–1227). Wiley Blackwell.

Lohmann, S. (1998). An Information Rationale for the Power of Special Interests. *American Political Science Review, 92*(4), 809–827.

Modern Ghana. (2014). ECOWAS Fails to Sign EPAs. 31 March. http://www.modernghana.com/news/532607/1/ecowas-fails-to-sign-epa.html#

Ngethe, N., & Olomo, J. (2010). Kenya. In A. Capling & P. Low (Eds.), *Governments, Non-State Actors and Trade Policy Making. Negotiating Preferentially or Multilaterally?* (pp. 214–248). Cambridge University Press.

Nigerian Federal Ministry of Trade and Industry. (2014). Why Nigeria Did Not Sign EU/ECOWAS. Retrieved February 12, 2016, from http://fmti.gov.ng/component/content/article/49-fmti-news/178-why-nigeria-did-not-sign-euecowas.html

Nzewi, O. (2009). Institutionalizing Participation in ECOWAS Policymaking. *Policy Studies Bulletin of CPS (Centre for Policy Studies), 10*(1), 11–14. http://www.cps.org.za/cps%20pdf/Syn10_1_May2009.pdf

OAU. (1991). *Treaty Establishing the African Economic Community*. Adopted on June 3, 1991 in Abuja and Entered into Force on May 12, 1994.

Ostry, S. (2002). Preface. In *Trade Policy-Making Process: Level One of the Two Level Game: Country Studies in the Western Hemisphere* (pp. i–iv). INTAL-ITD-STA, Inter-American Development Bank, Occasional Paper 13, Buenos Aires, Institute for the Integration of Latin America and the Caribbean and the Inter-American Development Bank.

Othieno, L., & Mampewo, D. (2012). *Opportunities, Challenges and Way Forward for Uganda's Trade in Education Services Within the East African Community*. Economic Policy Research Centre, Research Series No. 93, July. http://ageconsearch.umn.edu/bitstream/150475/2/series93.pdf

Páez, L. (2016). A Continental Free Trade Area: Imperatives for Realizing a Pan-African Market. *Journal of World Trade, 50*(3), 533–562.

Pérez-Esteve, M. (2010). The Influence of International Non-State Actors in Multilateral and Preferential Trade Agreements: A Question of Forum Shopping? In A. Capling & P. Low (Eds.), *Governments, Non-State Actors and Trade Policy Making. Negotiating Preferentially or Multilaterally?* Cambridge University Press.

Putnam, R. (1988). Diplomacy and Domestic Politics: The Logic of Two-Level Games. *International Organization, 42*(3), 427–460.

REPONGAC. (2015). *Lancement du Forum Régional des OSCs d'Afrique Centrale à Libreville*. Réseau des Plateformes Nationales des ONGs de l'Afrique Centrale, 17 November. http://www.repongac.org/sites/default/files/Article-Presse-Lancement%20du%20Forum-OSC-17-11-2015_Libreville.pdf

Stairs, D. (2000). Foreign Policy Consultations in a Globalizing World: The Case of Canada, the WTO and the Shenaningans in Seattle. *Policy Matters, 1*, 8.

Stephenson, S., & Walusimbi-Mpanga, R. (2015). Uganda's Higher Education Service Exports – An AUC Case Study. http://unctad.org/meetings/en/Presentation/ditc-ted-Nairobi-24082015-USAID-stephensoWalusi-4.pdf

Walumbisi-Mpanga, R. (2006). *Uganda's Services Coalition Finds Strength in Numbers*. International Trade Centre, International Trade Forum – Issue 1/2006. http://www.tradeforum.org/Ugandas-Services-Coalition-Finds-Strength-in-Numbers/#sthash.iOApvHVR.dpuf

Weldesellassie, I. K. (2011). IGAD as an International Organization, Its Institutional Development and Shortcomings. *Journal of African Law, 55*(1), 1–29. https://www.jstor.org/stable/41149838

Weston, A. (2005). *The 'Canadian Model' for Public Participation in Trade Policy Formulation*. North-South Institute.

CHAPTER 4

Addressing the Policy Disconnect of Services Trade: What a Development-Friendly Services Liberalization under the AfCFTA Should Consider

1 Introduction

Services in Africa are on the rise. From state-of-the-art telecommunication services to informal street vendors, the services economy on the continent has been gaining momentum. In 2016–2022 alone, the contribution of the sector in economic activity constituted more than half of the continent's total value added. The growth in the sector has overtaken that of the primary and secondary sectors, contributing to a steady "servisification" of the African economy.

Albeit or perhaps because of events such as the Covid-19 pandemic and the Ukraine–Russia conflict, several African countries over the recent years have been developing into competitive services hubs, sourcing their domestic, regional and even global markets with a range of services products, from transport and tourism to education and banking.

Indeed, be it by default or by design, several governments have also started to prioritize services, recognizing the role the sector plays in promoting economic growth and development. Among the various compelling reasons to do so, services have the potential to generate jobs and income for a rising African population, which is expected to double by 2050. Given the nature of labour and knowledge-intensive services, the motivation for

L. Páez, *The African Continental Free Trade Area*,
https://doi.org/10.1007/978-3-031-66605-6_4

harnessing these as part of a broad-based growth and development strategy is becoming increasingly attractive to African policymakers.

From a regulatory and policy perspective, however, it is difficult to target the sector. Services are often intangible and/or embedded and embodied in goods or even other services.[1] Unlike goods, they are difficult to touch, possess, accumulate or separate. All these qualities make it a complex task to design adequate policies which may foster the maximum economic and social contribution of services into the wider economy. This is why it is very important to articulate policies that really target services in view of the development needs and aspirations of Africa.

The continent has recognized the importance of services in various development blueprints, including in its *Agenda 2063: The Africa We Want*. And yet, though most African countries may prioritize services at the highest policy level (e.g. in their national development plans and strategies), this is not necessarily reflected in their trade policies, nor does it percolate into their sectoral and/or industrial policies. Hence, the various policy levels that may have a direct impact on services appear as disjointed and disconnected, making it difficult to advance the rise of a services industry and its associated growth and development benefits.

Against this backdrop, the AfCFTA services trade negotiations have been developing in parallel with trade in good negotiations.[2] Since the adoption of a Protocol on Trade in Services and the development of Services Negotiation Modalities (AU, 2018a, 2018b) that guide the negotiations of services liberalization commitments, this process carries important policy challenges for the AfCFTA membership that need attention. The present chapter therefore looks at the policy dimensions of services trade in Africa in the broader context of Africa's development and regional integration experience.

[1] **Embedded services** are referred to as the services that form part of the production and delivery of a good. **Embodied services** are those that are considered to be an integral part of a good or service that is being purchased and can be consumed at a later stage. An example of an embedded service could be the transport component to have a good shipped from the farm or factory gate to the market or a salespoint. An example of an embodied service can be access rights to download an update for a purchased software or application on a computer or IT device, or after-sale repair and disposal services which are offered as part of the warranty of a product.

[2] See discussion in Chapter 2.4.1 on objectives and guiding principles of the AfCFTA. See also AU (2015).

The chapter first conceptualizes services and services trade liberalization from a development policy perspective and discusses the motivations behind prioritizing services trade policy in Africa. The chapter then identifies policy dimensions and levels of disconnects across such policies and develops a framework for a subsequent policy mapping exercise of the various policy levels. After a review of services trade policies, the chapter explores how regional approaches could help bridge policy disconnects of the services policy landscape. It then proposes elements that need to be integrated into the implementation of the AfCFTA Services Protocol and liberalization process, to promote great policy consistency, so that the expected developmental gains from the AfCFTA can be maximized and realized.

2 Putting Services Trade on the Development Map

2.1 Understanding Services and Services Trade

In today's globalized world, services determine economic activity. It is virtually impossible to produce or sell anything without the involvement of services. Even the production of the smallest pin will require at the very least basic electricity, storage and transport services. From a ticket-vending machine to a state-of-the-art video conference call, services irremediably are part of our daily lives.

However, because of the nature of services, they are difficult to define, value and keep. This is what fundamentally distinguishes services from goods, which are tangible, quantifiable and can be stored. Services are broadly defined as economic exchanges between producers and consumers. As a result of these exchanges, the condition of the consumer (or good) receiving the service changes.[3] It is because of these quasi-public-goods quality that it is a very complex task to measure services.

Several methodologies exist to classify services, which categorize them into various sectors and subsectors. Most commonly known are the United Nations Central Product Classification (CPC) and the International Standard Industrial Classification of All Economic Activities (ISIC), the former focusing on a classification based on services products whilst the

[3] For further definitions and categorization of services based on the system of national accounts see UN (2009), pp. 96–97.

latter categorizes services into services activities. Most countries use either of these classifications and some may even derive their own.[4]

Services are often characterized as the "tertiary sector" of the economy, with the two other sectors being the primary sector (comprising agriculture forestry, fishing and mining), and the secondary sector referring to manufacturing and industrial activities. Nonetheless, services also form part of the various activities involved in the primary as well as secondary sector, hence this sectoral distinction may not be the best for measuring the contribution of services in the economy.

Irrespective of a country's level of development, services are needed for it to prosper. Services are important as they contribute to the economy with value generation and also support production in other sectors of the economy. For example, a firm producing photographic equipment may need to engage engineering and design services, as well as financial services, legal services and, lastly, commercialization and marketing services to reach its market.[5] These services will not only add value to the product, they will also engage other economic sectors in the various production stages of manufactures, which will ultimately also enable the firm to adequately market the product and capture the proceeds from the intellectual property and technology it generates.

Services sector development is therefore important for any economy, and especially if it is seeking economy-wide development and diversification. Services sector development refers to the deepening and widening of the scope and impact of services activity. The realization of progress in services development is generally accompanied by a direct effect on the economy, in terms of value added, employment generation, in addition to labour and productivity gains. Ultimately, as increased sophistication and wider range of services products is achieved through services sector development, consumers benefit from lower transaction costs and greater product diversity.

[4] For example, the General Industrial Classification of Economic Activities within the European Communities (NACE) is derived from the ISIC and thus enables comparisons.

[5] But because some of these services are far from the core activities of a firm and cannot be internalized, they may be outsourced. This is possible due to vertical integration possibilities of multinational enterprises (MNEs). Trade in manufactures have embedded services components implying outsourcing decisions beyond national borders and may be defined as the offshore trade in arm's length services. See Bhagwati et al. (2004) for a discussion.

In turn, services trade refers to the exchange of services across international borders. Traditionally, for services such as professional services, this would imply that the service provider crosses a border to deliver the service to the consumer, or vice versa. But with significant innovations in information and communication technologies (ICT), such as the internet and fintech, the scope for trade in services has greatly expanded. Historically, the cost of international services trade has also considerably shrunk. For example, the cost of international calls has dramatically dropped, in some cases at a faster rate than national calls, boosting trade through reduced business costs.

Nonetheless, services trade today is still often constrained by prevailing barriers both at national borders and also behind these borders (i.e. within domestic markets). These differences are often not easily identified by a foreign services provider from a distance. Hence, services trade liberalization responds to the need for dismantling of barriers both at the border and/or *behind the border* through domestic regulation, because most of the barriers to services trade are of regulatory nature.[6] These types of barriers raise operation costs and can act as a deterrent to enter a domestic market. In the face of such barriers, domestic services providers will have an unfair advantage over foreign ones. Accompanying measures and policy coherence regulating the domestic and tradable sectors may therefore be needed to ensure that market access is afforded to foreign services providers when services trade is liberalized.[7]

With the establishment of the multilateral trading system, members to the WTO have committed to progressively liberalize trade in services through successive multilateral negotiating rounds. When negotiating trade in services, reference is made to the *Services Sectoral Classification List*, a document which distinguishes 12 sectors and 117 subsectors, and is based on the CPC (WTO, 1991). Though the list is non-exhaustive and there are limitations in the classification,[8] it largely remains a reference for services trade negotiations in the WTO, as well as for African regional services trade negotiations.

[6] However, regulations which are deemed domestic can have extraterritorial effects, as discussed in Sect. 5, Box 4.2 of this chapter and also in Box 4.1.

[7] For a discussion on policy coherence and sequencing in services, see Páez (2011), pp. 131–132 and also pp. 78–84.

[8] Some countries have raised issues with the WTO classification and proposed alternatives. See South Centre (2003).

A per the General Agreement on Trade in Services (GATS Art. I:3), there are four modalities through which services may be internationally traded. Cross-border trade (mode 1), refers to exchanges of services across borders without the consumer or service provider needing to move. "Consumption abroad" (mode 2), implies the consumer crosses the border to consume the service. "Commercial presence" (mode 3) happens when a service provider has local representation (e.g. a subsidiary or branch) in the domestic consumer market to provide the service. Lastly, "presence of natural persons" (mode 4) refers to the service provider crossing a border to deliver the service.

Given the demise of the multilateral trade negotiations under the Doha Round which initiated in 2001, many countries have advanced trade integration through RTAs. Both the number and coverage of RTAs has expanded and include services. As a result, most WTO members are party to at least one RTA involving services (Roy, 2011). Africa is no exception and has various such RTAs. There is even a services-specific mega-regional FTA where an African country is participating, as exemplified in Box 4.1.[9]

Box 4.1 What the Trade in Services Agreement (TiSA) Could Look Like and Imply for Africa

In order to facilitate a potential future multilateralization, it is expected that the TiSA be based on the GATS and include key GATS-consistent provisions on the scope, definitions, market access, national treatment, exemptions and dispute settlement. So far, the TiSA negotiations have not been open to the public or to observers, nor have negotiating documents been made publicly available.

Since TiSA will include provisions on market access and national treatment, it is expected that the agreement be accompanied by schedules of commitments of the participating countries. There are mainly two different ways in which scheduling of such commitments

(*continued*)

[9] African RTAs such as EAC, COMESA, SADC and ECOWAS include services trade liberalization, as do various FTAs involving Africa, such as the Morocco-US FTA, EPAs and the TISA. Also see discussion in Chap. 8 more generally on the various mega-regionals and FTAs involving Africa.

Box 4.1 (continued)
is designed in trade agreements. First, there is the positive list approach, which is the approach used in the GATS, where only the sectors that governments explicitly choose will be included in the schedules and thus liberalized. The second approach, the former NAFTA-like negative list approach, which is common in FTAs with the US, covers all sectors except the ones that are explicitly excluded. This also means that sectors that do not currently exist will be covered by the schedules.

Though negotiations appear to have stalled in 2016 (Titievskaia, 2023), it is still unclear how the TiSA will be designed, it is believed that it will combine both the positive and negative list approach. This would go beyond what is currently agreed on in the GATS. Although a negative list approach is frequent in trade agreements where the US is involved, Morocco is the only African country involved in an FTA with the US. Other framework agreements between the US and other African countries on trade and investment have been discussed in this chapter, as well as Chap. 8 of this book).

Additionally, it is expected that the TISA contain a standstill clause, which would require governments to bind their existing levels of liberalization and not introduce new restrictions beyond these in the future, affecting the regulatory and policy space governments may have. Other provisions which may be included could relate to transparency obligations, which are often quite onerous in terms of compliance, especially if associated with CSR obligations, as mentioned later in Box 4.2.

In terms of standard setting, for financial services, the TiSA could contain provisions on the adoption of internationally agreed standards, such as those adopted by the G20, the Financial Stability Board (FSB), the Basel Committee on Banking Supervision (BCBS), the International Association of Insurance Supervisors (IAIS), the International Organization for Securities Commissions (IOSCO), the Financial Action Task Force (FATF) and the Organization for Economic Cooperation and Development (OECD). Depending on what is agreed, provisions could go well beyond what many African countries have committed in the context of the GATS and the Doha

(*continued*)

Box 4.1 (continued)

Round. Equally, negotiations could also consider a "prudential carve out" provision, which would allow countries to adopt measures for prudential reasons under special circumstances, similar to article 2 in the GATS annex on financial services. This could give governments some wiggle room, but this will ultimately depend on how the provision is phrased.

Not much has been heard about the advancement of TiSA negotiations since 2016. If the agreement is to go live at some point, it will have important implications on how Mauritius trades with Africa on services, both through its existing bilateral FTAs, as well as intra- and inter-regionally, and lastly also continentally, within the AfCFTA, which were highlighted in Table 8.1 of Chap. 8. Ex ante, MFN treatment preferences under the TiSA would imply that Mauritius cannot extend the receival of services imports from TiSA member States to its African FTA partners without the duties being paid. This would apply to SADC, COMESA, the TFTA and the AfCFTA partners.

Sources: Author's analysis based on the interpretation of the literature and references cited in the box.

However, in order to harness the potential benefits of services trade, countries need to operationalize the various services agreements and commitments they have signed on to. Beyond ratification, it requires that these agreements be domesticated through regulation and policy. This may entail the undertaking of services trade (policy) reviews, regulatory audits and subsequent reform of existing laws and policies, or, alternatively, the development of policies and regulation from scratch.

Services trade (policy) reform refers to a change in policies and regulation governing the exchange of services. It is intended to steer or change the course of commercial trade of a given services market, having implications for market actors and regulators alike. It is often argued that trade liberalization enables such trade policy reform, as countries commit to liberalize in return for market access elsewhere and are bound by the commitment to undertake necessary policy reforms to ensure their trading partners obtain the agreed (reciprocal) treatment.

Hence, in the context of services trade, liberalization may bring or lock-in a set of trade policy and regulatory reforms to enable compliance with a commitment made multilaterally or regionally. Nonetheless, liberalization does not automatically bring reforms. Certain conditions must be met for liberalization to enable reforms and their associated benefits. The liberalization experience in Africa remains at best mixed, as is discussed in the next subsections.

2.2 A Brief Retrospective of Services (Trade) Policy in Africa's Development Agenda

The African services sector has increasingly received attention from a development policy perspective and for good reasons. In many countries, it is a major contributor to output, employment and growth. However, not too long ago, the development discourse seemed to largely ignore services.

In the 1980s, the focus of Africa's development in the donor community and development partner as enshrined in the Berg Report (World Bank, 1981) was set on supporting the development of the tradable sectors of the African economy (i.e. commodities and agriculture). This was deemed to happen by switching the terms of trade in favour of the tradeable sectors and *against* the services sectors. Only services which were deemed as supportive of agricultural production were considered as relevant, such as education, water supply, and health (Please & Amoako, 1984, p. 49). The Lagos Plan of Action which laid out Africa's development roadmap for 1980–2000 gave prominence to the overarching objective of achieving self-reliance and food self-sufficiency, including industrial development, technological upgrading and agricultural development,[10] and to some extent, prioritized agricultural services in support of agricultural development (OAU, 1980).

During the 1980s and 1990s, development policies in the context of the Structural Adjustment Programmes (SAPs) which African countries were subjected to were steered towards promoting free market fundamentals. At the time liberalization was advocated for as well as privatization and deregulation of certain sectors of the economy. In this context, several

[10] See broader discussion in the context of the evolution of Africa''s regional integration process in Chap. 2.2 and its priority areas under the Lagos Plan of Action.

African countries undertook unilateral and substantial liberalization and privatization of various services markets, including sectors such as telecommunications, water and sanitation, electricity, finance, tourism and transport, and in some instances also health services. However, little attention was given to the developmental impact of such liberalization and this was heavily criticized.[11]

As a result, liberalization alone did not bring on the developmental gains that had been envisaged under the SAPs. It did not always translate into poverty reduction or development (Estache & Wodon, 2014; Vagliasindi & Nellis, 2009), and this was often associated with the absence of adequate policy frameworks for services, as was the case of financial liberalization of the banking sector in many African countries (World Bank, 2002, p. 80). In response to the failed policy recipes of the SAPs, some African governments re-regulated, resorted to nationalization and/or ended private participation in given sectors, at times with hefty legal and financial implications.[12]

Concurrent with the implementation of the SAPs, multilateral trade negotiations put services at the forefront of the international trade agenda. African countries taking part in the Uruguay Round of the WTO negotiated trade in services commitments, which resulted in substantial market access to their services markets. A total of 41 African countries[13] were part

[11] See, for instance, Carmody (1998) and Bromley (1995).

[12] This was the case of water distribution services in Tanzania. A round of privatizations in the late 1990s opened the sector to foreign participation under an arrangement with the Dar es Salaam Water and Sewerage Corporation. Biwater Gauff Limited was created as a British-German joint venture to provide water supply and sewerage services in Daar es Salaam. The company obtained a service operating contract in 2002 but was unable to meet the tariff collection targets and accumulated significant losses, leading to a termination of the contract, deportation of the management and seizure of assets. This activated a legal dispute under a bilateral investment treaty between Tanzania and the UK. See ICSID (2005).

[13] These were Angola, Benin, Botswana, Burkina Faso, Burundi, Cameroon, Central African Republic, Chad, Congo, Côte d'Ivoire, DRC, Djibouti, Egypt, Gabon, The Gambia, Ghana, Guinea, Guinea-Bissau, Kenya, Lesotho, Madagascar, Malawi, Mali, Mauritania, Mauritius, Morocco, Mozambique, Namibia, Niger, Nigeria, Rwanda, Senegal, Sierra Leone, South Africa, then Swaziland (now Eswatini), Tanzania, Togo, Tunisia, Uganda, Zambia and Zimbabwe. Cabo Verde, Seychelles and Liberia acceded after the Uruguay Round, and committed to services liberalization as part of their accession process.

of these negotiations, but their participation was documented as rather minimal (Laker, 2015). This led to a shared perception of poor performance in terms of negotiated outcomes from the Uruguay Round (Kessie & Apea, 2004, pp. 28–29). Indeed, many countries had virtually no experience in negotiating trade in services prior the Uruguay Round, unlike developed countries which had ample liberalization experience through negotiations of services in the OECD since the 1960s (Páez, 2011, p. 90–94) and which had initially pushed for the inclusion of services in the Uruguay Round (Roberts & Heydon, 2012, p. 173).

At the turn of the millennium, given the mixed experiences from the SAPs and the Uruguay Round, the trade paradigm shifted from liberalization to greater participation in international trade. The UN Millenium Development Goals (MDGs) endorsed in 2000 set the tone for a global partnership for trade development, wherein developing countries and development partners were on equal footing and had shared responsibilities towards achieving these goals, as per MDG 8. Though services trade was considered as part of MDG 8 targets, with ODA being channelled to trade development, as well as facilitating access to IT technologies. In addition, MDGs 1 to 6 also targeted aspects of social services, notably health, water and sanitation and education services.

Greater emphasis was placed by the development community on reducing barriers and costs associated with services trade and improving competitiveness, hence the focus on trade related infrastructure, trade facilitation and the reduction of adjustment costs associated with falling export revenue. Initiatives such as the Aid for Trade and (Enhanced) Integrated Framework (IF)[14] prioritized aspects of services trade by channelling resources to trade policy and trade-related infrastructure. Lastly, there was gradual incorporation of services trade issues in the design of Poverty Reduction Strategy Papers (PRSPs) and (DTIS) of African countries.[15]

[14] The IF started in 1997 as a joint programme of the United Nations Conference on Trade and Development, WTO, International Trade Centre, UN Development Programme, World Bank and International Monetary Fund. Its objective was to mainstream trade into development strategies of LDCs. The format of such strategies were PRSPs, used for conditional debt financing by the Bretton Woods institutions. The IF was relaunched as the EIF after a review in 2006, which recognized the failure of PRSPs and insufficient uptake of DTIS. See Saner and Páez (2006) for a critique.

[15] For example, Benin''s PRSP of 2011 prioritizes certain services trade sectors as does the PRSP of Burkina Faso (2012), Burundi (2012), Congo (2012) and the DTIS of Mali (2015) and South Sudan (2016).

Africa's major response to the failure of the SAPs[16] was enshrined in the context of the NEPAD (2001), which became a roadmap for Africa's development at the turn of the century. The NEPAD (and now AUDA-NEPAD)[17] covers infrastructure and transport services through its various programmes and initiatives, such as the Programme for Infrastructure Development in Africa (PIDA) and the African Transport Policy Programme (SSATP) and more recently the Single African Air Transport Market (SAATM). These specifically target infrastructure and transport needs of the continent and further promote transborder projects, as well as policies targeting sustainable transport sector development, transport connectivity as well as transit along African transport corridors.[18]

Furthermore, Agenda 2063 adopted in 2013 and which is the AU's development vision of 50 years, also prioritizes services. In addition to providing quality basic and public services, a major aspiration of this Agenda is to achieve free movement of services and connect Africa through 'world class' infrastructure, which includes transport, energy and ICT services (AU, 2013, para. 23 and 67(f)).

More recently, with the end of the MDGs and the adoption of the 2030 Agenda for Sustainable Development and its 17 Sustainable Development Goals (SDGs) in 2015, the global community places even greater emphasis on services. Not only are social services an area of focus, as previously with the MDGs (i.e. health, water and sanitation and education), as a means to achieve basic needs of subsistence. Other sectors feature, such as infrastructure (SDG 9), energy (SDG 7) and environmental services (SDGs 12–15), which bring on dimensions of economic empowerment and climate action.

This in itself is an entry point for the alignment of an Africa-owned strategy for development enshrined in Agenda 2063 and in the AUDA-NEPAD with that of the current global development agenda on services (Ighobor, 2015). Indeed, both these African strategies are viewed as integral parts of the 2030 Agenda (UN, 2015, para. 64). Going forward, a

[16] Another response to SAPs was the African Alternative Framework to Structural Adjustment Programme (ECA, 1990).

[17] In 2018 the NEPAD Planning and Coordination Agency was transformed into the African Union Development Agency (AUDA-NEPAD) as part of impact and operational efficiency reforms of the AU. See AU (2018c, 2019a).

[18] See also associated discussion on these infrastructure and transport initiatives in Sect. 5 of this chapter, as well as Chapter 8.4 in this book.

major issue is the mainstreaming of various services elements in the implementation and uptake of these two African initiatives at country and regional levels.[19] The AfCFTA could be a conduit for this, through the dismantling of barriers in the services market access negotiations. Hence, Africa faces a unique opportunity to harness services trade for its development. For this to happen, services trade policy has to be adequately designed, sequenced and aligned with the various policy dimensions affecting services.

In conclusion, services trade policy has experienced a shift: from a virtual non-existence to a certain degree of prominence in Africa's development agenda. This responds to the rise in relative importance of services and associated opportunities, as well as recent trends in Africa's development trajectory, as is discussed below.

3 The Status of Services Trade Policy in Africa: Importance, Trends, Evidence and Opportunities

There are several compelling reasons why services trade policy is important and should be a priority to Africa. The benefits from services trade liberalization can potentially go beyond the expected static welfare gains and bring on dynamic effects for the economy at large. However, for this to happen certain conditions need to be met and this often involves a policy dimension.

Africa is a small player in global services trade by any standard: its share of global services trade during 2000–2010 hovered between 2.2 and 2.4% (AU and ECA, 2015, Fig. 1.25).[20] However, the sector's contribution to Africa's output is quite substantial. During 2009–2012, the services sector grew at more than twice the world average, contributing to 49% of value added in the African economy and as much as 32% of total employment. (UNCTAD, 2015) This is consistent with research which corroborates that in many developing countries it is services that drives growth and at a more dynamic pace than manufactures (Ghani & O'Connell, 2014).

[19] Efforts in this regard have been made in the context of the AU-UN Framework on Implementation of Agenda 2063 and 2030 Agenda. See AU Decision 2018 and 2019.

[20] This did not change much in the next decade, as is later on discussed and depicted in Fig. 4.3 down below, given that on average, Africa's contribution to global trade remained steadily under 3% during 2016–2022.

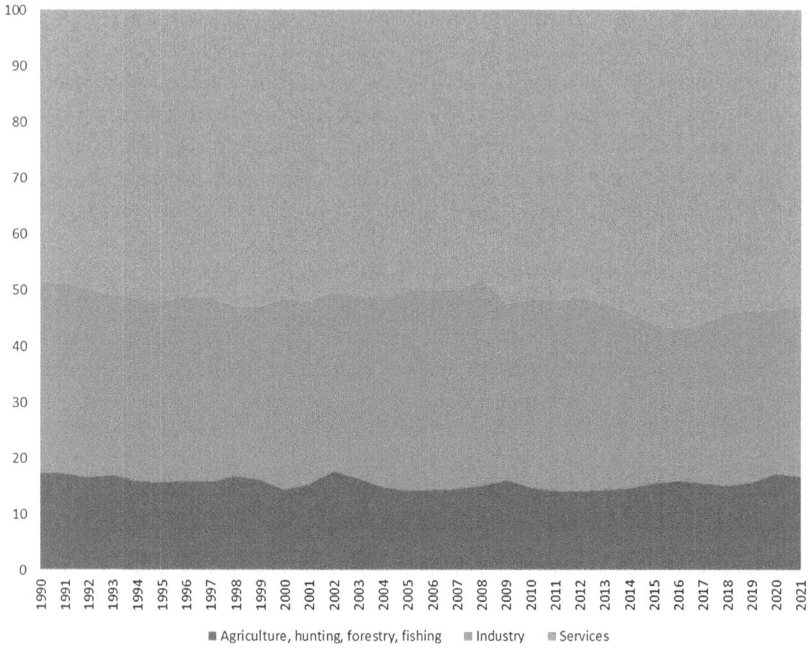

Fig. 4.1 Gross value-added contribution to GDP in Africa (1990–2021). (Source: UNCTADstat)

The observed growth trends are also explained by the main structural change the African economy has suffered since the 1960s. The continent experienced a shift from a traditional agricultural-based economy to a services-based one, with a gradual squeezing of the manufacturing sector. Some have named this phenomenon the "servisification" of the African economy. As can be appreciated in Fig. 4.1, when looking back at the beginning of the 1990s, the contribution to output of the agricultural sector hovered around 17%, manufacturing stood at 34% and services at 48% of GDP, respectively. Three decades later, services contribution to output has increased as depicted by the gradual widening of the services wedge in the graphic, and stood at 52% in 2021, gaining ground over the manufacturing wedge, which closed at 30% contribution from the manufacturing sector. Interestingly, the agricultural sector remains virtually unchanged, at 16% contribution to GDP in 2021.

This structural shift has also been characterized by a degree of deindustrialization (AU and ECA, 2014), and corroborating the notion that there may be limits to just how many workers can shift from the agriculture to the manufacturing sector and hence contribute to an industrialization-based growth (Rodrik, 2013). This is critical, at a time when automation and other technologies could substitute labour in developing countries that are seeking to develop via manufacturing. For example, the risk of job losses due to automation have been estimated at 65% in Nigeria, 67% in South Africa and as high as 85% in Ethiopia (Citi GPS, 2016), hence looking for alternative employment sources in light of these trends is crucial to ensure that structural transformation in Africa is inclusive.

Services offer such an alternative. The services sector in Africa has been consistent with the trend of creating more jobs than the manufacturing sector in many developing countries. If adequately harnessed, it could become the next growth escalator for many African countries, including latecomers (Ghani & O'Connell, 2014).

African demographics are very dynamic and play an associated role in Africa's growth and development trajectory. Given the current growth rates, Africa's workforce is expected to double from 1.2 billion in 2020 to almost 2.5 billion in 2050. With an estimated yearly entry of 10 to 15 million young Africans in the job market (AfDB, 2016), finding jobs for this youthful and growing population represents a challenge for African governments but also an opportunity in terms of fostering factor productivity gains driven through a capacitated labour force, as was seen in Asia in the 1960s.

Services have the potential to generate jobs and income for this rising population but investments in the sector as well as in human capital formation are needed to realize the opportunities it has to offer. The benefits of creating jobs in the services sector are manifold, especially if they add value and enable the growing population to expand their disposable income to make a decent living. If such expansion is coupled with the targeting of adequate levels of savings, a "demographic dividend"[21] of the growing population in Africa could be achieved.

[21] Refers to a relative increase in the working-age population vis-a-vis non-working-age population, which leads to a fall in the dependency ratio, with the potential to foster higher productivity and growth if the increased labour supply is absorbed and national savings are mobilized and channelled to expanding productive activities (AfDB, 2016).

Another associated demographic phenomenon with Africa's growth story is its "rising of the middle class", which in Africa is estimated at 370 million people (Ncube & Lufumpa, 2015). With higher disposable income, this population group is shifting its consumption patterns away from first necessities to a wider palette of goods and services. Indeed, the consumer market on the continent is expected to grow from $1.4 trillion in 2015 to $2.5 trillion by 2030 (Signé, 2018), which demands more and better services. Hence, the need for governments to define policies which expand the existing services base and services trade to satisfy that demand.

This expansion also represents an opportunity to reduce inequalities associated with the provision of (basic) services. These tend to be particularly overt in rural and remote areas in Africa. Furthermore, policies that target high-quality education and health services have the potential of reducing poverty and promoting inclusion. They have a bearing on productivity gains and hence need to be part of structural transformation strategies in Africa (AU and ECA, 2014).

In conjunction with ICT developments touched upon in Sect. 2.1 of this chapter, the tradability of services has increased over time. In Africa, this has not only reduced transaction costs of services trade, it has increased opportunities with major spin-off effects on inclusion. For example, mobile telephony has revolutionized access to finance and markets in remote areas, with important impacts on the agriculture and food value chains (Vodafone et al., 2011). Countries such as Kenya have been able to exploit social and economic gains of liberalized services associated with mobile banking in the form of greater financial inclusion (Jack & Suri, 2010).

However, the success of promoting financial inclusion in other countries has greatly been determined by policy and regulatory frameworks governing the financial and telecoms sectors (see Ondiege, 2015; EPRC, 2013; Africa Progress Panel, 2014). In sum, financial liberalization on its own is no guarantor for financial inclusion, and opening financial services trade in the absence of appropriate domestic regulations may not necessarily increase trade or generate greater efficiency in the provision of financial services (Páez, 2011).

More recently, another area making waves in Africa's services landscape in the wake of the Covid-19 pandemic has been associated with the digital realm, which encompasses digital trade and e-commerce, as well as many ICT-related services. Africa witnessed the coming of age of many services-related industries and also developed survival and resilience strategies supported by digital trade and e-commerce (ECA, 2021; ITC, 2020).

With the aegis of Industrialization 2.0 and the use of new technologies and innovations, including blockchain, internet of things, artificial intelligence, 3D printing and digital identification, there are unparalleled opportunities that Africa could exploit to jumpstart industrialization, as other continents and regions did in prior industrial revolutions. Indeed, many opportunities have been identified for an effective implementation of the AfCFTA, which could be a conduit for the continent's transformation through digitalization (AU, 2019a, 2019b). With the negotiation of the AfCFTA's Protocol on Digital Trade, the continent could inch closer to having a common regulatory framework for a digital single market that also responds to its digitalization objectives, as enshrined in the *AU Digital Transformation Strategy (2020–2030)*, endorsed in 2020 (AU, 2020).

Another more recent development which should also be taken into account by policymakers relates to commodities markets. Many African countries are commodity dependent and the recent observed fall in international commodity prices, notably oil, but also minerals and various soft commodities, have on repeated occasions raised concerns about the end of a commodities bubble, as was seen during the commodities supercycle in 2002–2003, which was mainly driven by China's growth (World Bank, 2015). In this context, it is also important to consider the associated procyclical risks of continued commodity dependency[22] and the need to diversify into other sectors.

Services represent an opportunity to reduce commodity dependency and exposure to boom-and-bust cycles of commodities markets. Indeed, Borchert and Mattoo (2009) argue that services trade are less prone to economic crises because demand for services tends to be less cyclical and the production of services is less dependent on external finance than manufactures. Nonetheless, the fact that Africa's participation in global trade is minimal, hovering at just under 2% of the global share, the sector has been growing, aligned with the global post-pandemic recovery. In 2022, Africa's services trade exports reached US$ 124.5 billion, with sectors such as transport and travel making up the lion's share of the continent's services trade, and this also points to an untapped services trade potential that is yet to be realized in terms of magnitudes, as well as sectoral diversification (see Fig. 4.2).

[22] See associated discussion in the context of LDCs, in Chap. 7, Sect. 3.

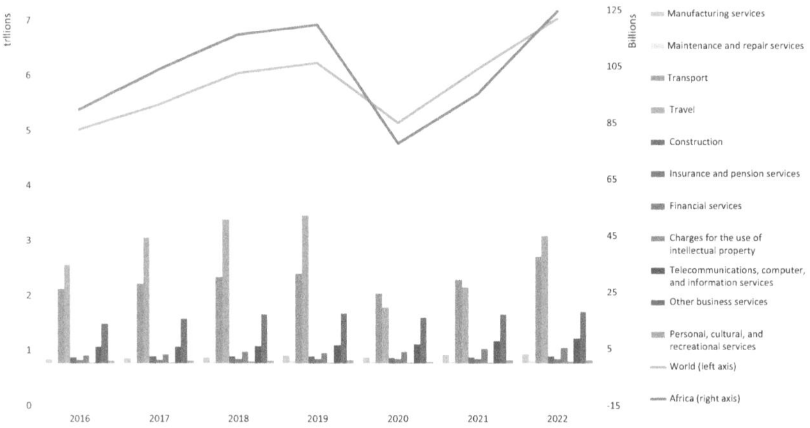

Fig. 4.2 Services trade exports in Africa, value and sectoral distribution (2016–2022). (Source: Author's representation based on WTO Stats (n.d.). Data includes commercial services and excludes government services)

More importantly, and despite the Covid-19 pandemic which almost led to a halt in international operations, today's trade is for the most part governed by the global value chains (GVCs), which may be characterized as production networks that source tasks and inputs from various geographical locations to produce goods and/or services. GVCs rely heavily on the vertical specialization, with various stages of production being separable (and also tradable) within and across countries. The services sector is critical to the overall cost structure and performance of countries participating in GVCs. This determines the global and regional sourcing decisions of multinational firms that constitute the GVC fabric (Francois et al., 2015).

Africa is yet to fully realize the vertical specialization required in GCVs that drive trade. This may be achieved by improving regulation that reduces (services) trade costs, as wells as transport-related infrastructure services (Hoekman, 2013). Encouragingly though, some African countries are already leaving a mark in selected services industries.

For example, there is positive evidence of some countries upgrading[23] in certain commodities and light manufactures GVCs, notably Botswana

[23] Gereffi (1999) describes upgrading as the dynamic movement within value chains of producers as they shift between different stages of the chain and characterized generally by a move into a subsequent stage in production (hence a move downstream). Upgrading can have various trajectories, as is further elaborated by Humphrey and Schmitz (2002).

in diamond processing and cutting (AU and ECA, 2013, Box 3.13), Cote d'Ivoire in cocoa processing (Douet & Mieu, 2016), and Kenya in the apparel industry (McKinsey, 2015a), which have received attention. Increasing the services component in such industries could support the much-needed diversification away from raw commodities trade and allow for upgrading and upskilling trade in more sophisticated tasks and services components.

An associated trend in Africa relates to upgrading *within* services value chains. For example, Gereffi and Fernandez-Stark (2010) find evidence of this in South Africa for business process outsourcing (BPO) services, as does Stephenson (2012) for information technology outsourcing (ITO) and BPO services in countries such as Egypt, Ghana, Kenya, Mauritius, Senegal and Tunisia. Carmel and Tjia (2005, p. 29) confirm the same in call centres in French-speaking North African countries, and in Mauritius and South Africa for Dutch-speaking customers, offering vital services for other services industries, such as travel and tourism, but also for internet and after-sale services.

Interestingly and despite all these encouraging developments, the major bottlenecks to African trade are still services trade related. Notably, infrastructure services which encompass road, rail, water and air transport, but also energy supply are known to be poorly developed in Africa and require heavy investment, with infrastructure financing needs estimated at US$ 130–170 billion a year. Though the continent is able to cover an important part through public funding, there still remains a financing gap to the tune of USD 68–108 billion (AfDB, 2018). This gap is felt in the cost of transport, which is known to constitute as much as 15–20% of import costs, doubling and sometimes tripling the cost in developed countries (Youssef, 2019). Furthermore, associated storage, cargo and freight services come at a prohibitive expense in Africa. As documented by Portugal-Perez and Wilson (2009), maritime freight costs on African exports are at times twice as high as in other regions and add up to 8.1% of costs of total value of trade due to inefficiencies in African ports.

Lastly, as with transport, energy supply as an input service to production of both goods and services is critical. Electrical power cuts in Africa are frequent; hence firms resort to electrical generator power, which costs four times as much as electricity from the grid (McKinsey, 2015b). This invariably diminishes the competitiveness of African products in the global economy.

In conclusion, there are compelling reasons for African countries to look at services trade policy from a development perspective. Some of the recent trends and their impacts on the continent present opportunities that call for a prioritization of the sector through targeted policy design.

4 Services Trade Policy in Africa: A Framework for Mapping Policy Disconnects

With the conceptual evolution of services being a tradable sector and the role it can play in economic development, as previously discussed in Sect. 2.2, so has the need to develop services trade policy in African countries, as part of their wider development objectives. But just how well are services trade policies articulated and how do they address policy outcomes that are congruent with wider economic policies? When policies are poorly articulated, they will not render the expected outcomes and impacts. In some circumstances, they may even hinder the attainment of the same.

The present section attempts to map out a policy framework for the services sectors that are considered *tradable* in Africa and tries to determine how well such policies are articulated and speak to each other. This is done with a view to establish where the policy realm on services trade appears as disjointed or disconnected. A *policy disconnect* may be defined as the absence of connectivity or rapport between the policy dimensions(s) required to bring on a change and fails to deliver the desired change outcome.

Policy disconnects are gaps or blind spots of policies' interactions. When a set of policies that are well articulated speak to and complement each other across different dimensions, there is policy connectivity. One may therefore consider policy connectivity as the glue that propels policy to their best possible outcome. This is particularly relevant for Africa's deeper integration into global trade, where a symbiotic relation between the services and manufactures markets are a requisite in GVCs as noted by Low (2013).

Poorly designed policies can lead to undesired outcomes and also bring on various negative externalities. For example, ill-designed policies are characteristically "policy blind", when they fail to target identifiable stakeholders (e.g. through a stakeholder mapping), which should be the natural beneficiaries of the policy. In turn, a poorly designed policy may be considered policy neutral, in that it neither creates the desired change nor does it worsen the situation of its targeted stakeholder. Though not harmful ex ante, there is an assumption of wastage of resources vested into that policy ex post. Lastly, "policy-relevant", may be those policies that are well designed in terms of targeting their policy constituents and bringing out the desired policy outcomes.

Countries may approach services trade along several policy dimensions. They may have *central* economic policy documents which define economic priorities in broad brushstrokes, either in the form of a national strategy, vision or plan. They may also have more specific *sectoral* strategies or plans, which may be national strategies or plans that focus on the tradable sector, where services trade may figure as a subsector alongside with trade in goods.

But beyond these two dimensions, services trade policy needs to be addressed integrally. This means the policy realm needs to cover policy interventions at the macro, meso and micro levels to effectively target and make the most of the sector. This implies that in addition to national and/or sectoral strategies which target the macro and meso levels of services trade, further policies which go beyond to target micro levels of sectoral specificity need to also be considered. Such policies may be either *flanking* or *transversal*. Such policies can *flank* services trade, when they establish forward and backward linkages into the economy within the services trade. They may include the domestic policy of any given services sector or of other economic sectors, and how they relate to the tradable side of services.[24] In turn, complementary or *transversal* policies may also contemplate the tradable dimension of the services sector in question by identifying the various linkages and contribution of services trade in their immediate

[24] Nonetheless, though sectoral policies targeting specific services such as transport, telecommunications and financial services, may be in existence, they may or may not target the trade dimension of services. In some countries, existing sectoral policies may be very much inward oriented, especially if the sector is not open to foreign participation. The notion of services being delivered "in exercise of a government authority" may prevail. Under such circumstances, services trade in that particular sector may not be open to liberalization and remains within the remit of a country's right to regulate. This could especially be the case of social and/or public services, such as health, education, or sanitation services, which would imply that these are not necessarily viewed as tradable sectors within a government's sovereign capacity.

economy remit. At the national level, this includes industrial or private sector development policies when they speak to services trade.

Lastly, services trade policy also needs to ensure there is policy coherence with international commitments made. This is a dimension that speaks to how trade policy may be addressed by *retrofeeding* external commitments and obligations that a country is bound to through the signing of FTAs with services chapters, and which require countries to domesticate or transpose such commitments through national legislation and policy. Such policies are very sector granular or specific, and so tend to address services trade at a micro level, without necessarily looking at the linkages with the wider economy.

It is only when all of these five dimensions are covered by policy that it is possible to speak of a comprehensive and cohesive policy environment, where the desired policy outcomes have a greater likelihood of being achieved. The greater the cohesion between the five dimensions, the greater policy connectivity, as is portrayed in the diagrammatic representation in Fig. 4.3.

In absence of such coherence and considering that there may be many other reasons why a given policy may not render the desired results beyond good policy design and calibration, some countries may be doing well in

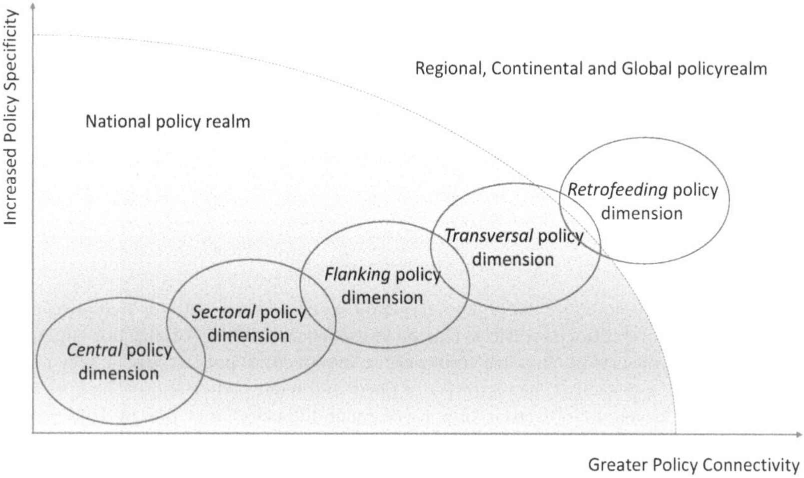

Fig. 4.3 A diagrammatic representation of policy connectivity. (Source: Author's own representation)

trade in services more by default than by design. This could mean they are missing out on opportunities to maximize their current services trade potential.

A mapping exercise of African trade policies at the national level may be conducted along the 5 policy dimensions of policy connectivity, namely *central, sectoral, flanking, transversal* and *retrofeeding*. As such, this approach can assist in determining the various "policy disconnects" that may exist along these dimensions by establishing the following:

1. Whether services (trade) forms part of the national development priorities (*central*),
2. Whether in the trade strategy of a country, services trade has prominence or, alternatively there is a specific services trade strategy (*sectoral*).
3. Whether services trade is mentioned in services policies or strategies (*flanking*).
4. Whether services trade is linked transversally to other economic policies or strategies (*transversal*).
5. Whether regional integration (e.g. RTAs with services chapters) form part of the central or sectoral policy levels (*retrofeeding*).

Though conducting a full-fledged mapping exercise for all countries goes beyond the remit of this book, such an exercise is key especially prior services trade negotiations, there is little evidence of exhaustive policy mapping in Africa at the national level. UNCTAD (2015) assessed policy disconnects of services trade policy at the national, regional and global levels in 30 African countries, reviewing some of the dimensions discussed in this section. ECA (2021), in the context of investment policy looked at prevailing policy disconnects in the investment sector in one country, considering the prospective needs of policy alignment towards the AfCFTA Investment Protocol.

Furthermore, some evidence of aspects of regulatory audits of services trade policy does exist. For example, in the context of Trade Policy Review Mechanism (TPRM) of the WTO, countries are regularly reviewed in terms of compliance with their international liberalization commitments under the GATT and GATS. For developing countries and LDCs, this happens at a slower cadence than for developed countries.[25] In the context of the AfCFTA Negotiations, the AfCFTA Secretariat has conducted regulatory audits in services sectors of all member countries.[26] These audits are somewhat narrow, in that they identify restrictions on market access and national treatment which affect the cross-border supply of services, following the Services Trade Restrictiveness Index, developed by the World Bank and the WTO.[27] Further work is also being advanced by the ECA (2022) on Digital Services Trade Restrictiveness Index, borrowing from the OECD methodology.

A policy mapping exercise would need to go beyond the regulatory audit, in that it would look at the elements of consistency and coherence across the policy and regulatory landscape. In conclusion, though there is some coverage, there is need for countries to conduct exhaustive policy review of their services trade policy landscape. Such reviews would need to look at all the dimensions of services trade policy discussed in this section, as an initial step to understand where policy interventions may be needed to overcome blind spots of policy, as well as counter ill-designed policies that work against realizing the full potential of services trade.

5 Bridging Policy Disconnects Through Regional Integration and the Role of the AfCFTA

With the AfCFTA and its remit to create a single market for services among others, some of the policy disconnects affecting services trade could be addressed. This speaks to the opportunity of *retrofeeding* existing commitments and regulation from the regional level into national policy of African member States. If done effectively, this can bring on successful reforms and change for the benefit of consumers and producers of the services markets alike.

[25] The cadence is established as per Annex 3 of the WTO agreement, on the basis of the magnitude of a country's contribution to world trade. For examples of the latest TPRs of African countries and regions in 2023, please see those of Southern African Customs Union, Botswana, Eswatini, Lesotho, Namibia, South Africa, Cameroon, Central African Republic, Chad, Gabon, Congo and Liberia. See https://www.wto.org/english/tratop_e/tpr_e/tp_rep_e.htm. Also see associated discussion on TPRs in Chapter 7.4 for LDCs.

[26] https://au-afcfta.org/2022/12/afcfta-trade-in-services-regulatory-audit-reports-launched/

[27] For information about the Services Trade Restrictiveness Index and its criteria, see https://www.worldbank.org/en/research/brief/services-trade-restrictions-database and also https://itip-services-worldbank.wto.org/default.aspx

A classic example of a region with a strong experience in this is the EU. Through its common trade policy, this regional integration body has been able to *retrofeed* commitments made at the EU level through the enactment and transposition of various directives and regulations in the internal market of the EU which comprises the domestic markets of the EU member States.

The EU experience has shown that this has been possible not only for the establishment of an internal market where there is free movement of goods. The same approach has been taken for trade in services, with very specific directives also *retrofeeding* commitments to ensure full market opening for sectors which tend to face complex behind-the-border regulations, such as telecommunications, and educational and financial services. Together with factor market mobility, notably, the free movement of persons, as well as substantial reforms of the educational system and the accreditation and mutual recognition of degrees, has further enabled the free movement of services providers in a range of sectors where special qualifications are required, such as health and professional services.

A more recent directive that not only targets the internal market of the EU has to do with Corporate Social Responsibility (CSR) with far-reaching implications for Africa. It is at the heart of transport, as well as other services that are embedded in goods and/or services supply chains. Known as the Supply Chain Directive, which is being domesticated in Europe, it serves as an example of how wide the net can be cast when policies *retrofeed* into national policy systems. As is further explained in Box 4.2, this Directive has the potential to not only enact policies pertaining to supply

Box 4.2 Extraterritoriality of EU Regulation Affecting Africa's Participation in GVCs

In 2022, the EU issued a new legislative proposal known as the "Supply Chain Directive" (Council of the EU, 2023; EC, 2000; European Commission, 2022), which seeks to ban the distribution of goods made with forced labour within the EU market. The rules apply to goods made in the EU and imported to the EU. In a nutshell, the Directive requires companies in Europe to undertake due diligence on their supplier from within and beyond the EU. A consumer in Europe can take to court an importer linked to a supply chain based on their view that there are human rights, or environmental concerns in the source country.

(*continued*)

Box 4.2 (continued)

The Directive is considered to already be domesticated or "transposed" in Germany through its German Supply Chain Due Diligence Act (2021), which came into effect beginning 2023, and other countries are expected to follow suit. Prior to this Directive, countries such as France, Germany and Portugal had legislation in place addressing various aspects of supply chains. Some sectoral regulation also exists in countries such as Austria, Macedonia and Sweden, whilst other countries such as Belgium, Spain and The Netherlands were in the process of passing similar legislation but are now revising their initial project laws for consistency and compliance with the Directive.

Already, EU members such as Austria, Croatia, Hungary, Malta, Slovenia and Slovakia, but also neighbouring countries whose main trading partner is Germany, such as Albania, Bosnia-Herzegovina and Serbia are reported to be directly impacted by the German legislation. Indeed, these latter countries provide a recent illustration of extra-territorial effect on third parties of EU regulation. These being relatively small countries with SMEs prevalent in their economic fabric are expected to have low adoption of the EU regulation (Mahillon & De Puydt, 2023).

Key provisions of the Directive require companies in the EU market to prevent, cease and remedy adverse impacts on human rights and the environment, and to publicly report on their due diligence. The provisions are far reaching in that they also entail electronic commerce (online) and distance sales, both domestic and imported products and their components. They look at production processes along the entire supply chain (from extraction or harvesting to manufacturing and distribution, implying services along manufacturing value chains can also be affected). Products found to not meet the standards will be suspended or refused circulation in the EU market. This can lead to import bans if such products or their inputs are sourced from abroad.

If approved, this Regulation[28] would complement EU efforts to include labour and environmental standards under (i) EPAs that

(*continued*)

[28] At the time of writing, the regulation was awaiting a first hearing the Parliament. See, Council of the EU (2023).

Box 4.2 (continued)
RECs and countries have strongly resisted, especially when it comes to specific indicators to monitor labour and/or environmental standards. This is part of a systematic approach of the EU to align trade concerns with non-trade policy objectives (NTPOs) (Manchin et al., 2023). It follows that this new Directive has far-reaching implications for Africa. It can lead to African SMEs laying off workers and even shutting down if EU companies stop sourcing from them in fear of the consequences. As with previous Directives that affect the EU internal market and which are considered to have extraterritorial effect, this adds on to the efforts of tightening compliance with processes and production methods (PPM) standards. In the realm of standard setting for trade, these are among the most difficult to comply with, and are often viewed as TBTs in disguise because they pose heavy administrative burdens that can lead to trade bans. They require taxing technological and financial resources, in addition to technical know-how. In Africa, there is substantial evidence that this particularly affects the textiles sector, where eco-and/or bio-labelling requirements are often present, but also in food and agro-processing, which are also service intensive (See Páez et al., 2010, pp. 18–19 for a discussion).

Sources: Author's analysis based on the references cited in the box.

value chains in the domestic market of EU members, it can also determine the way in which African countries which are currently part of supply chains operate, affecting their policy space.

When looking at the EU example, the argument that GVCs are in fact not global, but rather regionally and geographically concentrated around EU, US and Asia (Ferrarini, 2011; Baldwin & Lopez-Gonzalez, 2015), appears to hold when elements of CSR are considered. Indeed, Eurocentric value chains may affect the way in which Africa trades in a very deterministic way, as we will see with the EPAs in Chap. 8.

So what may be the alternative to Euro or Western Hemisphere or Asia-centric determinism? Services are well poised to emerge and become competitive as regional, rather than national services industries in the African context, given the small and fragmented topography of many African economies. The potential for regional value chains in Africa must not be understated. Known examples of emerging regional services are the financial services industries of Mauritius and Nigeria, the commercial air transport industry in Ethiopia, Kenya and South Africa, the educational services industries of Uganda and the health services of Ghana and Zimbabwe.

In some of these countries, these sectors are also taking up a lion's share of employment of both commercial as well as the public sector, as exemplified in Fig. 7.4 of Chap. 7. This again is a good signal that greater opportunities may lie in the services industries themselves or which serve as intermediary inputs that are embedded or embodied in the production and supply of goods and other services.

More importantly, regional cohesion around a services trade development agenda through an AfCFTA will also rebalance the status quo and reduce the likelihood of permeation of the policy space African countries experience, as was highlighted in the example in Box 4.2. The ability to move from fragmentation as individual countries and collude around services trade liberalization will build clout at the continental level, as is alluded to in Chap. 8, to make the most of trade.

Last but not least, regional integration developments in Africa also call for greater prioritization of services, as has been the case of several RECs through the implementation of their FTAs with services chapters. The next question will be what needs to be prioritized in terms of services trade policy in the AfCFTA? With the Services Protocol in place and the advancement of negotiations in services, to the point that a critical number of countries and RECs have submitted their schedules for verification,[29] the continent is inching at a solid pace towards the operationalization of a continental services market once the set of schedules are appended to the protocol and trade in services can start in earnest.

Sectors which need all the attention and must be prioritized are those which will render trade in a continental goods and services market a reality. These include backbone services which are embedded in both the

[29] At the time of writing, there had been a submission of 22 schedules which were in various stages of verification, and a total of 26 offers were still in different stages of negotiation (AfCFTA, 2023).

goods and services products that are subsequently traded. Some of these sectors do already form part of the so-called priority sectors of AfCFTA negotiations,[30] such as transport and financial services. But there are other sectors which also need to be frontloaded to get the most of services liberalization at the earlier stages of the AfCFTA going live in services. This is especially the case when we consider their expected dynamic effects, and what they could do to bolster the other two pillars of the AfCFTA, which are industrialization and infrastructure, as discussed in Chap. 2. Finally, there are also those enabling services sectors which would support the realization of the fourth freedom, namely, the free movement of persons. Those are all the services sectors and modalities that are embedded in and difficult to separate from the services provider. As was mentioned earlier, one of the qualities of services is inseparability of the service provider and the service itself. This is the case of many professional services, but also those services that require a very specialized expertise or that are labour intensive.

Advancing services trade at a regional-level policy, could bring on important possibilities for removing major bottlenecks and their associated costs in infrastructure services. Offering opportunities for private operators of these services could veritably increase trade, with important impacts on growth and development, including increased income for poor rural households, as demonstrated by Porto et al. (2011). This has been recognized by African governments, notably through the adoption of the BIAT Action Plan (AU, 2011), which prioritizes trade and transport facilitation as well as trade-related infrastructure as two of its main clusters for action, but also through targeted sectoral policies to facilitate transport such as the SSATP, and the SAATM, discussed earlier in Sect. 2.2 of this chapter. The implementation of these pan-African instruments will require policy interventions at continent, regional and country levels. As exemplified with what has transpired with the Yamassoukro Decision,[31] proper instrumentalization will require the engagement of the private sector to understand what the bottlenecks of aircraft carriers in Africa are and

[30] Priority sectors in the first round of AfCFTA services negotiations as defined in the services modalities are financial, business, communication, transport and tourism sectors, as per Annex X of the AfCFTA Protocol on Services.

[31] Though the Yamassoukro Decision came into force in 2000, following the Yamassoukro Declaration of 1999. However, implementation of the decision did not materialize as desired, which gave way to the SAATM as an initiative with measurable indicators and standards. See also discussion on the same in Chap. 2, Sect. 5.2.

effectively address these for a functional open-sky policy. Though not traditionally viewed as a trade agreement issue, commercial flights are part of trade in services and hence regulation which may pose tariff and non-tariff barriers to both cargo as well as passengers in this sector needs to be tackled holistically.

Equally so, the electrical power cuts require regional interventions. Efforts to overcome this are underway, through various regional power pools, notably operating in West and Southern Africa will require adequate policy grading so that regional grids not only offer a reliable service through the power pools, but also a means of economic empowerment for private operators that may tap into green technologies and propel a greener industrialization 2.0, as was mentioned in Sect. 3 of this chapter. Though not yet part of the services negotiations, this is an area that could find space under environmental services, once negotiations in this sector start in the AfCFTA which will in turn require policy and regulatory interventions both at the national and regional level.

Notably, the continent has made marked progress in facilitating labour mobility and migration, as well as free movement of services. For example, at pan-African level an African Migration Policy exists, which envisages the movement of persons, a conduit for services trade, as, for instance, businessmen and professional services providers will export their services through this modality. This has been recognized as a priority on the continent, since in 2018 and together with the launch of the AfCFTA, a Protocol on the Free Movement of Persons, Right of Residence and Right of Establishment was also adopted. Unfortunately, as with the Yamassoukro Decision, neither this Protocol nor the African Migration Policy have received adequate attention on behalf of the AU membership.[32]

Complementary to these efforts, for a successful circulation of workers and especially of the human capital embedded in these workers, as well as the business opportunities these may bring into a continental market, businessmen and women will require market access in order to have the incentive to move (under mode 4) and establish commercial presence (mode 3) in other locations beyond their domestic markets. This is

[32] Currently, only 4 AU member States have ratified the Protocol, which requires a total of 15 ratifications to enter into force. The African Migration Policy itself was subject to a major revision 10 years after its enactment in 2006 in Banjul and an associated action plan was requested in order to set it in motion.

essential for business services, especially those that are intensive in human capital, and that would bring on associated investments in other services and manufacturing sectors.

Hence, improving the conditions for African professionals and workers to be mobile invariably needs to consider services trade policy, and especially aspects of accreditation, mutual recognition and free exercise of professions. Though at the subregional level, there has been some considerable progress in this area, as exemplified by the negotiation of educational services at RECs level in Chapter 3.3.2 of this book, at the African level, there is urgent need to build on the experience and acquis of services trade negotiations on very technical aspects alluded to earlier and support wide-reaching liberalization of services in the AfCFTA market.

6 Conclusions

Until not too long ago, services as a tradable sector did not figure in Africa's development agenda, as well as in the discourse of Africa's development partners. Part of this silence could perhaps be attributable to the inherent complexity and characteristics of the services sector, which unlike goods, are often considered to be difficult to measure, store and separate from their providers. It is more recently, and thanks to the broader context of Agenda 2063 and 2030 Agenda, that an opportunity for aligning both international and African efforts to harness services trade for the continent's development could become a reality, in the context of the AfCFTA.

The dynamism of the services sector can and needs to be harnessed for Africa's development. However, for services trade to become a conduit for broad-based transformational growth and development, policies need to prioritize the sector. In particular, policies that directly target services, crowding in investment and promoting employment and human capital formation in sectors with trade potential are critical elements to unravel the full potential of services trade.

Furthermore, complementary policies which foster linkage development, especially between the services sector and other sectors of the economy which need services to thrive, are essential to backstop the development of services and ensure their sustainability, as these will create market conditions that are critical for industrialization, as well as greater opportunities to participate in the global economy through GCVs and RVCs.

Hence, Africa is showing a great potential that needs to be further bolstered and developed. As with manufactures, policy plays a critical role in supporting services development in value chains. But policies that could target services trade through various dimensions (*central, sectoral, flanking, transversal, and retrofeeding*), may appear as disjointed or disconnected. This policy disconnect, if left unattended, will stifle the complementary and dynamic effects that could be had of the symbiotic relation services and goods markets are predisposed to share, which are a requisite in RVCs and GVCs. Hence, efforts in designing (services trade) policy that may contribute to facilitating the process of upgrading and upskilling African services within services GVCs, especially in sectors where Africa may garner a comparative advantage, must be part and parcel of policy development and realignment. A starting point for this must be services trade policy mapping.

The present chapter proposed a framework for mapping services trade policy at the national level. Though there have been efforts to conduct regulatory audits, review trade policies and to measure the regulatory restrictions towards trade in services, these are only a part of the efforts required to fully understand what impedes the full realization of the benefits of well-designed services trade policy. The AfCFTA negotiations in services are advancing at a steadfast pace and offer opportunities for the rise of a veritable services industry that is continental.

Moving beyond issues of national treatment and market access for backbone services such as transport and finance, this chapter also looked at important interlinkages of policy dimensions that need to be teased out when prioritizing other sectors (such as education and environmental services), as well as modes of delivery (in particular for modes 3 and 4) for business and professional services. Given the complex nature and characteristics of services, which make them particularly difficult to measure and therefore also assess their impact, it will be particularly important to bring in adequate standardization, measurement and metrology of services into the AfCFTA. Against this backdrop, comparing the options of continental approaches towards harmonization, mutual recognition, approximation and standardization must also be weighed out in light of the efforts being made towards regulatory frameworks of services trade in the context of the evolving services trade agenda of the AfCFTA.

References

AfCFTA (2023), Final Report of the Fifteenth (15th) Meeting of the African Continental Free Trade Area (Afcfta) Committee of Senior Trade Officials (STOs), AfCFTA/STO15/REPORT/FINAL, October, Kigali, Rwanda.

Africa Progress Panel (2014), *Grain Fish Money. Financing Africa's Green and Blue Revolutions*, Geneva.

AU (2018a) Agreement Establishing the African Continental Free Trade Area. https://au.int/sites/default/files/treaties/36437-treaty-consolidated_text_on_cfta_-_en.pdf

AU (2018b), Decisions of the 31st African Union Assembly of Heads of State and Government in July 2018 (Assembly/AU/Dec.690(XXXI).

AU (2018c), "Modalities for Continental Free Trade Area Trade in Services Negotiations", of the Protocol of Trade in Services, Annex V, TI/CFTA/AMOT/3/TIS/MOD/FINAL.

African Union (AU) (2019a), "Towards the Entry into Force of the Agreement Establishing the AfCFTA and its Implementation", Final Report of Ministers, Second Specialized Technical Committee on Trade, Industry and Minerals, AU/DTI/STC-TIM/MIN/Final/Rpt, 11–12 January, Addis Ababa. https://au.int/sites/default/files/documents/36883-doc-ministerial_report-english.pdf

African Union (AU). (2019b). *Final Declaration, Second Specialized Technical Committee on Trade, Industry and Minerals, 11–12 January*. Ababa.

AU (2020) *The Digital Transformation Strategy for Africa (*2020–2030*)* https://au.int/sites/default/files/documents/38507-doc-dts-english.pdf

AU (2015), "Report of the Meeting of Ministers", Dedicated Session of Experts and Senior Officials followed by Ministers of Trade on the Continental Free Trade Area, at the AU on 8–15 May 2015, Addis Ababa.

AU. (2013). *Agenda 2063: The Future We Want*. African Union Commission.

AU. (2011). *Action Plan on Boosting Intra-African Trade and a Framework for the Continental Free Trade Area, Road Map, Architecture*. AUC and ECA.

African Union (AU) and United Nations Economic Commission for Africa (ECA) (2015), *Economic Report on Africa 2015: Industrializing Through Trade*, Addis Ababa.

African Union (AU) and United Nations Economic Commission for Africa (ECA). (2014). *Economic Report on Africa 2014: Dynamic Industrial Policy in Africa*. Addis Ababa.

African Union (AU) and United Nations Economic Commission for Africa (ECA). (2013). *Economic Report on Africa 2013: Making the Most of Africa's Commodities: Industrializing for Growth*. Jobs and Economic Transformation.

African Development Bank. (2016). *Jobs for Youths in Africa: Catalyzing Youth Opportunity across Africa*. Abidjan. https://www.afdb.org/fileadmin/uploads/afdb/Images/high_5s/Job_youth_Africa_Job_youth_Africa.pdf]

AfDB. (2018). African. *Economic Outlook, 2018*. https://www.afdb.org/fileadmin/uploads/afdb/Documents/Publications/African_Economic_Outlook_2018_-_EN.pdf

Baldwin and Lopez'Gonzalez (2015), "Supply-chain Trade: A Portrait of Global Patterns and Several Testable Hypotheses", *The World Economy* (2015): 1682–1721. https://doi.org/10.1111/twec.12189

Bhagwati, Jagdish, Arvind Panagariya and T. N. Srinivasan (2004), "The Muddles over Outsourcing", *The Journal of Economic Perspectives*, Vol. 18, No. 4 (Autumn, 2004), pp. 93–114, American Economic Association https://www.jstor.org/stable/3216794

Borchert, I. and Aaditiya Mattoo (2009), "The Crisis Resilience of Services Trade", *Policy Research Working Paper, No. 4917*, Washington DC, World Bank.

Bromley, S. (1995). Making Sense of Structural Adjustment. *Review of African Political Economy, No., 65*(1995), 339–348.

Carmody, Pádraig (1998), "Constructing Alternatives to Structural Adjustment in Africa", *Review of African Political Economy*, No. 75(1998): 25–46

Carmel and Tjia (2005), Offshoring Information Technology. Sourcing and Outsourcing to a Global Workforce, *Cambridge*, Cambridge University Press.

Citi GPS (2016), "Technology At Work v2.0. The future is not what it used to be". January, http://www.oxfordmartin.ox.ac.uk/downloads/reports/Citi_GPS_Technology_Work_2.pdf

Douet, Marion and Baudelaire Mieu (2016), "La Côte d'Ivoire rêve du chocolat" Jeune Afrique, N°2875, pp. 59–62, February.

Economic Commission for Africa. (2022). *Shedding new light on the evolving regulatory framework for digital services trade*. Addis Ababa. https://hdl.handle.net/10855/48750"

ECA. (2021). *Towards a Common Investment Area in the African Continental Free Trade Area: Levelling the Playing Field for Intra-African Investment*. Addis Ababa. https://repository.uneca.org/handle/10855/46741

Ghani, Ejaz and Stephen D. O'Connell (2014), "Can Service Be a Growth Escalator in Low Income Countries?", World Bank Group, *Policy Research Working Paper* 6971, July http://www-wds.worldbank.org/servlet/WDSContentServer/WDSP/IB/2014/07/22/000158349_20140722093642/Rendered/PDF/WPS6971.pdf

Estache, A., & Wodon, Q. (2014). *Infrastructure and Poverty in Sub-Saharan Africa*. Palgrave Macmillan.

European Commission (2022), Proposal for a Regulation on prohibiting products made with forced labour on the Union market, COM/2022/453 final, 14 September https://eur-lex.europa.eu/legal-content/EN/TXT/?uri=CELEX%3A52022PC0453

EC (2000), 2000/483/EC Partnership agreement between the members of the African, Caribbean and Pacific Group of States of the one part, and the European Community and its Member States, of the other part, signed in Cotonou on 23 June 2000 - Protocols - Final Act – Declarations. https://eur-lex.europa.eu/legal-content/EN/TXT/?uri=celex%3A22000A1215%2801%29

Council of the EU (2023), Progress Report on the Proposal for a Regulation on prohibiting products made with forced labour on the Union market, 2022/0269(COD), Brussels, 24 November 2023. https://eur-lex.europa.eu/legal-content/EN/TXT/?uri=CONSIL%3AST_15495_2023_INIT&qid=1702628204889

ECA (1990), *African Alternative Framework to Structural Adjustment Programmes for Socio-Economic Recovery and Transformation (AAF-SAP)*, Economic Commission for Africa: Addis Ababa. https://hdl.handle.net/10855/5670

EPRC (2013), "*Uganda 2013 FINSCOPE III Survey Report Findings: Unlocking Barriers to Financial Inclusion*", Economic Policy Research Centre, Kampala. November.

Ferrarini, Benno (2011), "Mapping Vertical Trade," *Asian Development Bank Economics Working Paper Series No. 263.*

Francois, Joseph, Miriam Manchin and Patrick Tomberger (2015), "Services Linkages and the Value Added Content of Trade", The World Economy.: 1631–1649.

Gereffi, G. (1999). International Trade and Industrial Upgrading in the Apparel Commodity Chain. *Journal of International Economics, 48*(1), 37–70.

Gereffi, Gary and Karina Fernandez-Stark (2010), Global Value Chain Analysis: A Primer, May 31, Center on Globalization, Governance & Competitiveness (CGGC) Duke University.

German Supply Chain Due Diligence Act. (2021) Lieferkettensorgfaltspflichtengesetz vom 16. Juli 2021 (BGBl. I S. 2959). Gesetz über die unternehmerischen Sorgfaltspflichten zur Vermeidung von Menschenrechtsverletzungen in Lieferketten https://www.gesetze-im-internet.de/lksg/

Hoekman, B. M. (2013). "Multilateral Institutions and African Economic Integration", *RSCAS Working Papers* 2013/67, European University Institute.

Humphrey, J., & Schmitz, H. (2002). How Does Insertion in Global Value Chains Affect Upgrading in Industrial Clusters? *Regional Studies, 36*(9), 1017–1027.

Ighobor, Kingsley (2015), "Sustainable Development Goals are in Sync with Africa's Priorities", *AfricaRenewal*, December: 3–5.

International Trade Centre (ITC). (2020). *Covid-19: The Great Lockdown and its Impact on Small Business, SME Competitiveness Report.* ITC.

International Centre for the Settlement of Investment Disputes (2005), Biwater Gauff (Tanzania) Ltd. v. United Republic of Tanzania (ICSID Case No. ARB/05/22). http://www.italaw.com/sites/default/files/case-documents/ita0095.pdf

Jack, W. & Suri, T. (2010) The Economics of M-PESA. Georgetown University and MIT Sloan. www.mit.edu/~tavneet/M-PESA.pdf

Kessie, E., & Apea, Y. (2004). Participation of African Countries in the Multilateral Trading System. In A. A. Yussuf (Ed.), *African Yearbook of International Law* (Vol. 12, pp. 9–66). Martinus Nijhoff Publishers.

Laker, Joan Apecu (2015), "African Participation at the World Trade Organization", *Development Policy Review, 33*(2). https://doi.org/10.1111/dpr.12101

Low, P. (2013). *The Role of Services in Global Value Chains.* Fung Global Institute.

Mahillon, L., & De Puydt, K. (2023). *The EU Supply Chain Act (Part 1).* Seeds of Law. https://www.lexology.com/library/detail.aspx?g=da9ca850-40db-4d39-a98a-1fb2ad005590

Manchin, M., L. Puccio, & A. Yildirim (Eds.) (2023), *Coherence of the European Union Trade Policy with Its Non-Trade Objectives,* World Trade Forum (pp. 263–270). Cambridge University Press. https://doi.org/10.1017/9781009308137.011

McKinsey (2015a), "Sourcing in a volatile world: The East Africa opportunity.", April.

McKinsey (2015b), "Brighter Africa: The growth potential of the sub-Saharan electricity sector," February 2015, http://www.mckinsey.com/~/media/mckinsey/dotcom/client_service/EPNG/PDFs/Brighter_Africa_The_growth_potential_of_the_sub-Saharan_electricity_sector.ashx

Ncube and Lufumpa. (2015). In M. Ncube & C. L. Lufumpa (Eds.), *The Emerging Middle Class in Africa, Routledge.*

OAU. (1980). Lagos. *Plan of Action for the Economic Development of Africa, 1980–2000.*

Ondiege, Peter (2015), "Regulatory Impact on Mobile Money and Financial Inclusion in African Countries - Kenya, Nigeria, Tanzania and Uganda", Centre for Global Development, March, http://www.cgdev.org/sites/default/files/Background-Paper-Financial-Inclusion-Ondiege.pdf

Páez, L. (2011). *Liberalizing Financial Services and Foreign Direct Investment: Developing a Framework for Commercial Banking FDI.* Palgrave Macmillan.

Páez, Laura, Stephen Karingi, Mwangi Kimenyi and Mekalia Paulos (2010), "A Decade (2000–2010) of African-US Trade under the African Growth and Opportunity Act (AGOA)", *ATPC Work in Progress,* No. 81, https://hdl.handle.net/10855/29212

Please, Stanley and K.Y. Amouako (1984), "The World Bank's Report on Accelerated Development in Sub-Saharan Africa: A Critique of Some of the Criticism", *African Studies Review, 27*(4): 47–58.

Porto, G., Depetris Chauvin, N., & Olarreaga, M. (2011). *Supply Chains in Export Agriculture, Competition, and Poverty in Sub-Saharan Africa.* World Bank.

Portugal-Perez, A., & Wilson, J. S. (2009). Why trade facilitation matters to Africa. *World Trade Review, 8*(3), 379–416.

Roberts, Christopher and Kenneth Heydon (2012), "Trade in Services", in Heydon, Kenneth and Stephen Woolcock (eds.), The Ashgate Research Companion to International Trade Policy, Ashgate Publishing Group; Abingdon UK, pp. 167–185.

Rodrik, D. (2013). Unconditional Convergence in Manufacturing. *Quarterly Journal of Economics, 128*(1), 165–204.

Roy, Martin (2011), "Services Commitments in Preferential Trade Agreements: An Expanded Dataset", Available at SSRN: https://ssrn.com/abstract=1957564 or https://doi.org/10.2139/ssrn.1957564

Saner, Raymond and Laura Páez (2006), "Technical Assistance to Least-Developed Countries in the context of the Doha Development Round: High Risk of Failure", co-authored with Raymond Saner, *Journal of World Trade, 40*(3): 467–494. https://kluwerlawonline.com/journalarticle/Journal+of+World+Trade/40.3/TRAD2006027

Signé, L. (2018). *Africa's consumer market potential: Trends, drivers, opportunities, and strategies.* Africa Growth Initiative at Brookings.

South Centre (2003), "Classification Issues In The Current GATS Negotiations: A Review Of The Different Proposals And Some Preliminary Considerations," Analytical Note, SC/TADP/AN/SV/1, April. http://www.southcentre.int/wp-content/uploads/2013/07/AN_SV1_Classification-Issues-in-the-Current-GATS-negotiations_EN.pdf

Stephenson, S. (2012). Global value chains and services: Implications for African countries. *Bridges Africa., 1*(4), 7–9.

Titievskaia, J. (2023). *Plurilateral Trade in Services Agreement.* Members' Research Service. https://www.europarl.europa.eu/legislative-train/package-multilateral-and-plurilateral-trade-agreements/file-trade-in-services-agreement-(tisa)

United Nations (2009), System of National Accounts 2008.

United Nations (2015), *Transforming our World. The 2030 Agenda for Sustainable Development, General Assembly*, A/RES/70/1 United Nations, New York.

UNCTAD (2015), Economic Development in Africa Report: Unlocking the Potential of Africa's Services Trade for Growth and Development.

Vagliasindi M and Nellis J (2009). Evaluating Africa's experiences with institutional reform for the infrastructure sectors. Africa Infrastructure Country Diagnostic Working Paper No. 23. World Bank.

Vodafone, Accenture and Oxfam (2011), "Connected Agriculture: The role of mobile in driving efficiency and sustainability in the food and agriculture value chain".

World Bank (2015), "Despite the End of the Commodity Boom, African Countries Can Sustain Their Economic Rise", April 21, http://www.worldbank.org/en/news/feature/2015/04/21/despite-the-end-of-the-commodity-boom-african-countries-can-sustain-their-economic-rise

World Bank (2002), Global Economic Prospects and the Developing Countries.

World Bank. (1981). *Accelerated Development in Sub-Saharan Africa: an agenda for action*. World Bank. http://documents.worldbank.org/curated/en/1981/01/438047/accelerated-development-sub-saharan-africa-agenda-action

WTO (1991), Services Sectoral Classification List, MTN.GNS/W/120, 10 July 1991.

Youssef, F. (2019). *Sustainable Transit and Transport Corridors in Support of LLDCs Trade and Regional Integration and Cooperation*. UNCTAD. https://unctad.org/system/files/non-official-document/cimem7p24_Frida%20Youssef_en.pdf

WTO Stats n.d.. https://stats.wto.org/

CHAPTER 5

Bilateral Investment Treaties and Regional Investment Regulation in Africa: Towards an African Continental Investment Area?

1 Introduction

Africa has experienced a surge in foreign direct investment (FDI) in recent years. Several factors have underpinned this trend, including the continent's growth performance, a rising middle class and consumer market, high rates of return on investment and the commodity boom and recent discoveries of minerals and fuel. In 2013, the continent reported US$ 57 billion FDI inflows. Prospects for this trend to continue are likely, as FDI inflows have continued to rise over the past years and in 2013 barely represented 3.9% share of world investment, hence there is room for growth (UNCTAD, 2014).

In an effort to boost such investments, many countries have reduced regulatory barriers applicable to foreign investment. Various measures undertaken by African States to improve the investment climate have included the promulgation of investment agreements, especially bilateral investment treaties (BITs). And yet, the impact BITs may have on

This chapter was originally published by the author of this book as an article entitled "Bilateral Investment Treaties and Regional Investment Regulation in Africa: Towards a Continental Investment Area?" in the *Journal of World Investment and Trade*, Vol. 18 (2017), no. 3: 1–35. This material has been reprinted with all rights and permissions from © Brill Nijhoff NV, with some amendments and updates.

L. Páez, *The African Continental Free Trade Area*,
https://doi.org/10.1007/978-3-031-66605-6_5

attracting greater FDI in Africa still remains contested. To the date, the role investment agreements may have in attracting FDI for greater economic development and transformation of the African economy still needs to be defined. This is imperative, as such agreements are often criticized for offering more protection and benefits to foreign investors, exposing African States to legal disputes and to foregoing viable potential investment opportunities from local or non-party investors that do not enjoy the same benefits.

This chapter seeks to contribute to the debate on how to reform the dispute settlement system and practice that is enshrined in investment agreements where Africa is partner. More broadly, it explores how harmonizing existing legal frameworks on investment at regional level emerging from the regional economic communities (RECs) may be instrumental in this process and discusses viable ways in which existing African institutions and legal frameworks can be used to create African jurisprudence of investment disputes that is coherent and consistent with the pan-African objective of attracting greater capital for Africa's economic transformation and development.

This chapter is structured as follows: Section 2 provides an overview of international investment regulation and resulting disputes affecting Africa. Section 3 focuses on existing regional investment regulation in Africa of the RECs. Section 4 critically looks at the elements conforming an emerging investment framework for Africa, including model laws and African institutions with a bearing on investment. Finally, Sect. 5 provides conclusions and policy recommendations.

2 International Investment Treaties involving Africa

International investment treaties—notably bilateral investment treaties (BITs)—have been on the rise over the past decades. The rationale underlying such instruments has mainly been to improve the regulatory environment for investment, albeit with mixed results. Various legal instruments have been developed bilaterally, regionally and even globally. Though the scope of these instruments varies significantly, they all share elements of investment protection and promotion and are mostly explicitly geared to attract FDI. African countries have been part and parcel of this process, and until very recently, in a secondary role.

This section studies the rise of BITs that are prevalent in Africa. It discusses two important and seemingly unrelated trends resulting from Africa's involvement in BITs, namely, the emergence of intra-regional BITs and increased number of investment disputes arising from BITs. Lastly, the section focuses the implications of BITs disputes on Africa and possible solutions.

2.1 *Overview of BITs Involving Africa*

Investment treaties have been prominently rising at a global scale, especially since the 1990s. According to the UN (UNCTAD, 2014) 2902 BITs are known to exist. These agreements form a complex (and competing) regulatory network for FDI around the world. Africa has been part and parcel of this process and today registers 780 BITs and is still counting. It is interesting to note that Africa has been signatory to these types of agreements since as early as 1947, but only experienced a marked increase in the number of BITs since the 1990s (see Fig. 5.1).

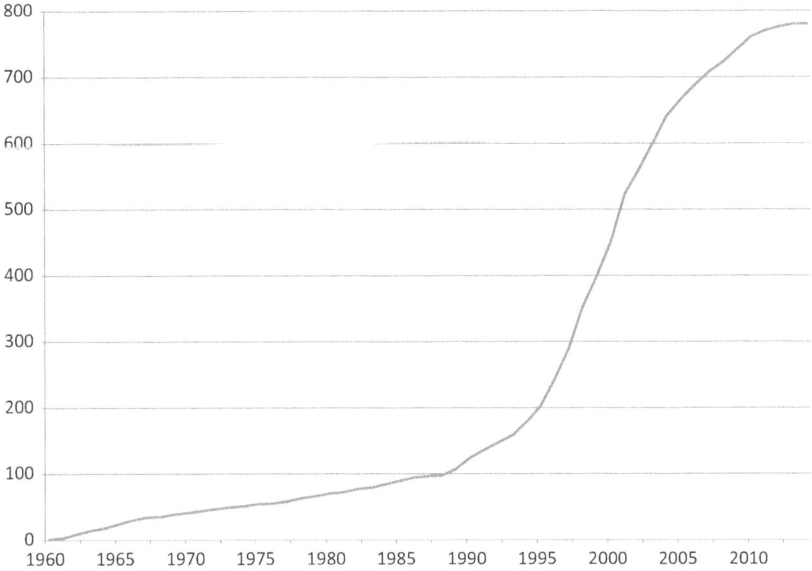

Fig. 5.1 The rise of African BITs (1947–2014) (cumulative by date of signature, includes also terminated agreements). (Source: Constructed with data from UNCTAD's Investment Policy Hub)

Some of the early or first-generation BITs have been the basis (or model) for investment agreements and instruments that govern FDI in many African countries today. From a historical perspective, the surge of these agreements in Africa, at least initially, has been driven by traditional trade and investment partners of the continent, reflecting the colonial linkages and heritage, rather than by economic development priorities of the nascent African States. First-generation BITs primarily sought to protect and lock in investment interests of developed country partners already present in the region, in particular in sectors that portrayed typical features of enclave economies, such as minerals, fuel and other commodities, in order to guarantee and sustain the export of primary inputs for the industry of the source country after independence. These initial agreements also responded to strategic asset seeking FDI priorities of source countries, seeking to lock in market benefits and control competition of new entrants. The rationale was similar to that of the trade regimes colonial partners established in Africa, such as the Lomé Convention of 1958, which dictated the pattern and specialization of trade from Africa to Europe up until today.

Indeed, some of these BITs emerged as African nations gained independence and became sovereign States, a process which lasted well into the 1980s. Having acquired legal personality in the international community, many African countries hastened to exercise their rights according to international public law and gain legal recognition by signing of these agreements. For African countries, these agreements were therefore a means to ascertain themselves in global international settings. The ability to legitimize their rights vis-à-vis other States on investment issues, which had previously been managed under the hood of the colonial administrations in place, took the forefront, relegating the need to establish and tailor investment provisions that would speak to the investment concerns and realities of the young African nations to a secondary concern.[1]

Subsequently, in the 1990s, which was the decade in which the lion's share of these BITs were signed, the emphasis was set on affording greater investment protection as a means to attract more FDI and its related benefits to the host country. African countries rushed to sign BITs with

[1] Indeed, many of the BITs at the time followed templates of existing French, British, Belgian, German or Swiss BITs, and were often duplicated word for word across Africa. Hence, African States were minimally involved in the actual drafting of these first-generation agreements.

external partners, in the hope that this would attract greater FDI inflows, and to some degree also in response to the policy advice of the Structural Adjustment Programmes (SAPs), in many Sub-Saharan countries, which advocated for the liberalization of markets.[2] Though the continent has been experiencing a surge in BITs in recent years, whether or not this has resulted in greater FDI remains inconclusive and has been subject to much debate in both academic and policy circles.[3]

Though a causal relationship cannot be inferred, the rise in BITs in Africa also has coincided with the general trend of growing FDI inflows. Indeed, despite the panoply of BITs and other initiatives that have been put in place to attract greater capital, Africa's share of global FDI inflows is still one of the lowest in the world at 3.9%, in 2013 compared to 29.4% and 20.1% for Asia and Latin America, respectively (UNCTAD, 2014). Part of this low share is explained by the perceived risks of investing in Africa, even though the continent has the highest rate of return compared to other regions.[4]

When studying the geographic distribution of these BITs, a great majority (81% of a total of 780 BITs) have been celebrated with non-African parties. This trend is of course partly explained by the evolution of the historic relationship the continent has had with former colonial powers. Further, there is a relative high geographical concentration of these BITs, as over two thirds of these agreements have been enacted by a subgroup of 17 African countries. As shown in Fig. 5.2, among the most prolific countries signing BITs with non-African parties have been North African countries: Egypt (with 71 BITs), followed by Morocco (47), Tunisia (38) and Algeria (36).

More recently, however, and as the number of possible BITs pairings of African countries with non-African parties is exhausted, this trend may be reversed in the future, especially given the fact that African countries are gradually signing more investment treaties with each other. An important

[2] SAPs in Sub-Saharan Africa during the 1980s and 1990s focused on four major policy premises, namely: macroeconomic adjustment, trade and investment liberalization, de-regulation and privatization. Hence, BITs were used as conduits for investment liberalization. See associated discussion in Chapter 4.2.2.

[3] See, for example, ECA (2014a), Swenson (2013), Páez (2008), Hallward-Driemeier's (2003) and Egger and Merlo (2007).

[4] Africa's rate of return in 2011 was 9.3% compared to the 7.2 % reported at the global level and higher than emerging markets such as Asia and Latin America at 8.8% and 7.1%, respectively (UNCTAD, 2013).

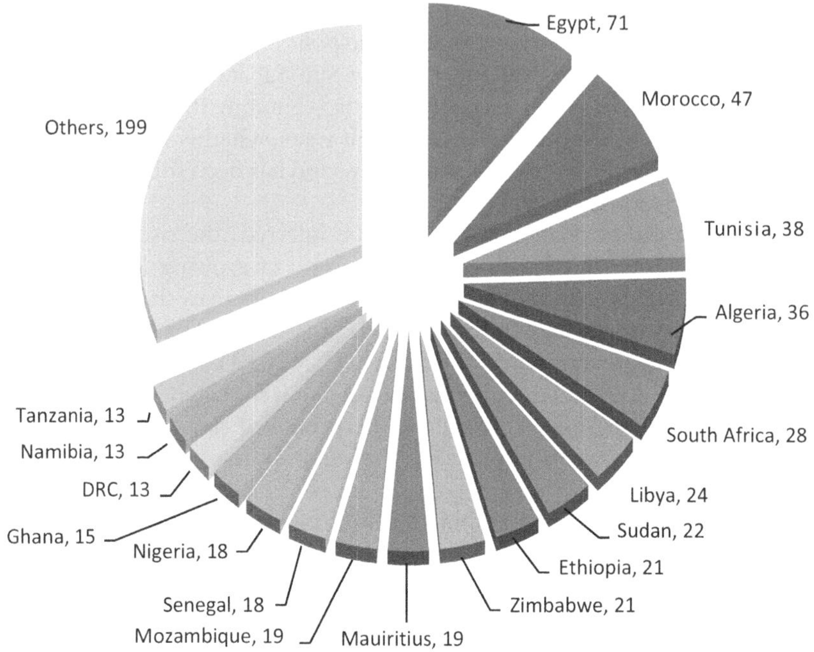

Fig. 5.2 Distribution of African BITs with non-African parties (2014). (Source: Based on the UNCTAD IIA Database of BITs concluded as at 1 June 2014)

dimension that could also be explaining this trend is the deepening of regional integration between African nations, both bilaterally as well as in the context of the agenda of regional economic communities (RECs), which are also developing regional investment regulation and policies, as discussed in Sect. 3 of this chapter.

2.2 *Characterizing Intra-African BITs*

Africa roughly accounts for over a fourth of existing BITs around the world. As was highlighted previously, the promulgation of these agreements intensified in the late 1990s and early 2000s, in an effort to boost investor confidence and attract greater FDI. Of smaller magnitude, but steadily increasing, is the number of intra-African BITs, which involve two

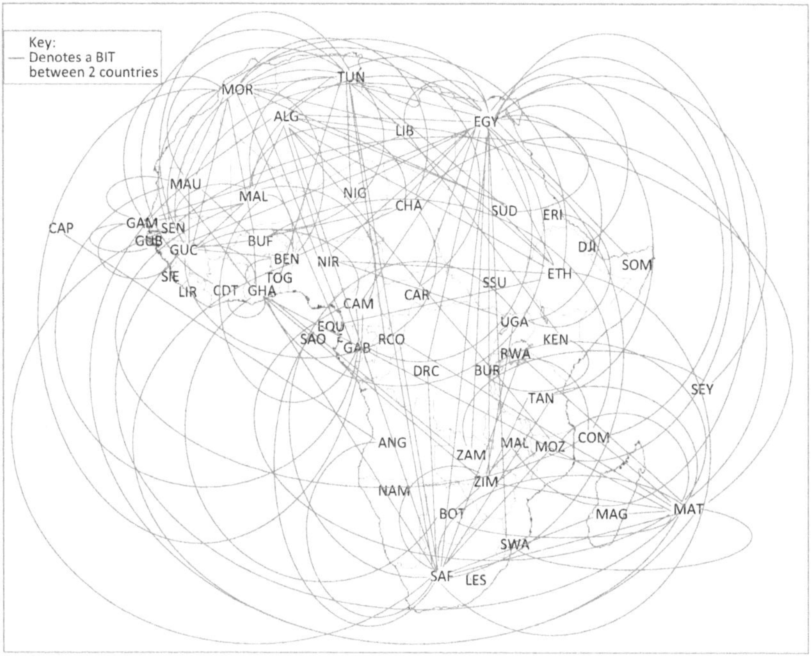

Fig. 5.3 Mapping intra-African BITs: a spaghetti bowl of investment regulation. (Source: Based on the UNCTAD IIA Database of BITs concluded as at 1 June 2014)

African parties. There are 145 intra-African BITs representing roughly one-fifth of the total BITs signed by African countries, depicted in Fig. 5.3.

Though African countries were more actively involved in BIT practice during the 1960s than any other region (UNCTAD, 2000), it was only in 1982 that the first BIT between two African countries was signed between Egypt and Somalia. At the time, African countries had already signed a total of 110 BITs with non-African homologues since 1960 (when the first BIT between Chad and France was signed, after becoming independent from the French). Hence, intra-African BITs have a relatively recent history.

Only in the late 1990s did intra-African BITs gain currency, following the global trend shown earlier in Fig. 5.1. An important distinction with intra-African BITs as opposed to BITs signed by African countries with the rest of the world is that the former grew more dramatically within the continent well into the early 2000s, whereas the latter's growth slowed down since 2002, after an initial explosion between 1987 and 1997. As illustrated by the steep curve in Fig. 5.4, BITs picked up in Africa since 1997, more than tripling in numbers in the span of a decade. Therefore, though intra-African BITs came about at a later stage and have a relatively low base, they are catching up with BITs signed by African countries with the rest of the world.

A major motivation reflecting the prevailing the global view during the 1990s that BITs were the optimal instrument for investment protection and promotion, as was corroborated by the global trend of BITs quintupling during the 1990s (UNCTAD, 2000). Furthermore, BITs between African countries mainly responded to two additional motivations, namely: like-minded States sharing a need to regulate investment both through domestic and international law-making, and the recognition of investment regulation as a means to attract greater investments and deepen regional integration, with a view to ultimately contribute to development objectives. Though there ample is evidence of investment regulation being enacted in

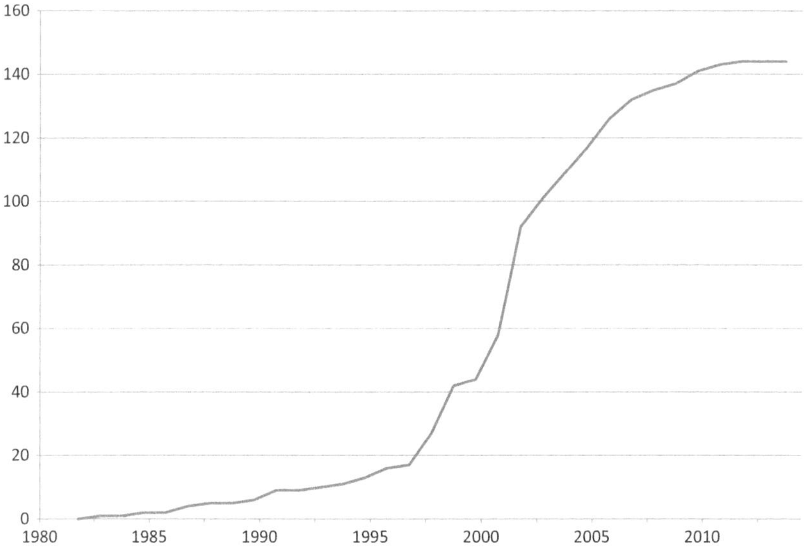

Fig. 5.4 Number of BITs signed between African Countries **(cumulative by date of signature)**. (Source: Authors calculations on the basis of UNCTAD IIA Database for BITs)

the aftermath of independence in African countries, it was only in the 1990s that many African countries actually incorporated FDI in their national development plans and strategies, hence raising the relevance of such flows in their vision documents. [5]

At country level, some African nations have been particularly prolific in signing intra-African BITs. Leading this process is Egypt, followed by South Africa and Mauritius in second place, Tunisia, Morocco and Guinea, as shown in Fig. 5.5. Lagging behind in the signing of BITs are five African countries, namely Lesotho, Liberia, Namibia, Sao Tome and Principe and Sierra Leone, which at the time this chapter was finalized had not yet signed a single intra-African BIT.

It is also worthwhile noting that intra-African BITs show similar concentration to that of BITs with the rest of the world (in both Figs. 5.2 and 5.5, Egypt, South Africa and Morocco are among the top 5 countries). Nonetheless, there are other countries that do not appear to be as prominent in signing BITs with non-African parties, but that have been very active in signing intra-African BITs, namely Togo, Guinea Bissau and Mali, as can also be appreciated in Fig. 5.5. There appears to be some country and even regional specificity in these three cases, as these three countries are from West Africa.

There are also some interesting regional particularities when it comes to the distribution of intra-African BITs by common language, common border and/or shared membership to a regional group is assessed. Of the 145 agreements, a total of 45 BITs exist between francophone countries and 41 between Anglophone countries, leaving 59 agreements that can be categorized as "mixed" BITs, meaning the parties to these BITs have different official languages (either English, French or Portuguese).

The language split can be done more rigorously to incorporate Arabic and Portuguese, but in essence it is noteworthy that there are by far more African countries with BITs that do not share a common language than those that do. Hence, language does not appear to be a decisive factor in the promulgation of intra-African BITs. Furthermore, this seems to suggest that though a given language grouping could follow a particular legal

[5] See Ahooja (1964) for a discussion on the prevailing disconnect between development plans after independence and investment law and Akiwumi (1975) on how inconsistency in the law actually hindered economic development in Africa.

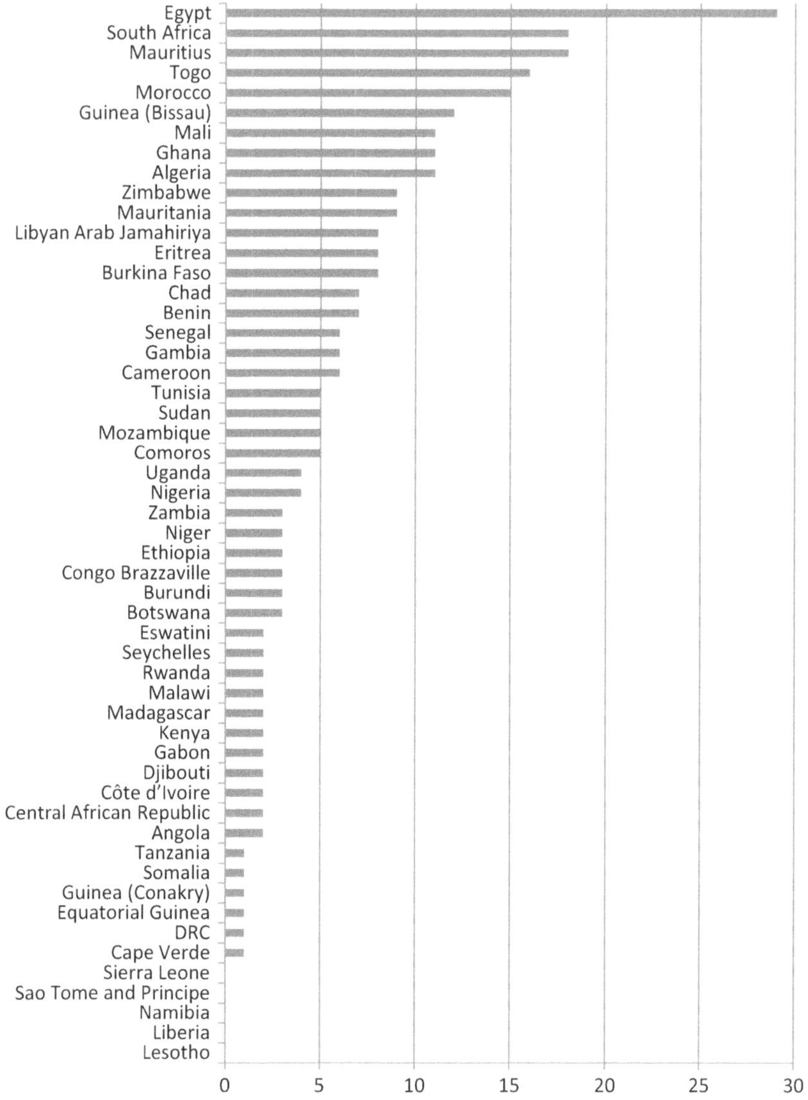

Fig. 5.5 Ranking of intra-African BITs by signatories (2014). (Source: Authors calculations on the basis of UNCTAD IIA Database for BITs)

tradition[6] (i.e. roman legal tradition as opposed to Anglo-Saxon), this has not deterred countries from signing "mixed" BITs.

In the case of a common border, a total of 18 BITs have been signed by neighbouring countries. Hence, the prevalence of BITs between two African neighbouring countries is rather low, at 12%. The lion's share of these agreements—a total of 127 BITs—has been signed between countries that do not have a common border in Africa. Therefore, as with common language, a common border does not appear to be a decisive element in the promulgation of intra-African BITs.

A completely different story appears to be the case when regional integration is considered. For example, when membership in an existing regional group is considered, over two thirds of intra-African BITs (99 of the 145) have been signed between countries pairs that share the same membership in at least one regional economic community (REC), as illustrated in Fig. 5.6.[7]

Given the regional "spaghetti-bowl" of overlapping memberships in the RECs, which is very prevalent in Africa, some countries with a BIT often even share two common REC memberships. Just to give an example, this is the case of Djibouti and Egypt, which are members to both CENSAD and COMESA.

When studying the distribution of intra-African BITs between RECs members (i.e. intra-RECs BITs), some regions appear more prolific than others. The blue bars in Fig. 5.7 capture this distribution in absolute terms, which is characterized by a high variability across the different RECs. Nonetheless, some regional groupings do appear to be more intertwined through shared BITs, whilst others are barely active. For example, among the most prolific regions where members have signed BITs are

[6] Traditionally, African countries have inherited either the roman legal tradition though the colonial administrations of France, Italy, Belgium, Portugal and Spain, or the Saxon legal tradition from the British Empire. However, as most of the agreements today, follow international public law foundations and international customary law, legal tradition does not appear to have a bearing on who is partnering with who to sign a BIT in Africa.

[7] The eight recognized RECs by the African Union are: the Arab-Maghreb Union (AMU), Community of Sahel-Saharan States (CENSAD), the Common Market for Eastern and Southern Africa (COMESA), the East African Community (EAC), Economic Community of Central African States (ECCAS), Economic Community for West African States (ECOWAS), Inter-Governmental Authority on Development (IGAD) and Southern African Development Community (SADC).

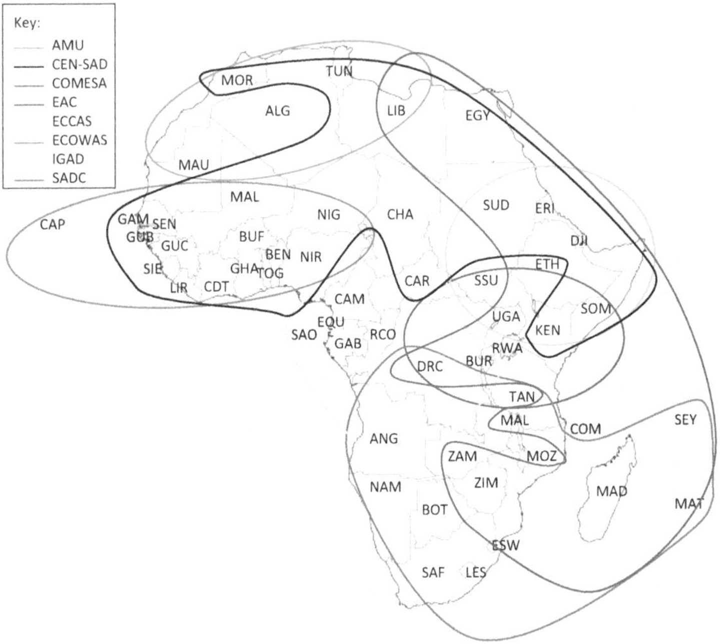

Fig. 5.6 Overview of RECs memberships in Africa. (Source: Author's illustration based on AU (2014b) and RECs official cites and legal instruments)

CENSAD (with a total of 61 BITs) and COMESA (21 BITs), followed by SADC and ECOWAS (18 and 13 BITs, respectively).

Equally, when the Tripartite agreement between the members of three RECs is considered and which came into force in July 2024, there is already a high degree of connectivity in investment matters. A total of 45 BITs exist between member countries of the COMESA, EAC and SADC. This corroborates the expectation of an extended market, as the region spanning over these three RECs constitute a market of 600 million people and a combined GDP of US$ 1 trillion.

Less actively engaged in this process are the Central African countries members to ECCAS, which have not yet signed a single BIT among each other. Similarly, in the EAC region, only Burundi and Kenya share a BIT, whereas IGAD members share two BITs and finally the AMU region has total of eight BITs.

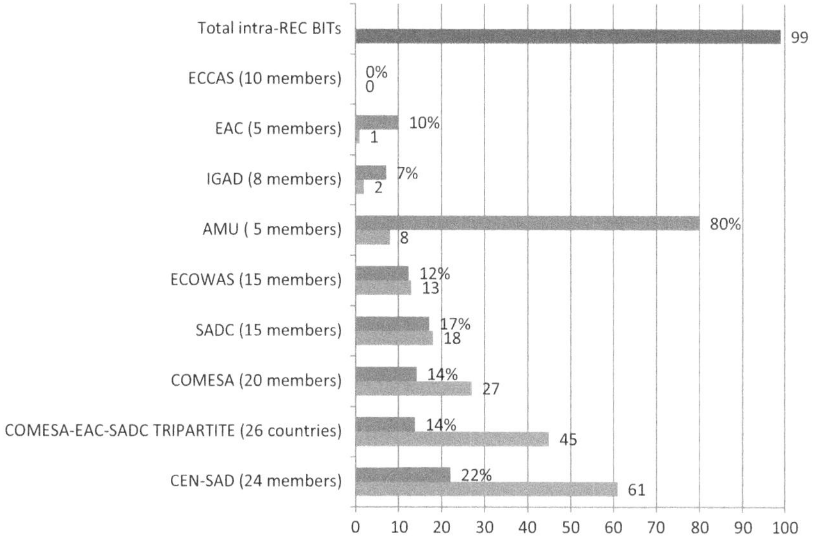

Fig. 5.7 Number of Intra-REC BITs and participation rate (%). (Source: Author's calculations based on data on 2016 BITs data from UNCTAD. Does not reflect the current membership)

Because comparisons in absolute numbers may skew results in favour of the RECs with a larger membership, it is also important to assess the prevalence of actual BITs participation weighted against the potential maximum participation in the context of each RECs (i.e. a participation rate). Figure 5.7 depicts this participation rate within each REC in percentage terms in the red bars. Results show that *in comparative terms*, the regions where intra-RECs BITs are more prevalent are AMU (with a participation rate of 80%), followed by CENSAD (with a 22% participation rate) and SADC (17% participation rate).

Overall, the strong prevalence of intra-RECs BITs reflects the shared notion across many African countries of the potential pull factor an extended market has for FDI. Especially when market-seeking FDI is trying to realize economies of scale and scope, investment agreements may have a role to play in attracting this type of FDI. All of the eight RECs have programmes of market integration, and many have made considerable progress in establishing free trade areas, customs unions and some are even moving towards the consolidation of common markets. This creates opportunities for investment in sectors where a larger consumer market can be tapped as a result of the extended market effect of the RECs.

In conclusion, when intra-African BITs are characterized, it becomes apparent that regional integration is an important dimension in a significant part of these agreements, particularly for market-seeking FDI. Although from a regional perspective BITs are not the optimal approach to developing a regional legal framework for investment, they provide for a network of investment protection for foreign investment, as it allows the market-seeking type of FDI to "jump tariffs" and in conjunction with an FTA, may also bring on related benefits of the dismantling other trade barriers in the region conformed by the two signatories of the BIT.

Furthermore, the increasing prevalence of intra-African BITs has come hand in hand with a spectacular rise in intra-African investment over the last couple of years (UNCTAD, 2014). Indeed, as will be discussed in the next section, some regions in the continent are trying to rationalize the proliferation of these bilateral instruments and are promulgating regional instruments that span over a whole region, in response to the need of a more coherent framework for regulating investment.

3 Regional Investment Regulation in Africa

Since the 1990s African countries have been making important strides towards the accomplishment of an ambitious regional integration agenda. Many RECs, which are the pillars of regional integration in Africa, have made progress in establishing free trade areas, customs unions or, in the case of the EAC, even a common market. All of this forms part of the efforts towards the realization of an Africa Economic Community, as envisaged in the Abuja Treaty (OAU, 1994) which is the *carta magna* of Africa's regional integration process.[8]

In this context, the promotion of investment at the REC level has also received increased attention, as shown by the relatively recent emergence of investment protocols, which are regional legal instruments norming this type of capital flow. Coupled with the recent growth in intra-African

[8] The Abuja Treaty of 1994 is the foundational backbone of Africa's regional integration process. It lays out a roadmap for Africa's regional integration in successive stages and designates the RECs as the pillars on which this process relies on. See discussion in Chapter 2.2.3.

investment, with greenfield investment projects alone growing to 18% between 2009 and 2013 from 10% between 2003 and 2008,[9] the continent has been witness to a raised relevance of regional investment regulation.

Against this backdrop, this section analyses the regional investment regulation in Africa. It first discusses the regional investment protocols in four of the eight RECs, namely COMESA, ECOWAS, SADC and UMA, looking at some of the major legal provisions with a bearing on FDI. It also looks at some of the emerging soft law in the EAC and SADC regions, highlighting how these instruments also contribute to the development of a regional body of law on investment in Africa.

3.1 *Regional Investment Protocols*

In relative recent years, some RECs have been developing regional investment regulation. The AMU, COMESA, ECOWAS and SADC members within their respective regions have either signed a regional protocol or some regional regulation that is related to investments. There is the *Convention on the encouragement and protection of investments between the countries of the AMU* (AMU, 1991), the *Investment Agreement for the COMESA Common Investment Area* (COMESA, 2007) the *Supplementary Act adopting Community Rules on Investment and the Modalities for their Implementation with ECOWAS* (ECOWAS, 2008), and the *SADC Protocol on Finance and Investment* (SADC, 2006).[10]

As can be appreciated in Fig. 5.8, these regional protocols cover a vast majority of countries through their respective RECs (a total of 46 out 54 African member States), representing a complex regulatory web for investments, at both the national and regional level. Furthermore, and as discussed in the previous section, because of the multiple membership some countries have across the RECs, some are even subject to more than one protocol on investment, as is the case of DRC, Libya, Madagascar, Malawi, Mauritius, Seychelles, Eswatini, Zambia and Zimbabwe. All of these countries are bound by the protocols of COMESA and SADC, except for Libya which is bound by COMESA and AMU legislation.

[9] Intra-African investment has increased significantly, especially from countries such as South Africa, Kenya, and Nigeria, and this trend is especially being observed in the context of the EAC and SADC regions (UNCTAD, 2014).

[10] A comparative summary of the main legal elements of these four agreements is found in Table 5.1 in the annex to this chapter.

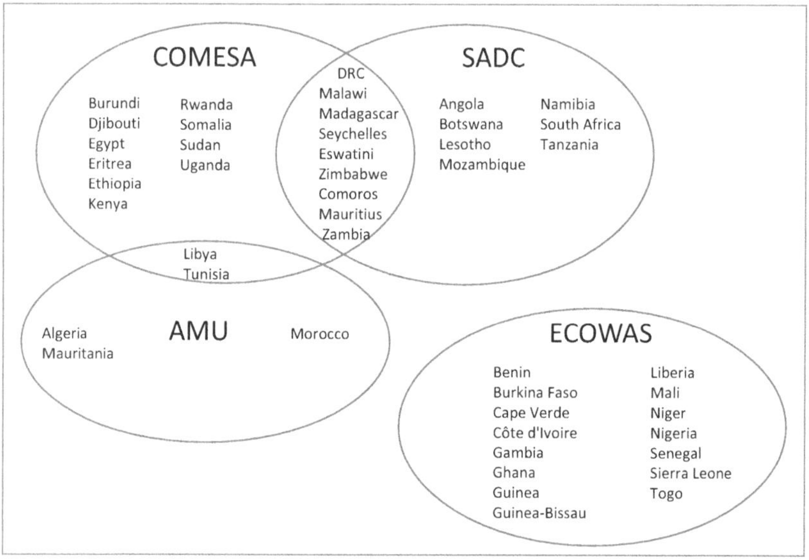

Fig. 5.8 Mapping of the membership of regional investment protocols within the RECs. (Source: Author's representation on the basis of WTO RIA Database and RECs official cites and legal instruments)

Though implementation of some of these protocols at country level may take time, investments are already being targeted through them. Furthermore, some regions do not yet have a regional protocol but do envisage cooperation and integration in investment in the near future. For example, in the case of the EAC, a model law has been developed to that effect, as will be discussed in greater detail in subsection 3.2.

Given the prevalence of regional investment regulation in Africa and its potential overlap with some intra-African BITs, it is important to assess the content and key provisions of these regional protocols, as well as the resulting obligations and rights that have a bearing on intra-African investments. The present section looks at some of the binding instruments developed and endorsed by the member countries of the AMU, COMESA, ECOWAS and SADC, as well as some of the model laws that have emerged in the COMESA, EAC and SADC regions.

3.1.1 AMU Regulation on Investment

The *Convention on the encouragement and protection of investments between the countries of the AMU*[11] is an investment agreement dating back to 1991 between five Northern African countries. Its main objective is to encourage investment among AMU members and is deemed to contribute to the programme of work of the AMU, in particular in relation to the promotion of trade in the region.

The agreement has five chapters dealing with definitions, investment deals, transfers and convertibility of investment, expropriation and guarantees and dispute settlement. A major highlight of the AMU convention is that the definition of investment is conditioned by what is conceived as capital. Chapter 1 of the convention defines capital very broadly, ranging from financial and material assets to intellectual property and non-material assets. Hence, the scope of protection on investment is quite broad.[12]

3.1.2 COMESA Regulation on Investment

The *Investment Agreement for the COMESA Common Investment Area*[13] adopted by the COMESA Council of Ministers at the Twelfth Summit of COMESA Authority of Heads of State and Government, held in Nairobi in 2007. This agreement envisages a COMESA Common Investment Area (CCIA) as a consequence of the creation of the COMESA Free Trade Area (FTA) in 2000. Its main aim is to increase the flow of both intra-COMESA investments as well as non-COMESA investment, as well as promoting the CCIA as an attractive investment area. Beyond this specific aim, the ultimate goal being pursued is the realization of the COMESA Common Market.

The agreement has various key provisions on definition of investment, scope, standard of treatment, expropriation, dispute settlement and transparency. The main highlights of these provisions are summarized in Table 5.1 in the Annex of this chapter.

A salient feature of the agreement is that it makes direct reference to the laws and practices of its member States. For example, the Agreement only applies to investments of COMESA investors that have been specifically registered pursuant to the Agreement with the relevant authority of the Member State in which the investment is made. In addition, the CCIA

[11] From here on referred to as the AMU convention.

[12] See Annex Table 5.1 for a summary of the key elements of the agreement.

[13] From here on referred to as the CCIA agreement.

Agreement specifies that investments are admitted in accordance with national laws and regulation and, according to article 13, COMESA investors and their investments shall comply with all applicable domestic measures of the member State in which their investment is made. Pre- and post-establishment are also subject to national rules and regulations.

3.1.3 ECOWAS Regulation on Investment

The *Supplementary Act Adopting Community Rules on Investment and the Modalities for Their Implementation with ECOWAS*[14] was adopted by the ECOWAS Head of States in December 2008. This Act is instrumental to the implementation of the Regional Common Investment Market, as it contains the key provisions designing the main features of this market and has the objective to promote investment that supports sustainable development in the region.

The Community Rules cover aspects such as definition of investment, scope, pre- and post-establishment requirements, standard of treatment, performance requirements, transfers, expropriation and dispute settlement, among other elements.[15] All investments made by an investor before or after the entry into force of the Act are covered, provided that an investor is any individual or company of any Member State of ECOWAS or a company that has invested or is making an investment in the territory of an ECOWAS member State. In addition, they provide three different levels of treatment: the national treatment, the most-favoured-nation treatment and the minimum regional standards. The national treatment will be granted to investors on a case-by-case basis, after an examination to determine if the "in like circumstances" concept is respected (national investor and foreign investor need to be in the same situation). The inclusion of the most-favoured-nation treatment does not oblige an ECOWAS State to extend privileges resulting from a customs union, a free trade area, a common market or an international agreement on taxation. The minimum regional standard includes fair and equitable treatment, as well as the prohibition of discrimination.

Lastly, a distinctive characteristic of the Community Rules is that they go farther than some other protocols by addressing issues that are not typically part of African BITs. These issues are corporate governance and practices, corporate social responsibility, minimum standards for

[14] From here on referred to as the Community Rules on Investment.

[15] See Annex Table 5.1 for a summary of the key elements of the agreement.

environmental, labour and human rights protection, as well as fight against corruption.

3.1.4 SADC Regulation on Investment

The *SADC Protocol on Finance and Investment* was adopted in 2006 by the SADC countries and entered into force in 2010.[16] It was developed to foster harmonization of the financial and investment policies of the State Parties, facilitate regional integration, create a favourable investment climate with the aim of promoting and attracting investment in the region, as stated in Art 2. of the SADC Protocol. The Protocol also provides some key provisions that can help the States to move towards the harmonization of their investment regimes. Though the scope of the agreement is quite broad and includes various types of asset-based investment, a salient characteristic is that member countries have the possibility to exclude short-term portfolio investments, sensitive sectors or activities with potential negative effects on the economy. This provision is further supported by the flexibility for member countries to grant preferential treatment to qualifying investments and investors, in order to achieve national development objectives on a non-MFN basis. Hence, some degree of policy space is afforded to development concerns related to investment in the SADC region.

3.2 Emerging Model Laws on Investment at the Regional Level

An important and relatively recent development in African relates to model investment agreements within RECs. The intention is that such agreements orient the member countries of the RECs when they engage bilaterally with other countries, in the continent and beyond.

Model laws on investment are recognized as a tool often used to ensure consistency among the various investment agreements and existing investment regulation.[17] They help take due account of existing obligations within the domestic jurisdiction as well as commitments resulting from

[16] From here on referred to as the SADC Protocol.

[17] A recent example of model law at international level is the Commonwealth's guide entitled: *Integrating Sustainable Development into International Investment Agreements: A Guide for Developing Countries*, which mainly affects the Anglophone African countries that follow the British legal tradition and which also takes into account the existing investment agreements discussed in the previous section of SADC and COMESA. Also see model laws alluded to in Chapter 8.3.

existing treaty law of a particular country or region. Because of all these qualities, a model law is also often perceived as an important instrument for harmonization of existing treaty law (e.g. in the form of BITs or other agreements), as well as other regulation and policies.

An important characteristic of model law is that it is a soft law instrument, which is not binding in nature. This is the case of the *EAC Model Investment Code* and the *SADC Bilateral Investment Treaty Template* (SADC, 2012). Therefore, member States which adhere to these agreements are doing so on a voluntary basis, as is expressly stated in these agreements. As was the case with the binding regulation contained in the of the RECs discussed previously, here too, there is a small overlap in the membership, as Tanzania is both member to the EAC and SADC.

The *EAC Model Investment Code* (EAC, 2006) was adopted in 2006 by the then Partner States of the EAC, and subsequently also by Rwanda and Burundi which joined the EAC in 2009. As stated in the preamble of the Code, the Partners States seek to harmonize their investment laws and the Code is recognized as a tool to assist them in raising the standard of their national laws and policies and also in enabling them to attract better quality and quantity of investment into the region.

The EAC Model Code contains six parts dealing with various aspects of investments, including preliminary issues (including definitions, application and scope of the code), right of establishment, investment promotion agencies, special economic zones and miscellaneous issues pertaining to regulation. An important singularity of the EAC Code is that it does not contain articles per se, rather, sections and subsections that are phrased in the form of provisions. Member States have the option to adopt any or all of the provisions of the Code, as stated in Section 3(1).

The most salient aspect of the EAC Model Code is that it goes beyond traditional aspects of investment protection and promotion in the context of investment treaties. It incorporates provisions on special economic zones in Part IV of the Code. These provisions are informed by an Annex which list types of fiscal and non-fiscal incentives. In a sense, these provisions attempt to level the playing field among investors of different origin, such as domestic and foreign investors, whilst also recognizing in the preamble of the Code that competition as a result of differing incentive structures across the Partner States works against the regional objective of establishing a common investment zone. Hence, this agreement is quite progressive in its nature and compared to other existing regulation on investment at REC level.

In turn, the *SADC Model Bilateral Investment Treaty Template* was issued in 2012 and in an effort to address the overall goal of the SADC Protocol on Finance and Investment to promote harmonization of the Member States' investment policies and laws. This model BIT allows member countries to design BITs which include any or all of the proposed provisions. An exhaustive commentary is also included, cautioning on the implications of the choice of language contained in each of the provisions, particularly with regards to treaty interpretation in the context of investment arbitration.

The *SADC Model BIT Treaty Template* (SADC, 2012) is a comprehensive instrument dealing with investor rights post establishment, rights and obligations of investors and State parties, general provisions, dispute settlement and final provisions. All the provisions are linked and build on the SADC Protocol, which underscores the particular importance that is being given to consistency between existing regulation at the regional level and future regulation that may come to being through a BIT.

Both the EAC and SADC model agreements treat major aspects of investment treaties and seek to provide guidance to the membership of their respective RECs. These two model laws establish a clear link with the existing trade integration agenda in the regional space in which the RECs operate, and hence are viewed as complementary to the development of a common market at the REC level. Further, they make an effort in providing regional investors the same standard of treatment as national investors and no less favourable treatment than that afforded to foreign investors. This also prioritizes the relevance of levelling the playing field for new entrants operating and investing from within the region, which are growing. Lastly, this nexus draws attention to the role investment can play in the agenda of a developmental regionalism that is Africa based and that is translating the vision of the Abuja Treaty into concrete action.

In conclusion, there are emerging model laws in the continent that are seeking to set the tone and guide the emergence of comprehensive legal frameworks on investment regulation in the African subregions. These instruments are linked to existing community laws and by extension, form part of a broader set of policies and regulation that are being enacted to deepen and support regional integration through the attraction of greater investments. Despite their relevance, a major handicap of these instruments is their non-binding nature. Hence, RECs are faced with the inability to enforce them, meaning progress in harmonizing existing investment agreements currently relies on the particular and voluntary interest of member States.

4 Towards a Regional Investment Framework in Africa

Having reviewed the major investment instruments prevalent in Africa, this chapter now focuses on the central question of what prospects for regional integration in the investment arena in the African context exist and how these may be harnessed. This section explores answers to these questions in two ways: first, in the context of how much progress has been made in harmonizing investment regulation in the RECs. Second, the section also looks at the scope and plausibility of a continental investment area, as a means to catalyse the creation of the African Economic Community in years to come.

4.1 Building an African Regional Approach for Investment

There is a growing body of instruments dealing with investment in Africa, both at the national and regional level. African countries and RECs are actively involved in developing regulation at both the bilateral and regional level through BIT and investment protocols, as well as through the relatively recent emergence of model laws on investment. At present though, the regulatory environment for investments in Africa appears somewhat cluttered and unorderly given the numerous BITs. This does not convey a harmonized approach to investment. Some RECs, such as ECOWAS, SADC, COMESA and the EAC, have acknowledged this regulatory weakness and have partly tried to address it by promulgating common investment regulation as well as model laws. More interestingly, there is a growing importance of intra-African BITs, especially predominant in the geographic space of already existing RECs. Together with the recent growth of intra-African investment, all these trends pose both challenges and opportunities for the continent.

In terms of opportunities, the body of regulation which emanates from bilateral and/or regional instruments is also having a direct bearing on the capacity of African governments to govern investment. Some of the opportunities of this regulation are yet to be capitalized on, especially the fact that some model agreements are being developed to assist member States and RECs in levelling the playing field for investors with different origins. A major challenge in this regard has to do with being able to "read" across the various incentives that the panoply of BITs have created for foreign investors versus domestic or regional investors, with a view to eliminate forum shopping practices by foreign investors who tend to go for a location with the most attractive incentive structure across these BITs, and often resulting in a crowing out of domestic and regional investors that do not have access to such incentives.

A second opportunity pertains to a common element present in the various regional investment protocols. It relates to the notion of a wider economic space as a powerful means for attracting greater investment for the regional market. This regional market is presented as a fully integrated economic space in which investors can operate, rather than individual national markets. The economic rationale behind this idea is that economies of scale could be fully reaped given the attractive size a regional market represents for investors, in particular in regions where the national markets are rather small and fragmented. An important condition for the full economic benefits of economies of scale to be reaped would require that trade barriers, including non-tariff barriers, be completely removed among the countries conforming the regional space. Investment which is attracted to these regional markets could hence also raise the availability of funds for regional integration and development projects.

A third opportunity relates to the soft law instruments of recent date and which seek to influence and shape the design of future investment treaties and regulation. These "soft law" instruments present an opportunity to harmonize and add consistency to the legal treatment of FDI. While the models for investment treaties are useful for harmonization, they also pose a major challenge given their non-binding nature. Policymakers at the regional level have recognized that there are limits to what RECs can do and that there is need for the development of an African regional approach through standard models for negotiating contracts and investment treaties.[18] Adding to the constraints is the related challenge of implementing RECs' investment regulation against the backdrop of the multiple and overlapping memberships, which add greater complexity to existing regional efforts.

In this context, African senior officials dealing with trade have initiated a dialogue in the context of the AU on the role of international investment agreements, especially with a view to support a regulatory environment

[18] See Final Communiqué of the 18th Session of the Intergovernmental Committee of Experts (ECA, 2014b).

that fosters Africa's industrialization and transformation process, and, in particular, does not reduce the necessary policy space to undertake such transformation.[19]

All of these efforts point to the timid emergence of a regional investment framework which for the time being remains disarticulated. However, both regulations emerging from the RECs as well as from the AU follow a top-down approach, meaning that supra-national bodies are driving this process. However, if efforts to harmonize investment regulation are to gain ground, African countries themselves have to institute and drive change and do so in consultation with their main stakeholders.[20]

In conclusion, a transformed and transformative investment regulatory framework in Africa will entail regulatory reform, including the revisiting and even the phasing out of some of the existing BITs. Re-regulation of investment in some instances may also be necessary. A bottom-up process of validation driven at the national level, where there is the buy-in of policymakers, parliamentarians and the whole array of stakeholders in the investment field, is a prerequisite if this framework is expected to transcend. Lastly, it will also demand a greater degree of "mainstreaming" investment and in particular FDI, into national development plans in a manner that is consistent with national and regional development priorities and greater consistency with adopted pan-African and regional positions and regulations on investment issues.

4.2 *Towards an African Continental Investment Agreement?*

The recognition by African constituents that there are limitations to what can be done in a regional context, as highlighted in the previous subsection, calls for the question of whether an African Continental Investment Area (ACIA) would be desirable. A related question would focus on what could be some of the prerequisites in terms of the institutional, legal and policy framework required for the constitution of an ACIA and does Africa already fulfil some of these requirements?

A first major element in the constitution of an ACIA pertains to the institutional framework that needs to be set up. The African Union (AU) has made some progress in this regard, creating a governance structure that could also serve an ACIA. As per the Constitutive Act of the AU, part of the institutional setup for an African Common Market includes three

[19] See AU (2013a, 2013b).

[20] See discussion on stakeholder consultations in Chap. 3.

institutions, namely the African Investment Bank (AIB), African Central Bank (ACB) and the African Monetary Fund (AMF). Investment is hence expected to figure prominently in regional integration of the AU, as the mandate for the AIB is to "Promote investment activities of the public and private sector intended to advance regional integration of the member States of the African Union". Though the AIB is not fully operational, the AUC has been mandated to fast-track its operationalization, as per a Malabo Declaration of the last Summit of Heads of State and Government held in June 2014 (AU, 2014a).

Two other African institutions dealing with investment in the context of the AU are the African Union Commission on International Law (AUCIL) and the recently created African Institute of International Law (AIIL). These are bodies that could be in a capacity, at least from their mandate to articulate the necessary provisions that could guide the process of designing (and at a later stage interpreting) the legal provisions of the ACIA, a process that would ultimately be driven by the African Union and which would count with the support of the RECs.

Lastly, the African Court of Justice (ACJ), which is one of the AU's principal organs on jurisprudence would also be in a capacity to interpret the relevant ACIA provisions when a dispute arises, given its mandate of adjudication of legal disputes involving African member States. Indeed, the ACJ forms part of the governance structure of the African Continental Free Trade Area (AfCFTA) that is to be established in 2017. Hence, the possibility of having a redress mechanism for trade disputes arising in the context of the AfCFTA is already part of the process which would lead up to the AEC.[21]

Hence, from an institutional perspective, Africa already has some of the necessary institutions in place to cater for the ACIA. As the continent moves on towards the creation of an African Common Market, as per the Abuja Treaty and which envisages an economic space where there would be free movement of capital, it will be a prerequisite that all the institutions mentioned are up and running, vested with the necessary delegated authority by the member countries of the AU and adequately resourced to govern over regional investment issues in the continent. Equally important will be that these institutions enjoy sufficient political independence

[21] In the Roadmap establishing the CFTA the proposed governance structure envisages that disputes are to be addressed by the African Court of Justice. See AU and ECA (2012), pp. 50–51. Furthermore, a Protocol on the Dispute Settlement mechanism of the AfCFTA was adopted as part of the Agreement establishing the AfCFTA (AU, 2018).

and autonomy, which will require the ceding of some power from both national and regional authorities, as well as efforts geared to institutions building. The latter is particularly important for the legal bodies so that they may enjoy judicial independence in the interpretation of and ruling on investment law at pan-African level. This has been subject to much attention and critique in the past, especially in the light of a recent arbitration case in the SADC region.[22]

A second major element in the establishment of an ACIA that would need to be addressed is the legal framework of the ACIA. This would consist of a constitutive act or agreement of the ACIA, which would set the scope, main purpose and objectives of the ACIA, as well as the resulting obligations and rights of its membership. Accompanying this backbone agreement could be a set of specialized or sectoral agreements dealing with aspects that are critical to investment in various sectors (e.g. infrastructure, energy, agriculture, industry), and possibly also schedules of investment liberalization schemes of each of the integrating members. This legal framework would be subject to negotiation and approval by the members, as is standard in many trade and investment agreements.

If we are to judge by the recent experience of the efforts to negotiate the EAC-COMESA-SADC Tripartite Agreement which recently came into force in July 2024 and, in a pan-African context, the African Continental Free Trade Area (AfCFTA), the approach towards negotiating an ACIA could be incremental, building on the acquis of existing investment regulation that has been negotiated at the REC level. This approach forms an integral part of the Roadmap of the AfCFTA, which builds on the progress made in the context of the RECs.

Furthermore, with the negotiation and recent adoption of a Protocol on Investment in 2023, it should be noted that African countries have far from been shy of including investment as a prominent item in their common agenda. This is already a step towards envisaging an ACIA and is

[22] Legal redress in the SADC region is managed by the SADC Tribunal, which in 2008 ruled on the investment dispute *Mike Campbell (Pvt) Ltd and Others v. Zimbabwe*. The Tribunal's award was in favour of the contestant for the confiscation of his land under the Zimbabwean agrarian land reform and dictated Zimbabwe to afford just compensation. Subsequently the heads of SADC States temporarily suspended the SADC tribunal in 2010 at the behest of Zimbabwe, setting a bad precedent of trumping compliance with their legal obligations and undermining efforts to project regional institutions in Africa as credible alternatives to international arbitration. See Ewelukwa (2014) for a discussion and also see associated discussion in Chapter 8.3.

encouraging and will contribute to greater harmonization in African investment regulation in years to come.[23]

Finally, a third major element in the constitution of an ACIA relates to the policy framework. There is little done at the pan-African level on this front. A first attempt has been the inclusion of investment in the agenda for discussion of the AU Conference of Ministers of Trade, held in December 2013, and research has been commissioned to gain a better understanding of how BITs may help Africa in its quest for economic transformation (AU, 2013a).

Against this backdrop, economic policy analysis will need to inform the process of constituting a policy framework that serves an ACIA. This will require that all stakeholders involved in the process of establishing an agenda have a common understanding of the critical issues that underlie investment in the continent and provide for greater dissemination and advocacy of sustainable investment policies that strike a balance between the responsibilities linked to FDI protection and promotion and the necessary policy space to address development concerns.

5 Conclusions

The present chapter discussed whether the issue of international investment regulation where Africa is involved. It reviewed the panoply of BITs which have been signed by African countries and also extensively characterized intra-African BITs which clutter the investment regimes in Africa. The chapter also discussed emerging regional investment regulation in the continent as a tool for harmonizing the cluttered "spaghetti-bowl" of investment regimes. The chapter discusses the merit and viability of an African Continental Investment Area as an alternative to the existing investment regime, in favour of a more harmonized and developmental approach to that builds on existing regional institutions and processes. Overall, the findings and results of this chapter suggest that there are elements for greater regional harmonization of investment regulation in the context of the RECs and that this could be a fundamental building bloc to a unified continental space for investment under the aegis of an African Continental Investment Area, through the AfCFTA Investment Protocol.

[23] Also see discussion in Chapter 6.5 on the Pan-African Investment Code and the AfCFTA Investment Protocol.

Annexes

Table 5.1 Legal elements of regional investment protocols in the RECs

ELEMENTS	*AMU Protocol*	*COMESA Investment Agreement*	*ECOWAS Community Rules*	*SADC Protocol*
DEFINITIONS	Investment definition is informed by what is considered as capital, including, among others: moveable and immovable property, claims to money, goods, services or other performance having economic value, stocks and bonds; real estate and intellectual property, contractual rights, concessions and non-material assets.	Investment definition is linked to national laws and regulations on investment of member countries. An indicative list includes moveable and immovable property and related property rights such as mortgages, liens and pledges; claims to money, goods, services; stocks, shares of companies; intellectual property, technical processes, know-how, etc. In addition, business concessions conferred by law or under contract and such other activities that may be declared by the Council as investments. Excluded are goodwill market share and loans to a member country.	Investment is defined broadly by a positive list which includes: a company; shares, stock and other forms of equity participation in a company, and bonds, debentures and other forms of debt interests in a company; contractual rights, construction or management contracts, production or revenue-sharing contracts, concessions; real and intangible property, including rights, such as leases, mortgages; rights conferred pursuant to law, such as licenses and permits. Portfolio investments are expressly excluded.	Broad definition of investment comprising: moveable and immovable property and related property rights such as mortgages, liens and pledges; claims to money, goods, services or other performance having economic value; stocks, shares and debentures of companies and interest in the property of such companies; intellectual property rights, technical processes, know-how, goodwill and industrial property rights; rights conferred by law or under contract. Short-term portfolio investment of speculative nature or in sensitive sectors may be excluded.

SCOPE	Applies to investments made by citizens of the AMU region, who can be natural or legal persons and who enjoy nationality in accordance with the applicable laws of the member country.	Applies only to investment that has been registered with the relevant authority of member countries where it was made. COMESA investors are nationals or judicial persons of member countries. A judicial person owned or controlled by a foreign national must maintain substantial business activity to qualify as investor.	Applies to all investments made by an investor before or after the entry into force of the Community rules, provided that the investor is an individual or company of an ECOWAS member country who has or will make an investment in the ECOWAS region.	Party and non-Party investments and investors. For non-Party investments, coverage is provided in as far as the investment has been admitted to or made in a member country.
ADMISSION	Admission of investments in accordance with national laws and regulations,	Admission of investments in accordance with national laws and regulations.	Admission of investments in accordance with national laws and regulations.	Admission of investments in accordance with national laws and regulation.
TREATMENT	Fair and equitable treatment, national treatment and MFN treatment,	Fair and equitable treatment, national treatment (does not apply to Temporary Exclusion and Sensitive List) and MFN.	National treatment, MFN treatment and minimum regional standards are the three levels of treatment offered.	Fair and equitable treatment and MFN treatment are offered.
TRANFERS	All transfers and convertibility of investments can be made freely and in accordance with national law and regulations	Investors have the right to transfer assets (returns, proceeds from compensation, payments, unspent earnings of expatriate staff) as per national law and regulations	All transfers related to an investment can be made freely and without delay. Exceptions to this rule are expressly listed	Repatriation of investments, returns and capital movements are allowed in accordance with national laws and regulations

(continued)

Table 5.1 (continued)

ELEMENTS	*AMU Protocol*	*COMESA Investment Agreement*	*ECOWAS Community Rules*	*SADC Protocol*
EXPROPRIATION	Expropriation only for public purpose, under due process of law, on a non-discriminatory basis and subject to prompt, adequate and effective compensation (Hull formula).	Expropriation only for public purpose, under due process of law, on a non-discriminatory basis and subject to prompt, adequate and effective compensation (Hull formula).	Expropriation allowed only for public purpose, based on due process of law, non-discrimination and subject to prompt, adequate and effective compensation (Hull formula).	Expropriation only for public purpose, under due process of law, on a non-discriminatory basis and subject to prompt, adequate and effective compensation (Hull formula).
RULES OF ORIGINS AND KEY PERSONNEL PROVISIONS	Right to hire qualified persons from any country (priority given to qualified workers of member countries).	Right to hire qualified persons from any country (priority given to qualified workers of member countries).	Prohibition to require that Senior Management and Boards of Directors of an investment be of a given nationality.	Engagement of key personnel regardless of nationality when skills missing in the region, and possibility of skills transfer.
RESERVATIONS AND EXCEPTIONS	Agreement is not applicable in the areas or sectors that each AMU country reserves.	Agreement is not applicable to taxation measures (unless there are allegations of expropriation). A member country can take measures to fulfil international obligations), protect security interests or safeguard the balance of payments.	State parties can take measures to avoid or abate a balance of payments emergency. Laws that have the purpose to promote equality or protect people whom suffered long-term discrimination are not affected by the Community rules.	State parties may grant preferential treatment to qualifying investments and investors in order to achieve national development objectives.
DISPUTE RESOLUTION	Investor to State disputes have recourse to national courts, prior activation of ad hoc arbitration mechanism. Other international dispute mechanisms also mentioned.	State-to-State disputes have recourse to negotiation, mediation, independent arbitral Tribunal, COMESA Court of Justice. Investor to State disputes also have ICSID, UNCITRAL or other as agreed.	Mediation (through national mediation centres), national courts, the ECOWAS Court of justice. No express mention of UNCITRAL or ICSID rules is made.	State-to-State disputes are covered by SADC Tribunal. In addition, investors to State disputed have recourse to SADC Tribunal, ICSID, Ad hoc Tribunal or UNCITRAL Rules.

PERFORMANCE REQUIREMENTS	No specific performance requirements are mentioned.	No specific performance requirements are mentioned.	Performance requirements are allowed to promote domestic developments benefits from investments and can cover exports, preference to goods produced, volume or value of imports and exports, restrictions on sales of goods and services.	No performance requirements mentioned.
INCENTIVES	Various incentives are listed, including the facilitation of land purchase or lease, a waiver on investment related fees and the provision of public facilities and services, among others.	Not mentioned.	Member States shall avoid competition through incentives.	Local and regional entrepreneurs can receive support from the State (skills development programmes, SME development; investments in supporting infrastructure; and other supply-side measures to enhance competitiveness).
PRE- AND POST-ESTABLISHMENT	Not mentioned.	Pre- and post-establishment are subject to national rules and regulations. Protection offered by the agreement covers both phases.	Environmental and social impact assessment to be conducted by the investor and shared with the local community prior establishment. Post-establishment obligations are respect of rules related to hygiene, security, health, social welfare, human rights and labour standards.	Pre- and post-establishment are subject to national rules and regulations. Protection offered by the agreement covers both phases.
TRANSPARENCY	Not mentioned.	Member countries must publish all relevant measures which pertain to, or affect, the operation of the Agreement. Transparency is also required in the application and interpretation on national laws, regulations and administrative procedures.	Transparency is mentioned in the protocol in the context of dispute settlement procedures.	Predictability, confidence, trust and integrity are promoted. Enforcement of open and transparent policies, practices, regulations and procedures related to investment.

Sources: AMU Convention, Investment Agreement for the COMESA Common Investment Area (CCIA) 2007, Supplementary Act A/SA.3/12/08 Adopting Community Rules on Investment and the Modalities for their Implementation with ECOWAS and SADC Protocol on Finance and Investment

References

African Union (2018), *Agreement Establishing the African Continental Free Trade Area*. https://au.int/sites/default/files/treaties/36437-treaty-consolidated_text_on_cfta_-_en.pdf

African Union (2014a), *Malabo Declaration On Accelerated Agricultural Growth And Transformation For Shared Prosperity And Improved Livelihoods*, Doc. Assembly/AU/2(XXIII), Twenty-Third Ordinary Session 26–27 June 2014 Malabo, Equatorial Guinea.

African Union. (2014b). *African Union Handbook*. Ababa.

African Union (2013a), "A Concept Note to Initiate a Dialogue on the International Investment Agreements Among the African Union Members August 2013", 8th Ordinary Session of the Conference of AU Ministers of Trade, 21–25 October 2013, Addis Ababa.

African Union (2013b), "Report of the Meeting of Trade Senior Officials", 8th Ordinary Session of the Conference of AU Ministers of Trade, 21–23 October 2013, Addis Ababa.

African Union and ECA (2012), "Boosting Intra-African Trade, Issues Affecting Intra-African Trade, Proposed Action Plan for boosting Intra-African Trade and Framework for the fast tracking of a Continental Free Trade Area", Assembly/AU/2(XVIII), http://ti.au.int/en/sites/default/files/Boosting%20IAT%20Assembly%20AU%202%20%28XVIII%29%20English.pdf

Ahooja, Krishna (1964), "Investment Laws and Regulations in Africa", *The Journal of Modern African Studies* 2.2 (1964): 300–303.

Akiwumi, A. M. (1975), "A Plea for Harmonization of African Investment Laws", *Journal of African Law* Vol. 19, No. 1/2, International Conference on Banking Law and Development in Africa (Spring–Autumn, 1975), pp. 134–153.

ECA (2014a), "Foreign Direct Investment vs. National Champions?: The Role of FDI and Domestic Firms in Catalyzing Structural Transformation in Eastern Africa", Background Paper ECA/SRO-EA/ICE/2014/6, 18th Meeting of the Intergovernmental Committee of Experts (ICE), Kinshasa, 17–20 February.

ECA (2014b), *Final Communiqué*, 18th Meeting of the Intergovernmental Committee of Experts (ICE), Kinshasa, 17–20 February.

Egger, Peter and Valeria Merlo (2007), "BITs and FDI Dynamics", *World Economy*, 1536–1549.

Ewelukwa Ofodile; "Africa and the System of Investor-State Dispute Settlement: To Reject or Not to Reject?", *Transnational Dispute Management*, TDM 1 (2014).

Hallward-Driemeier, Mary (2003), "Do Bilateral Treaties Attract FDI? Only a Bit and they Could Bite", World Bank.

Páez (2008), "Regional Trade Agreements and Foreign Direct Investment", Aussenwirtschaft The Swiss Review of International Economic Relations, September 2008. http://papers.ssrn.com/sol3/papers.cfm?abstract_id=1276246
UNCTAD. (2014). *World Investment Report 2014: Investing in the SDGs: An Action Plan*. UNCTAD.
UNCTAD. (2013). *World Investment Report 2013: Global Value Chains. Investment and Trade for Development.*
UNCTAD (2000), *Bilateral Investment Treaties 1959-1999*, UNCTAD/ITE/IIA/2, United Nations Conference on Trade and Development.
SADC Model BIT Treaty Template (2012)
Swenson, Deborah (2013), "Bilateral Investment Treaties and International Integration", Mimeo, University of California, Department of Economics, Working Paper.

DATABASES:

UNCTAD International Investment Agreements (IIAS) Database. http://unctad.org/en/pages/DIAE/International%20Investment%20Agreements%20(IIA)/IIA-Tools.aspx
Investment Policy Hub. http://investmentpolicyhub.unctad.org/IIA/IiasByCountry#iiaInnerMenu

LEGAL TEXTS:

OAU (1994), Abuja Treaty Establishing the African Economic Community, 1994
AMU (2007), Convention on the encouragement and protection of investments between the countries of the AMU. 1991 *Investment Agreement for the COMESA Common Investment Area*, 2007 http://vi.unctad.org/files/wksp/iiawksp08/docs/wednesday/Exercise%20Materials/invagreecomesa.pdf
SADC (2006), SADC Protocol on Finance and Investment, 2006 http://www.sadc.int/files/4213/5332/6872/Protocol_on_Finance_Investment2006.pdf
SADC (2012), SADC Model Bilateral Investment Treaty Template, 2012. http://www.iisd.org/itn/wp-content/uploads/2012/10/sadc-model-bit-template-final.pdf
ECOWAS (2008), Supplementary Act adopting Community Rules on Investment and the Modalities for their Implementation with ECOWAS, 2008. http://www.ecobiz.ecowas.int/en/pdf/cim-vision-english-version.pdf
EAC (2006), The East African Community Model Investment Code, 2006. http://www.eac.int/invest/index.php?option=com_docman&task=doc_view&gid=9&tmpl=component&format=raw&Itemid=70

CHAPTER 6

Has the African Growth and Opportunity Act Promoted US FDI in Africa? Reflections on a Post-2025 AGOA on Investment

1 Introduction

The African Growth and Opportunity Act (AGOA) is a unilateral preferential trade agreement (PTA) of the Unites States (US) which confers duty free access to US markets to exports from over 30 Sub-Saharan African countries. Enacted in 2001, the AGOA has undergone a number of renewals and amendments, including multiple changes to its list of beneficiaries.

The latest proposal for the renewal of the current AGOA, which is expected to expire in November 2025, may bring on an extension from 2025 for another 16 years until 2041. This new phase, if approved by the US Congress, could constitute a major turning point in the history of the preferential trading scheme. To put things into perspective, the previous renewal for AGOA V was passed on 22 July 2014, through an act of the US President with representatives of the US Congress. This was possible only after the much contested Trade Promotion Authority (TPA) was approved, giving the President a special dispensation to pass the renewal. This much expected renewal came at the nick of time, as the AGOA's expiry was in September 2015.

From its inception, trade has been at the forefront of the AGOA initiative. Investments have also been an integral part of a broader US–Africa business agenda, though they have received considerably less attention

L. Páez, *The African Continental Free Trade Area*,
https://doi.org/10.1007/978-3-031-66605-6_6

(and support) than trade. This has partly explained the relatively low US foreign direct investment (FDI) flows to Africa in recent years, at a time when the continent has been receiving an important influx of FDI from other world regions. Nonetheless, accompanying initiatives to the AGOA have been the celebration of bilateral investment treaties (BITs) and Trade and Investment Framework Agreements (TIFAs), which the US has signed in with several African countries and regions, as well as the former outlined US Strategy toward Sub-Saharan Africa which also featured investments more prominently.

Much of the research focus of the relationship between FDI and AGOA has been in the textile sector, where this type of capital flow has been mainly driven by Asian textile companies based in Africa. Indeed, there is a wealth of documentary evidence on the presence of Asian firms in various African countries which are AGOA beneficiaries, and which have taken advantage of their participation and linkage to textile global value chains, relocating to Africa in pursuit of lower labour costs and duty-free access to the US apparel markets for their exports.

Despite this attention, there is relatively little empirical evidence on the overall impact of AGOA on (US) FDI and the nature of the relationship between this preferential trade agreement and FDI in Africa, or the effects BITs (and in particular TIFAs) may have had in fostering such flows from source FDI countries which have taken advantage of preferential trade under AGOA.

The research presented here seeks to shed light on some of these dimensions by studying the nexus between AGOA and investment in Africa during the first 15 years of existence of this preferential agreement. As such, the chapter is organized as follows: Section 2 provides an overview of the AGOA, its evolution, elements and conditions, as well as related US investment agreements with Africa. Section 3 discusses the theoretical underpinnings of the relationship between trade and FDI in the context of preferential trade agreements, followed by an analysis of the composition and nature of AGOA trade and (US) FDI and existing empirical evidence on the impact of AGOA on trade and investment in African beneficiaries. Subsequently, Sect. 4 develops a gravity model to empirically assess the nature of the relationship between investment and the AGOA. Finally, Sect. 4.4 develops policy recommendations based on the results of the empirical analysis and considers elements for a revised AGOA which may promote Africa's development of (regional valued chains) and deeper integration into existing global value chains through regional investments that may take advantage of existing regional (factor) markets.

2 A Retrospective on the AGOA

2.1 A Synopsis of the Evolution of AGOA and Its Framework Agreements

The AGOA is a US legislation which provides for preferential treatment of exports from Africa in the form of duty-free and largely quota-free access for approximately 7000 product items. Originally signed into law by President Clinton as part of the US Trade and Development Act on 18 May 2000, the AGOA has been the blueprint of US–Africa trade relations since the beginning of this century. The AGOA has undergone a number of amendments and extensions, as reflected in Section 3108 of the Trade Act of 2002, AGOA Acceleration Act of 2004 and the African Investment Act of 2006 (referred to as AGOA, II, III and IV, respectively). The last of these was the passing of the *Trade Preferences Extension Act of July 2015*, which marks the fifth extension of this unilateral trade preference agreement (henceforth AGOA V) which is still valid until 2025.

The various amendments and extensions have involved some substantial changes to the original provisions of the legislation. Notably, a major amendment of AGOA II was the inclusion of an apparel provision and the third country fabric provision, which allowed beneficiary countries that fulfil a given criteria to enjoy duty-free access to US markets for manufactured textile and apparel products out of yarn from anywhere in the world. Under AGOA III and IV these preferences were again extended. Other amendments have dealt with the incorporation of various apparel-related provisions, as is discussed in more detail in subsequent sections. Since AGOA's inception, various countries have also experienced the withdrawal (and sometimes reinstatement) of their beneficiary status under it.

These various amendments at different points in times have resulted in unsynchronized deadlines of the various preferences. Together with the withdrawal of preferences, this has often been cited by African countries as an impediment to fully taking advantage of the AGOA, especially since this deprives them of the necessary foresight required to attract long-term investments (Karingi et al., 2011). Indeed, without predictable conditions and longer time frames, long-term investments are not likely to materialize and support the building of productive capacities.

Taking due consideration of one of these limitations, the last extension contained in the AGOA V synchronized and streamlined all preferences which is now expected to end in 2025. The US government has argued that this will generate a stable environment to attract investments (Kelley 2015). In contrast, African countries in the run up to this last extension had been advocating for a 15-year extension, arguing that this time frame would provide investors with incentives to adequately recoup their investments (Njiraini, 2014).

However, among the most notable amendments in AGOA V is a section dealing with out-of-cycle reviews. This allows the president to fast-track reviews at any given point in time during a calendar year, and to withdraw the AGOA beneficiary status of any country which is found not to meet the requirements of the legislation (AGOA V, Section 105). To date, the president would undertake a review on a yearly basis and announce countries which were withdrawn or suspended from the benefits of AGOA. This new mechanism has actually added to the existing uncertainty of investors as the possibility of automatic withdrawal of preferences after a poor review outcome takes away some of the predictability required to attract and retain investments in the long term.

Finally, another amendment to the legislation worth mentioning is the inclusion of a provision on AGOA utilization strategies. It requires African countries (and regional economic communities, at the behest of the USTR) to prepare utilization strategies deemed to assist them in tapping into the potential benefits under AGOA and encourage greater regional integration (AGOA V, Section 107). In order to take advantage of this, the East African Community has prepared a joint regional strategy to exploit AGOA (EAC, 2016), which looks at elements of regional value chains in light of the regional industrialization policy of that REC (Ligami, 2015). In addition, substantial negotiations between this REC and the US have been underway to deepen trade ties, as exemplified by the signing of a cooperation agreement with the US (ICTSD, 2015). This has also been the case with other broader framework agreements between the US and other African countries and regions, as is discussed in the next section, as well as in Chapter 8.2 and 8.3 of this book.

Acknowledging that the objectives of AGOA cannot be met through market access alone, the US has also worked closely with African governments and businesses to help maximize AGOA trade benefits by launching other trade-related initiatives. Accordingly, the centrepiece of US support for building trade capacity was the African Global Competitiveness Initiative (AGCI), a 5-year programme which supported African countries to access trade opportunities available under AGOA. It was implemented by four USAID-funded regional hubs in Botswana, Ghana, Kenya and

Senegal (Páez et al., 2010a). These hubs have been reported to facilitate various transactions in the textile and apparel, specialty food, cut flowers and other product categories under AGOA, which were worth US$ 178 million of AGOA trade through 2010 (USAID, 2011).

AGCI was superseded in 2011 by the African Competitiveness and Trade Expansion Initiative (ACTE) with an initial pledge worth US$30 million per year for 4 years to support trade capacity building under AGOA. In total, since 2001, a total of US$4 billion have been invested in trade capacity building under this initiative in AGOA countries by various US government agencies. (Brock, 2014).

The AGOA is also related to the Overseas Private Investment Corporation (OPIC), which supports private equity investment to afford more investment opportunities under AGOA in the region. OPIC was reported to have raised US$ 250 million for two private equity investment funds in 2005 and its total exposure in the region was estimated at more than US$ 2 billion in 2008 (Jones, 2010, p. 21).

Other initiatives related to AGOA have included the signing of Trade and Investment Framework Agreements (TIFAs), Trade, Investment and Development Cooperative Agreements (TIDCAs) and Bilateral Investment Treaties (BITs) with African counterparts. As will be discussed in the next subsection, the US has signed an impressive number of these agreements with African countries and regional economic communities (RECs).[1]

A new amendment which would constitute a sixth extension (AGOA VI) could breathe life into the current status quo of underutilization of this preferential scheme. A draft of a bill to renew AGOA has been put forward in Congress, in the aftermath of the last AGOA Forum which took place in November 2023 in South Africa. This bill, known as the *AGOA Renewal Act of 2023*, has been circulated by a US senator,[2] and needs enactment from the Senate during the 118th of Congress, that is to adjourn its session in January 2025. This critically coincides with the expiry date of the AGOA V and hence its timeliness.

What is more compelling lies in the substance of this bill. The changes being proposed could bring in some of the needed flexibilities that AGOA

[1] Also see the discussion associated with this in Chap. 8 and Table 8.1.

[2] For particulars on the proposed bill see https://www.coons.senate.gov/news/press-releases/senator-coons-releases-draft-of-agoa-reauthorization-act-to-deepen-us-africa-economic-relationship#:~:text=The%20AGOA%20Renewal%20Act%20would,and%20reduce%20dependence%20on%20China and https://agoa.info/downloads/legal/16382.html

I to V have often been criticized for lacking. Notably, the proposed amendments would allow for more flexible rules of origin, where regional cumulation across the whole of Africa (including non-beneficiaries), and 3-year rather than yearly reviews, which would allow some countries to retain their eligibility, given their vulnerabilities due to fluctuations in their income levels.

But there are important challenges that are yet to be mastered. First, the current US administration does not count with the TPA, described earlier at the beginning of this chapter.[3] In past administrations, this has become a major sticking point for the advancement of trade agreements, as was the case during the Clinton Administration (Wright, 2004). Secondly, a number of countries (Rwanda, Tanzania and Uganda, for example in 2017) have been subject to out-of-cycle reviews introduced under AGOA V, described earlier in this section. Sometimes such reviews have led to ineligibility. Furthermore, a significant number of other countries have become ineligible over the past couple of years for various (political) reasons (e.g. Cameroon in 2020, Ethiopia, Guinea and Mali in 2022 and Gabon, Central African Republic, Niger and Uganda in 2024). With a dwindling number of beneficiaries, it will be difficult for the continent as a whole to take advantage of a revamped AGOA VI. Lastly, what perhaps is also missing is the formulation and or revision of existing framework agreements, that also see eye to eye with the reality of the AfCFTA, that has come to stay, in order to reap the maximum and associated benefits of trade and investment through AGOA.

2.2 *The Relationship between Investment Agreements and the AGOA*

Investments have been an integral part of the AGOA agenda, though arguably less clearly articulated and prioritized at its inception. Indeed, under AGOA I, investments were mentioned in conjunction with trade, but in hortatory language, as exemplified by (sec. 102 (8) and (9)), and which hardly represented a commitment to promote US investments.

In recent years, a clearer formulation of an investment agenda has gained currency in the context of AGOA. Indeed, the US Strategy toward Sub-Saharan Africa presented by President Obama in 2012, has further

[3] Under the Biden administration, the prior TPA expired on 1 July 2021 and has not been renewed. See Congressional Research Services (2022).

bolstered the role of investments in AGOA beneficiaries. The strategy gives priority to promoting regional integration, and lauds the work conducted in the context of the East African Community Trade and Investment Initiative, to help reduce barriers to trade and investment in the continent. It also seeks to encourage trade and investment of US companies in Africa by launching a Doing Business in Africa campaign and providing business facilitation support for companies which are interested in investing in Sub-Saharan Africa (The White House, 2012).

More recently, the "Trade Africa" initiative, was aimed at promoting Africa's regional and international trade. Initially launched in the East African region, this initiative is expanding to other African countries and also focusing on investment-related trade promotion.[4]

The AGOA V in Section 108 formally spells out the US policy on trade and investment with Sub-Saharan Africa. It mentions the negotiation of investment and trade agreements as instruments to deepen and expand existing ties both with individual countries and RECs and vests such agreements with the catalytic role of facilitating greater trade and investment flows with the region.

This policy is consonant with the US foreign policy on trade and investment, which in recent years has aggressively pursued various trade and investment agreements with countries and regions around the world (see US GAO, 2004, p. 3 and 26), and especially since the stalling and death of multilateral discussion on investment in the WTO Doha Round.[5] There are three types of investment agreements the US has celebrated with Africa, namely TIFAs, TIDCAs and BITs. The former two may be characterized as cooperation agreements between parties. They are forward looking, generally outline cooperation modalities, and contain an indicative agenda of work towards developing and deepening trade and investment relations. They are also known to precede FTAs with the US, such

[4] See https://www.usaid.gov/tradeafrica for further information.

[5] The multilateral trading system in the context of WTO trade negotiations does not formally include investment in its mandate, except for trade-related investment measures. Many countries at the time the Doha Round was launched had the expectation to advance on several issues which arose in the context of the Singapore Trade Ministerial of 1996. These issues were trade facilitation, competition, government procurement and notably investment. They were named the "Singapore Issues" and were included as part of a built-in agenda for discussion upon the launch of the Doha Round. Today, only progress has been made with regards to trade facilitation, the other three issues were formally dropped from the current Doha Round. See Páez (2011), pp. 88–93 for an exhaustive discussion.

as bilateral FTA with Morocco and plurilaterally with SACU which also have a TIFA agreement with the US.[6]

In turn, BITs are traditional investment protection and promotion agreements. They contain legal obligations which are binding for its signatories and conform with the *Vienna Convention on the Law of Treaties* (1969). Correspondingly, differences in the interpretation or administration of such agreements can be resolved through international dispute settlement mechanisms, notably under the International Court of Justice (ICJ), the United Nations Commission on International Trade Law (UNCITRAL) or the International Centre for the Settlement of Investment Disputes (ICSID). Indeed, all of these three avenues are expressly mentioned in the various US-Africa BITs.

As shown in Table 6.1, during the period under review (2000–2014), the US had a total of 9 BITs with African countries, 4 TIFAs with RECs which span over a total of 35 countries, 11 TIFAs with individual countries, and finally 1 TIDCA with SACU, comprising 5 Southern African countries. This renders an impressive total of 24 investment agreements between the US and Africa. Furthermore, it is interesting to note that there is considerable overlap in terms of membership. Several countries have some bilateral agreement with the US, and given their multiple memberships in RECs, also have repeated TIFAs in place. This is the case of DRC, Egypt, Ghana, Liberia, Libya, Kenya, Rwanda and Senegal. Hence, an intricate web, or "spaghetti bowl", of investment agreements with the US seems to have been formed, which is consistent with the general pattern of BITs Africa has with the rest of the world (Páez, 2017).

Another interesting highlight is that these investment agreements are widespread across African countries, irrespective of whether they are AGOA beneficiaries or not. The only countries which currently did not have an investment agreement with the US during the said reference period are Gabon, Equatorial Guinea, Central African Republic and Somalia, with the latter three not being AGOA beneficiaries at the time.

Indeed, virtually all of the BITs (with the exception of the US-Rwanda BIT) predate AGOA and go as far back as 1983. It follows that none of the older BITs would establish a formal link to AGOA, but neither do the TIFAs and TIDCA which superseded the AGOA. Hence, though the

[6] More recently, a plurilateral trade in services FTA known as the Trade in Services Agreement (TiSA) is in the process of being negotiated between 23 countries, including Mauritius and the US.

Table 6.1 Mapping of AGOA benefits and investment agreements with the US (2000–2014)

Country	*AGOA Beneficiary*	*General/Special rule Beneficiary*	*Bilateral BIT/ TIFA*	*COMESA TIFA*	*EAC TIFA*	*ECOWAS/ WAEMU TIFA*	*SACU TIDCA*
Algeria			○				
Angola	●		○				
Benin	●	●/○				●/○	
Botswana	●	●/○					●
Burkina Faso	●	●/○				●/○	
Burundi	●			●	●		
Cameroon	●	●/○	●				
Cape Verde	●	●/○				●	
Central African Republic							
Chad	●	●/○					
Comoros	●			●			
Congo Brazzaville	●		●				
Côte d'Ivoire[b]	●	●/○				●/○	
DRC[a]			●	●			
Djibouti	●			●			
Egypt			●/○	●			
Eritrea[a]				●			
Ethiopia	●	●/○		●			
Equatorial Guinea							
Gabon	●						
Gambia[a]						●	
Ghana	●	●/○	○			●	
Guinea (Conakry)[b]	●	●/○				●	

(*continued*)

Table 6.1 (continued)

Country	*AGOA Beneficiary*	*General/Special rule Beneficiary*	*Bilateral BIT/ TIFA*	*COMESA TIFA*	*EAC TIFA*	*ECOWAS/ WAEMU TIFA*	*SACU TIDCA*
Guinea (Bissau)[b]	●	●				●/○	
Kenya	●	●/○		●	●		
Lesotho	●	●/○					●
Liberia	●	●/○	○			●	
Libyan Arab Jamahiriya			○	●			
Madagascar[b]	●	●/○		●			
Malawi	●	●/○		●			
Mali[b]	●	●				●/○	
Mauritania[b]	●						
Mauritius	●	●/○	○				
Morocco			●/○				
Mozambique	●	●/○	●/○				
Namibia	●	●/○					●
Niger[b]	●	●				●/○	
Nigeria	●	●/○	○			●	
Rwanda	●	●/○	●/○	●	●		
Sao Tome and Principe	●						
Senegal	●	●/○	●			●/○	
Seychelles	●			●			
Sierra Leone	●	●/○				●	
Somalia							
South Africa	●	●					●

Sudan				•			
South Sudan[a]				•			
Eswatini[a]				•			•
Togo	•					•/○	
Tunisia			•				
Uganda	•	•/○		•	•		
Tanzania	•	•/○		•	•		
Zambia	•	•/○		•			
Zimbabwe				•			

Source: Author's representation based on Brock (2014), USTR and Trade Compliance Centre https://ustr.gov/trade-agreements/trade-investment-framework-agreements and US International trade administration http://trade.gov/agoa/eligibility/index.asp

[a]Country has lost eligibility and not regained it; [b]Country has lost and regained eligibility during 2000–2015

AGOA may seek to promote trade and investment, its relationship with these agreements is yet to be spelled out. This, however, is not to say that AGOA may not have been instrumental in attracting investment to Africa. There is indeed documentary evidence of this in the textile and apparel sector, as will be further elaborated in subsequent sections.

2.3 Requirements and Conditionalities under AGOA and Their Implications on FDI in Africa

AGOA eligibility requirements and conditionalities are contained in Section 104 of the AGOA legislation (AGOA V). Section 104 also spells out various political and human rights conditions as well as labour standards eligible countries have to comply with. Eligible countries are defined and listed as Sub-Saharan African countries. Out of the 48 possible beneficiaries listed, a total of 38 countries enjoyed this status during the period of study (2000–2014), as shown in the first column of Table 6.1. This number has suffered various changes over time, as eligibility is assessed yearly by the US president on the basis of established criteria in the law. A number of countries have lost eligibility in the past, such as DRC and The Gambia, Eswatini and South Sudan, whilst others have been able to regain it, most recently Guinea Bissau and Mali in 2014. Furthermore, a country which had graduated under the AGOA is Seychelles, and had to exit the beneficiaries list in 2017.

In addition, countries are eligible to more beneficial rules of origin if they meet the economic development criteria of a "lesser developed" economy, defined by a threshold of US$ 1500 GNP per capita in 1998. This criterion allows them to benefit from the Special Rule for apparel under AGOA, which gives market access to apparel produced with fabric that originates from anywhere in the world, as opposed to the General Rule which requires that apparel sources yarn and fabric inputs either locally or from other SSA countries or US markets. Mauritius to has been in the limelight for surpassing this criterion in recent years, which would be catastrophic for its textile industry.

The AGOA has often been criticized for the very ambiguous application of this rule, as Botswana and Namibia have been granted this status though they surpass the given threshold. In addition, the fact that only Sub-Saharan African countries are considered to be eligible for AGOA beneficiary status leaves North African countries out of this preferential trade arrangement, though arguably some could comply with the special rule[7] and Morocco, Tunisia and Egypt could also be potential sources for fabric and yarn inputs and hence benefit from the AGOA general rule.

Equally, a number of additional and very specific rules of origin apply to those countries which qualify for various apparel benefits. The main rule relates to transshipment which requires a certificate of origin for textiles and apparel. Eligible countries must adopt a visa verification system for transshipment to be granted the apparel preferences under the General Rule. Other and very complex apparel provisions which were introduced in AGOA IV relate to handloomed, handmade, folklore articles and ethnic printed fabrics (so-called category 9 benefits). The granting of duty and quota free benefits for this type of apparel is subject to an exhaustive review and consultation with the interested beneficiaries.

Of the 38 beneficiaries under AGOA V, 29 have access to the General Rule (as shown earlier in Table 6.1), 28 in total have access to the Special Rule, and 21 enjoy the additional preferences under category 9 apparel.[8] Only 4 countries (Benin, Burkina Faso, Nigeria and Tanzania) enjoyed all the apparel-related benefits under AGOA in the review period (2000–2014). This, however, has not necessarily translated into taking full advantage of these apparel benefits. Indeed, it has been reported that only a handful of countries, mainly Kenya, Lesotho and Mauritius have been able to significantly realize the apparel benefits under AGOA (Brock, 2014), and have also experienced associated foreign direct investment (FDI) in their apparel sectors (Lall, 2003; Gibbon, 2003).

As a result of the stringent and sometimes heterogeneous application of AGOA criteria, SSA countries have often complained about the arbitrariness of its conditionalities and its impact on their ability to benefit from the promise of greater trade and investment under AGOA and have indeed requested for greater transparency and foresight in its application. Furthermore, concerns have also been voiced as to the extent to which AGOA has met its objectives in terms of increasing Africa–US trade, diversifying and adding value to African exports and more specifically, attracting FDI to support these processes. In conjunction with this, concerns

[7] According to the *World Development Indicators*, out of the five countries in question, GNP per capita in 1998 for Egypt and Morocco were indeed under the reference threshold, whilst Algeria was just over the threshold by US$30. http://data.worldbank.org/indicator/NY.GNP.PCAP.CD?page=3

[8] Information on AGOA eligibility for apparel is found on the website of the US Department of Commerce: http://web.ita.doc.gov/tacgi/eamain.nsf/6e1600e39721316c852570ab0056f719/8a3cec919226ed0f852573940048b050?OpenDocument

have also been raised on the ability of AGOA beneficiaries to tap into regional value chains which would enable them to source intermediate products from other countries in the region, even if they do not meet the stringent rules of origin of AGOA. This could be an opportunity in itself to promote regional value addition and develop existing regional value chains which could attract greater FDI (See Páez et al., 2010b; Karingi et al., 2011). But in order to achieve this, the existing rules of origin and transshipment requirements would have to be relaxed, something which has long been advocated by African constituents of AGOA but so far not been translated into an amendment of the existing legislation.

Equally so, countries that enjoy the various fabric provisions appear to have a less favourable impact on the attraction of US investment. Once again, though causality may only be inferred, this could be an indication of the more stringent conditionalities for the apparel and textiles provisions having a dampening effect on FDI. Indeed, recent research seems to suggest that the Special Rule under AGOA has been counterproductive to building skills and attracting investment into the apparel manufacturing sector of African countries (Edwards & Lawrence, 2013).

A pertinent question which arises in this context is whether the two major objectives of AGOA of increasing trade from African countries and attracting greater FDI into Africa are indeed interrelated and mutually supportive or exclusive. In sum, the question of whether AGOA has been instrumental to attracting greater US FDI in the region needs to be answered empirically, which is the focus of the next two sections.

3 Relationships Between AGOA Trade and FDI

3.1 Composition and Nature of AGOA Trade and US FDI to AGOA Countries

The AGOA preferences cover over 6000 product items, after the extension of GSP preferences to a further 1800 product lines. These include numerous food products, handbags, gloves, footwear, iron and steel items, automotive components and vehicles and notably, apparel and textile products. Thus, more than 7000 products, with the exception of certain textile and apparel products which are subject to quota restrictions, enjoy duty-free and quota-free access to the US.

When looking at the figures during the reference period (2000–2014), aggregate trade data on AGOA reveals that since its inception, a total of

US$ 208 billion cumulative trade entered US markets under AGOA I to IV. Figure 6.1 below depicts AGOA export performance during the reference period. As can be appreciated, peak years for African exports were 2008 and 2011, which have been associated with the commodity boom of international commodity prices, as AGOA countries are highly commodity export dependent.[9] The two major slumps of total trade were in 2002 and 2009, both in the aftermath of international financial crises which waned US demand of imports as the economy receded. Since 2011, total trade has been falling sharply, down to pre-2004 levels, and is partly explained by the end of the commodities bubble, as is further also exemplified later in Fig. 6.3 with oil and fuel commodities.

It appears that AGOA preferential trade suffered from less volatility than total exports from the AGOA region, as shown by the more normalized curve in Fig. 6.1. Peak AGOA years were 2005 and 2008. In 2006, AGOA trade retracted noticeably and contrary to the behaviour of total

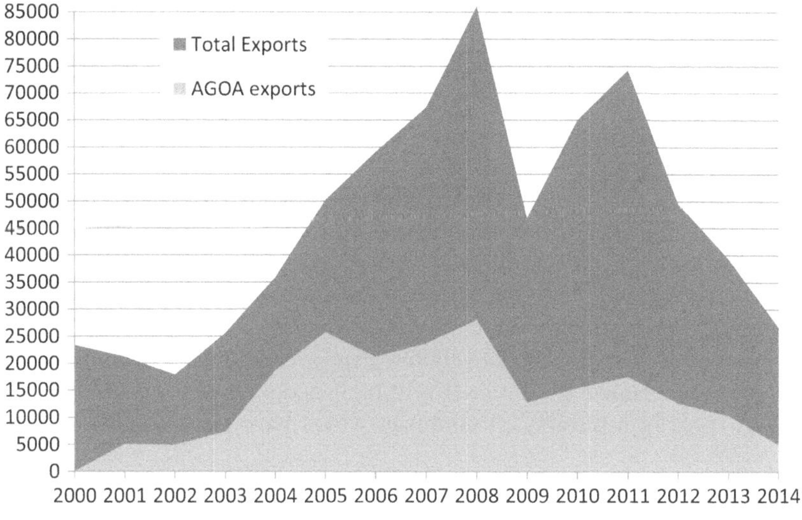

Fig. 6.1 Exports to the US from AGOA beneficiaries 2000–2014 (customs value in US$ million). (Source: Author's representation, on the basis of data from U.S. Department of Commerce and USITC)

[9] The continent has experienced the greatest increase in export concentration, with an export concentration ratio nearly doubling from 0.27 in 1995 to 0.48 in 2008 (UNDP, 2011).

US trade from the AGOA region widened the gap considerably and pointing to various root causes. Furthermore, 2009 saw a contraction in line with total trade after the financial turmoil, followed by a sluggish recovery until 2011. Since then, AGOA trade has been retracting, reaching an absolute low in 2014, comparable to pre-2004 AGOA levels.

Especially since 2006, AGOA preferential trade appears to have been losing out on non-AGOA trade to the US from the same beneficiary region. This loss in preferential trade responds to several factors, including the lack of predictability of the beneficiary status, as many countries have lost (and in some instances not regained) eligibility, as shown earlier in Table 6.1. It also relates to the aforementioned stringent rules of origin and visa requirements, in particular for textiles and apparel exports, as well as increased competition in apparel export markets since the prevailing quota system under the Multifibre Agreement (MFA) was eliminated in 2005.[10]

A second important dimension of characterizing AGOA trade relates to its sectoral composition. When classified by major product categories, the lion's share of AGOA exports (87%) is concentrated in mineral fuels and oils, as shown in Fig. 6.2. The almost perfect correlation of the total trade curve with the curve of this export category denotes that changes in AGOA trade are mainly explained by fluctuations of trade in these energy-related products.

Oil trade is followed by textiles and apparel (7%) and transportation equipment (3.5%). Further, though other products have also successfully been exported to the US, such as metals, agriculture and food products and chemicals, and represent an important source of revenue for some countries, their aggregate share of AGOA trade is less than 3%. This heavy concentration of trade in relatively few export categories is also mirrored and partly explained by the relatively high geographic concentration of AGOA trade in a number of countries which have been able to exploit

[10] The MFA under the WTO established a temporary regime for trade in textiles, which allowed member countries to apply quota restrictions to avoid surges of textiles and apparel imports through "grandfather clauses". The MFA was phased out in December 2004. Its expiry was supposed to help African and other developing countries ensure market access to those countries which had "grandfather clauses" for their domestic market. However, the downward trend of Africa's trade in these markets after the phase-out of the MFA is indicative of a loss in market share to other competitors, once the playing field for textile trade was "levelled". Thus, contrary to the general perception prior to the MFA phase-out, it was only beneficial for the more competitive Asian exporters and not for Africa as a whole.

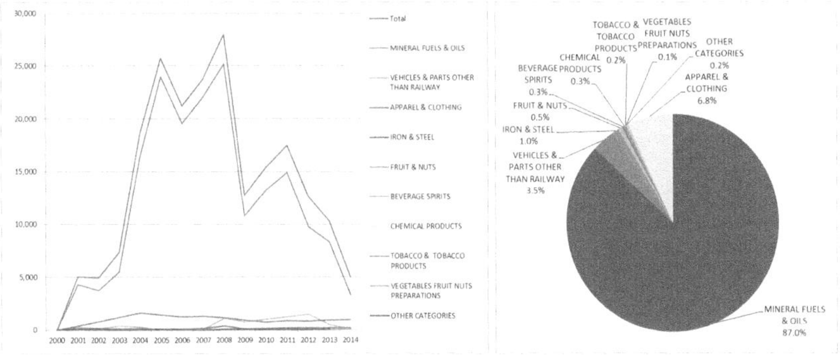

Fig. 6.2 Composition of AGOA exports by main export category 2000–2014. (customs value in US$ million and % shares). (Source: Author's representation, on the basis of data from U.S. Department of Commerce and USITC)

AGOA benefits. For example, the modest growth portrayed in the textiles and apparel exports relates to the increasing number of AGOA-eligible countries that between 2000 and 2005 were able to meet the apparel-related visa provisions and therefore export, followed by stagnation after 2005 given the increased competition of textile exports after the expiry of the MFA, whilst the rise in transport equipment exports is exclusively explained by South Africa's activity in this category.

During the reference period 2000–2014, the major beneficiary under AGOA has been Nigeria, concentrating almost two-thirds of AGOA trade, followed by Angola (18% share), South Africa (6% share) and Republic of Congo (3%), as is depicted in Fig. 6.3.

Variations do not necessarily respond to outliers gaining ground over established AGOA exporters. For example, Nigeria's smaller share in 2014 (and the dropout of Gabon) compared to the aggregate AGOA period (2000–2014) responds to the fall in oil prices, whilst Madagascar's disappearance from the top exporter list responds to the withdrawal of benefits during 2010–2014, whereas Lesotho's and Kenya's performance defined by their increased share in AGOA trade, as well as Eswatini's appearance on the top 10 list, responds to important increases in their apparel trade.

A closer look at AGOA utilization rate of the top 10 exporters during 2000–2014 further corroborates that countries that have had the best performance in AGOA are apparel exporters (Lesotho, Kenya, Madagascar and Mauritius) rather than those exporters specialized in trade (Nigeria,

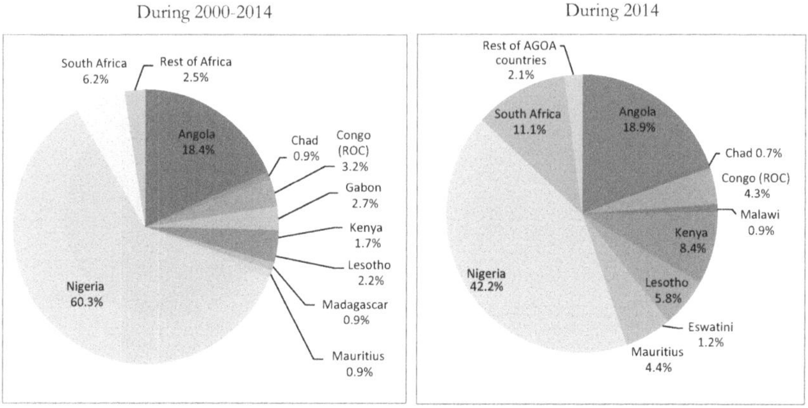

Fig. 6.3 Top 10 AGOA beneficiary exporters 2000–2014 (% shares of customs value) During 2000–2014. During 2014. (Source: Author's representation, on the basis of data from U.S. Department of Commerce and USITC)

Angola, Congo and Chad). It is also noteworthy to mention that the most diversified of AGOA exporters (South Africa) has the second lowest utilization rate after Chad, as almost 90% of this country's exports to the US do not enjoy AGOA benefits. Overall utilization of AGOA preferences is 30% of total exports to the US of the AGOA region, which underscores that it is underutilized. The situation is even starker now that some of the main exporters under AGOA V, such as Ethiopia, Mali and Guinea were suspended in 2022, Burkina Faso in 2023 and Central African Republic, Gabon, Guinea and Uganda in 2024. Equatorial Guinea and Seychelles have also graduated in the interim, reducing the current list to 31 beneficiaries (Fig. 6.4).

At the other extreme of the spectrum are AGOA beneficiaries which have not been able to take advantage of AGOA benefits. These are Benin, Burundi, CAR, Comoros, Liberia, Sao Tomé, Seychelles and South Sudan. These countries have no recorded US imports categorized under AGOA preferential trade, though virtually all do export goods to the US that do not benefit from AGOA preferences, implying that these countries have been missing out on potential export revenue gains.

When characterizing US investment in the continent, Africa received a total of cumulative investment flows during the reference period (2000–2014) worth US$ 48 billion and US investment stock in 2014 for

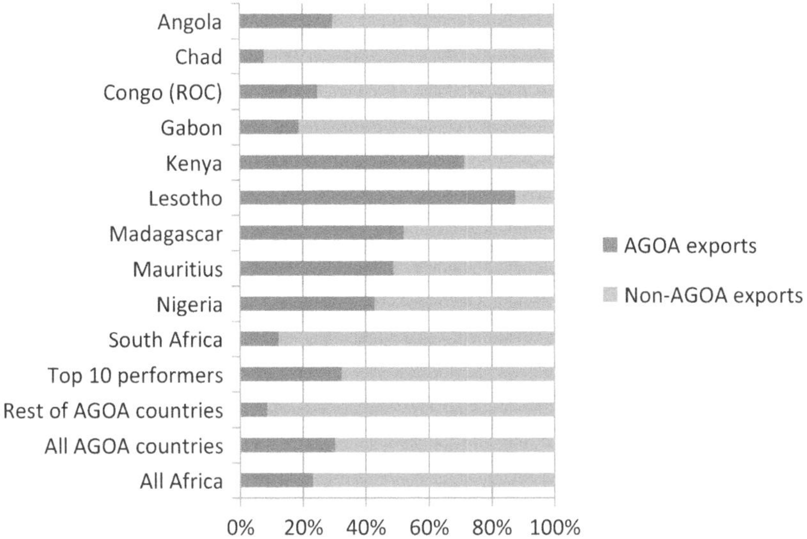

Fig. 6.4 AGOA utilization rate (Utilization rate is defined as US imports receiving duty-free and quota-free access under AGOA over the total import value from the country(ies) to the US, expressed in percentage terms) by top 10 AGOA exporters 2000–2014 (% share of customs value). (Source: Author's representation, on the basis of data from U.S. Department of Commerce and USITC)

the continent amounted to US$ 56 billion. Though the general trend during 2000–2009 was marked by a rapid rise in US FDI flows, this has been characterized by a high degree of volatility, as shown by the curve in Fig. 6.5. Since 2009, this trend has noticeably reversed, with FDI flows continuously decreasing and hitting its lowest point in 2012. Notable retractions in FDI flows transpired in 2002, 2008 and 2012 in response to the global financial meltdowns triggered by the bursting of financial bubbles in the IT, real state and commodities markets, respectively.

AGOA FDI flows also portray a high degree of volatility, the overall pattern of these flows are not perfectly aligned with US African FDI. There is indeed a relatively high degree of variance, especially in the first 8 years of the AGOA. For example, AGOA FDI plummeted in 2005, at a time when overall US FDI flows to Africa was on the rise. Equally, as US FDI to Africa receded during 2006–2008, US FDI to the AGOA region experienced an increase. It was not until 2008 when these two flows became

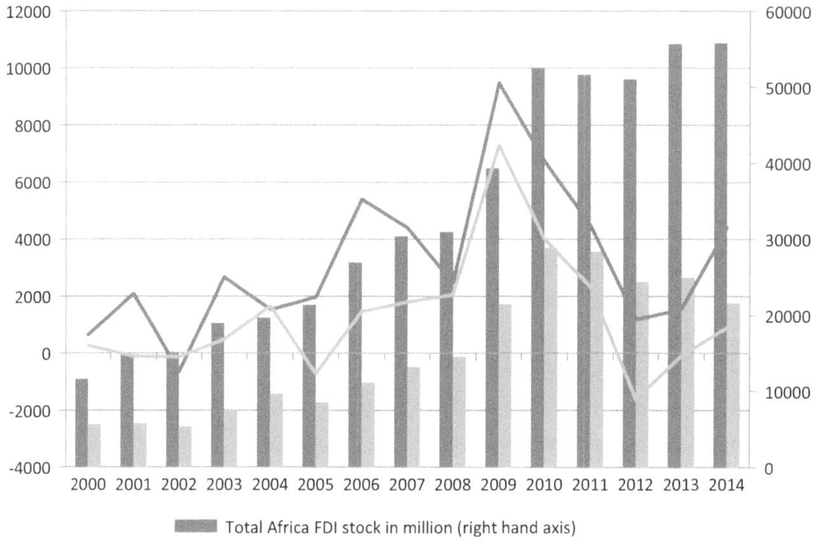

Fig. 6.5 US FDI in Africa and AGOA region compared 2000–2014 (stock and flows in US$ million). (Source: Author's representation, on the basis of data from U.S. BEA)

more aligned in terms of magnitude and direction, which is also partly explained by the significant growth of US FDI stock to the AGOA region between 2008 and 2010.

Almost two thirds of total US FDI flows in Africa during 2000–2014 were attracted by three countries. These were Egypt, which registered a 36% share, followed by Nigeria and South Africa, each with a 12% share of cumulative FDI flows for the reference period. The remaining one-third of US FDI flows is distributed across the rest of Africa countries. The AGOA subregion was a major recipient of US FDI flows, with an aggregate US$ 20 billion during the reference period, and of US$ 22 billion in US FDI stock, representing 40% and 39% shares of aggregate US investment flows and stocks to the African continent, respectively.

As with AGOA trade, when US investment to the AGOA region is disaggregated geographically it also portrays a relatively high concentration in a few countries. Topping the list of US FDI stock in 2014 is South Africa with a 27% share of US FDI to the AGOA region. It is closely followed by Mauritius and Nigeria, as can be appreciated in Fig. 6.6. Other

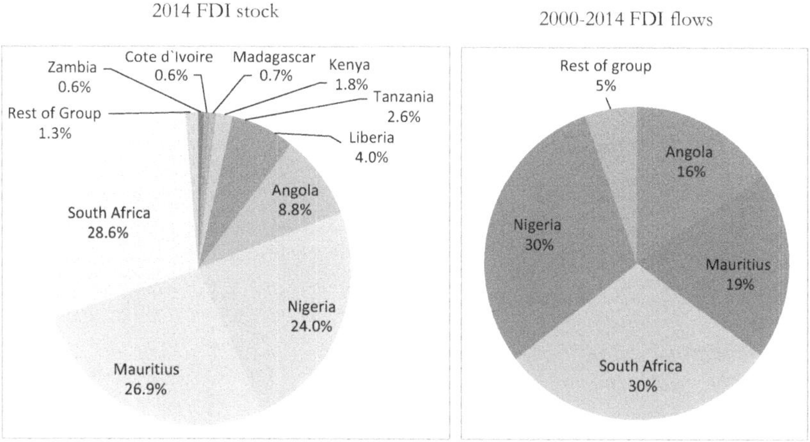

Fig. 6.6 Top hosts of US FDI flows and stocks to the AGOA region 2000–2014 (% share) 2014 FDI stock 2000–2014 FDI flows. (Source: Author's representation, on the basis of data from U.S. BEA)

top hosts of US FDI stock are Angola, Liberia, Tanzania, Kenya, Madagascar, Côte d'Ivoire and Zambia. The remaining 19 AGOA beneficiaries barely accumulate 1.3% of total US FDI to the AGOA region. Another important characteristic of this ranking is that with the exception of Nigeria and Gabon, which specialize in oil exports to the US under AGOA, the other top FDI hosts which concentrate the lion's share of US investment stock to the AGOA region have a relatively more diversified exports base.

US FDI flows during 2000–2014 portray an even higher concentration than stock, because some countries also experienced disinvestments during the period of study which stocks over time may mask. Given these disinvestments, a relatively larger number of AGOA countries (25) barely hold 5% of US FDI flows in the AGOA region. The lion's share of 95% goes to the same top four countries mentioned earlier, with Nigeria in second place, leading over Mauritius.

US FDI in Africa heavily concentrated in the minerals sector, which in part also determines investment in certain host countries. Figure 6.7 illustrates this concentration in the mining sector, which receives almost two-thirds of total US FDI stock. Nigeria, for example, receives 7% of total US investment stock in the mining sector.

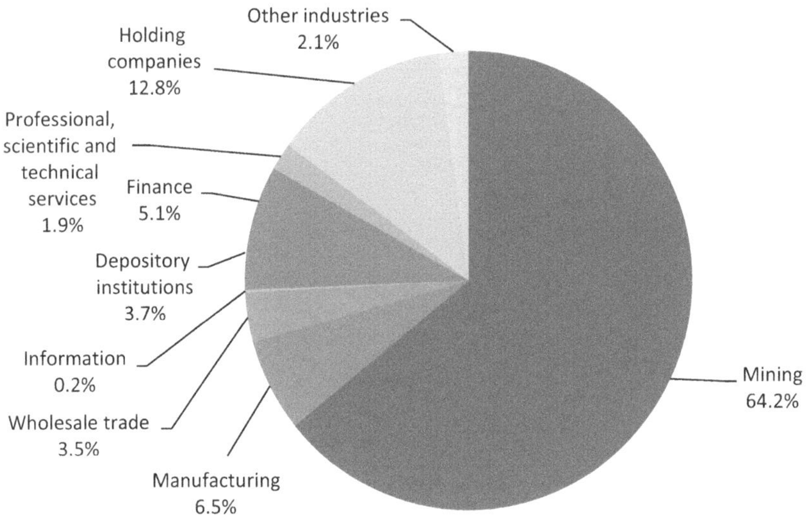

Fig. 6.7 US sectoral breakdown of FDI stock in Africa 2000–2014 (% shares). (Source: Author's representation, on the basis of data from U.S. BEA)

Given that both AGOA trade and investment in the AGOA region depict a relative high concentration of a few sectors, it is important to also empirically assess at sectoral level whether the relationship between AGOA trade and US FDI stock in Africa is of complementary or substitutive nature, as will be done in the next section.

3.2 Theoretical and Empirical Underpinnings of the Relationship Between Trade and FDI

The theoretical literature on the relationship between trade and FDI is well established. Various theoretical models explain this relationship from the perspective of the operations and undertakings of multinational enterprises (MNEs), notably Hymer's (1976) "theory of international operations of national firms", Akamatsu's (1962) "Flying Geese Paradigm", Vernon's (1966) "Product Life-Cycle Theory" and Dunning's "Eclectic Paradigm"(1979), as well as their various adaptations and iterations.[11]

[11] See Páez (2008, 2011) for a summary and evolution of these theories.

More recently, the literature contextualizes trade and investment relationships in the context of global commodity or "value" chains (GVCs), which explain the formation of industry clusters through FDI in various geographically distant locations which are interconnected through sourcing relationships and the trading of tasks and intermediary inputs (Gereffi, 1999).

The relation between trade and investment can be explained in terms of complementarity, substitutability or a combination of both. Determining the nature of the relation is necessary to determine economic justifiability for RTAs' protection of FDI. Intuitively, if trade and FDI flows are substitutable, an RTA that promotes trade will negatively impact FDI. Hence, investment protection in this setup may not have much pertinence. On the other hand, in the presence of complementarity, further trade would also promote FDI, which makes the inclusion of investment rules in an FTA appealing, in particular for countries seeking to attract greater FDI (Páez, 2008).

Exporting firms that decide to shift the location of their production abroad through investment in a plant to supply their foreign markets through that plant are said to be substituting exports for FDI. The main rationale behind substitution is to circumvent foreign trade barriers (e.g. tariffs), which generally reduce profits. Given that a FTA leads to the elimination of tariffs between its partners, a foreign firm will have the additional motivation to "tariff jump" to source the extended market that FTA may represent by investing in a country which is member to that FTA.

Internalization theory assumes substitution as transaction costs in the form of trade (tariff) barriers are internalized through FDI. Several authors have undertaken empirical testing for substitution, notably Williamson (1975), Belderbos and Sleuwaegen (1998), Svensson (1997) and Head (2001). Alternatively, a firm may decide to source a foreign market through both trade and investment, rather than through exports or FDI exclusively. For instance, a subsidiary of the firm may be built to source foreign markets (and also third markets), and even import some of their foreign production back to their country of origin or source. Thus, trade and investment flows are considered "complementary" in this situation and portray a certain level of vertical integration and confer proximity advantages, as is discussed in the early literature on complementarity, notably Lipsey and Weiss (1984), Swenson (1997) and Brainard (1997).

3.3 Evidence of AGOA's Impact on Trade and Investment

There is a wealth of empirical studies which assess the impact of AGOA in terms of trade and its associated investments. For example, Phelps et al. (2009) conducted a survey at enterprise level representative of the Kenyan clothing industry and found that the AGOA has in some respects geared the local Kenyan textiles manufacturing industry towards exports, but that the way in which investments have entered this industry has resulted in a relatively low linkage development and poor developmental impact. The survey also provides firsthand evidence of the origins of the FDI stemming mainly from Asian MNEs.

Edwards and Lawrence (2013) find that in AGOA countries, there has been a certain degree of trade determination in low-value-added and low-quality products as a result of the quota restrictions, first under the MFA agreement, which has been subsequently further exacerbated under the AGOA preference structure because LDCs are further encouraged to specialize in clothing products with high fabric costs, and discouraging linkage development and the sourcing of cheaper fabric sourced from poorer countries. From this analysis, it follows that investment in the AGOA apparel sector in Africa, has greatly determined specialization in low-value-added apparel exports.

Other studies for countries such as Kenya, Lesotho, Mauritius and Madagascar and also regional studies, notably Lall (2003), Rotunno et al. (2013), Tati (2014), Morris and Staritz (2014) and McKinsey (2015) share common findings on the complementary relationship between AGOA trade and FDI (and the associated job creation) in the garment export industry, but at the forefront of these discussions is Asian and not US FDI.

Other literature also corroborates the fact that US FDI has been elusive. For example, Karingi et al. (2011) provides survey material and Páez et al. (2010b) documentary evidence on the limited US investment associated to AGOA. From these analyses, very few countries have reported investments originating from the US. Such investment has mainly concentrated in the textiles and apparel sector in countries that figure as apparel exporters under AGOA.

Given the evidence compiled in the literature surveyed, the question arising in the context of this research is whether AGOA has also been investment creating and whether there is evidence of both bilateral trade and investment between the US and Africa under this preferential trade agreement can be characterized as a mutually supportive endeavour, as the US seeks to promote. The next section tackles these queries empirically, through the application of a gravity model.

4 Empirical Study

Having reviewed the empirical literature on AGOA's impact, some critical questions arise in the context of the ability for African countries to attract investment under AGOA. First, is there an observable relation between the AGOA and US FDI into Africa? Second, has benefiting from the Special Rule of the AGOA helped beneficiaries attract greater US FDI in the apparel sector? And third, does regional integration in Africa play a significant role in attracting US FDI? The present section seeks to answer these inquiries empirically through a gravity model specification which looks at US FDI stock in African countries during 2000–2014, as is explained below.

4.1 Description of Methods

As a starting point and in order to consider the questions raised above, a gravity model is developed to measure if there is any observable relationship over time between investment flows that have entered Africa and the AGOA preferences. Gravity models have been extensively developed in trade literature to assess trade and factor movements across borders. Originally introduced by Tinbergen (1962), Anderson (1979) was the first to develop a theoretical foundation of gravity models for international trade. Gravity equations relate bilateral trade flows with variables such as GDP, distance, transport costs and trade barriers to infer how these flows may be affected under the presence of a customs union or preferential trade area. Such models have also been used to measure the impact of regional integration on investment flows, notably, Levy Yeyati et al. (2002), Head and Ries (2008), Eaton and Kortum (2002), Rueda Maurer (2003), De Sousa and Lochard (2011) and Páez (2008, 2011).

In this chapter a gravity model is proposed to assess the effects of AGOA on US investment in Africa, and a set of parameters reflecting the relationship between US FDI and the AGOA are considered in the model. The selected period is relevant for the study, given that the AGOA initiative was launched in 2000 and has been extended on several occasions, most recently to 2025. During the observable period of study, Africa experienced a surge in FDI stock whilst various countries gradually became AGOA beneficiaries, and a subset of these countries also became beneficiaries of the Third Country Fabric provision, the two main apparel-trade-related benefits. Hence this allows for observing whether changes in FDI stock were in any way associated with the AGOA. The period also allows a general observation of what happened to FDI in countries which were suspended from AGOA trade preferences, as well as in countries which have never benefited from the AGOA. Lastly, during this observable period, the US also had several investment agreements in place with African countries and regions, which confer legal protection to US investments or provide a framework for promoting these in the future. The model also allows observing the relationship between these instruments and FDI, which are considered by some of the literature as determinants of investment.

4.2 Statistical Parameters and Variables

There are three major statistical sources used in the present study. These are the *Bureau of Economic Analysis Statistics*, the *USITC trade statistics* and the World Bank's *World Development Indicators*. What follows is a description of the selected parameters used as variables for the model and what they are expected to capture in the empirical analysis.

Foreign direct investment: The dependent variable is US FDI stock, obtained from the *Bureau of Economic Analysis Statistics*. In the model, the expectation is that an increase in FDI is explained by the AGOA variables if the relationship between AGOA trade and investment is complementary. Alternatively, if the relationship is negative, this may point to a substitution relationship.

Gross domestic product: GDP of both the source country (the US) and host countries (Africa) in current US dollars have been taken from *World Development Indicators*, as well as the current GDP per capita of the source country. The expectation in this type of analysis is that GDP and also GDP per capita (which denotes the relative wealth of the source markets) are positively related to investment.

Distance: The CEPII distance measure between the country pairs is used, which provides the Great Circle distance between capital cities of two countries in kilometres. Traditionally, the distance variable is expected to be negatively related to investment, meaning, the further away the host country the more likely investors will substitute investment for trade (See Mayer & Zignago, 2011).

Non-AGOA trade: Is the customs value of total exports stemming from Africa to the US in current US dollars from the *World Development Indicators*. This parameter is expected to show a positive relationship with FDI.

AGOA trade: This is defined as the value of total US imports stemming from Africa that received duty-free treatment under the AGOA in current US dollars from the *USITC trade statistics* database. This parameter is expected to show a positive relationship with FDI. Thus, an increase in the value of AGOA imports is presumed to lead to an increase in FDI in the presence of complementarity between trade and investment flows in AGOA countries. The contrary will happen if the relationship between these two flows is of a substitutive nature. In addition, two variables denoting oil and apparel imports under AGOA are also drawn from the same database at HS 2 level.

AGOA beneficiary: This is a dummy variable which reflects AGOA beneficiary status. As with the previous dummy, it takes the value of "1" when a country obtains beneficiary status under the AGOA and "0" whenever such preference is withdrawn or is not conferred. It is expected that in the presence of a complementary relationship between FDI and trade, this variable is positive, meaning it explains the rise of investments in AGOA countries and negative if the relationship between AGOA trade and FDI is of a substitutive nature.

General and special apparel provision: These two dummy variables denote the granting of the apparel preferences for AGOA beneficiaries which have been able to comply with the stringent rules of origin for apparel, notably having a visa system in place. Correspondingly, the general rule dummy takes the value of "1" when a country is granted duty-free access for their apparel trade and "0" whenever such preference is withdrawn or does not apply. The same applies to the special rule dummy. It is expected that in the presence of a complementary relationship between FDI and AGOA trade, these variables are positive, meaning that countries benefiting from the apparel provisions have been able to attract FDI, especially given the abundant literature on how countries benefiting from textile trade under these rules have harnessed FDI in their apparel sector.

Bilateral Investment Treaties, TIFAs and TIDCA: These are three dummy variables that denote membership to an investment agreement with the US. They receive the value of 1 when this is the case and 0 when there no such agreement in place. These variables also capture the effect of regional integration in the context of the RECs, as the US has signed some of these agreements on a regional basis with countries members of RECs such as COMESA, EAC, ECOWAS, WAEMU and SACU. These variables also indirectly capture the extended market effect resulting from the FTAs within these RECs, in addition to investment protection in some of these RECs' regulation. These variables are expected to reflect positively on investment in the context of major African regional integration initiatives, especially if the relationship between AGOA trade and FDI in Africa is of a complementary nature.

All monetary variables have been normalized in constant terms, using the US consumer price index as a deflator with 2005 as base year obtained from the *WDI* database. In addition, as is standard with gravity models, all nominal variables have been logged using natural logs.

4.3 The Model

The gravity model proposed regresses US FDI against a set of explanatories which seek to assess the nature of trade and investment relationships as a result of the AGOA. The following base specification is considered in the analysis:

$$Ln\left(FDI_{ij}+1\right)=\alpha_{j}+gdp_{j}+gdpic_{j}+gdpc_{j}+dis_{ij}+tx_{ji}$$
$$+ax_{ji}+agoa+grule+srule+bit+tifa+tidca+\varepsilon$$

Where:

FDI_{ii}	is the log of FDI+1 of country *i* (US) in country *j* (AGOA country)
α_j	is the constant term for country *j*
dis_{ij}	is the distance in kilometres between the capitals of countries *i* and *j*
$gdp_{i,j}$	is the GDP of country *i* and country *j*, respectively
$gdpc_i$	is the GDP per capita of country *i*
tx_{ji}	is the total exports from country *j* to the US
ax_{ji}	is the total AGOA imports of the US from country *j*
agoa	is a dummy reflecting access to AGOA benefits for country *j*
grule	is a dummy reflecting access to General Fabric Provision benefits for country *j*

srule is a dummy reflecting access to Special Fabric Provision benefits for country *j*

bit is a dummy reflecting a bilateral investment agreement between countries *i* and *j*

tifa is a dummy reflecting an investment agreement between countries *i* and *j*

tidca is a dummy reflecting an investment agreement between countries *i* and *j*

ε is the error term

Since we want to observe how FDI behaves when regressed over a set of time-varying explanatory variables, the chosen estimation method is fixed effects. This allows the random correlation of the unobserved effects with the explanatory variables in each time period. Given that we are working with a multiple linear regression model, all of the unobserved effects which determine the dependent variable and are not explained by the independent variables are captured by the error term (ε).

Fixed effects also allow us to study the effect of a big dummy set on the dependent variable, in the present model, unlike random effects models which result inadequate for our analysis, because they assume that the unobserved effects behave independently of all the explanatory variables in all time periods, and hence are uncorrelated to the parameters we are using to explain FDI.[12] Further, in random regression models the effects of the groups (i.e. of all dummy variables in the model) are assumed to be fixed. Thus, the overall effect of the dummies is not quantified. This can lead to observation biases as the dummy set used in this model changes over time, as denoted by the various withdrawal of AGOA benefits and the various changes in the context of Africa's regional integration, which needs to be quantified and observed.

Given the numerous zero variables, data gaps due to undisclosed or unrecorded information and negative investment records for various countries (portraying disinvestment in a given year), the regression is run with FDI stock data and not FDI flow data. The investment position quantifies the stock of investment over time, hence allows the elimination of running logs of FDI zero variables which tend to be numerous on FDI flow data, and which would otherwise be dropped. This eliminates most

[12] For details on the chosen estimations methods see Wooldridge (2006), pp. 497–501 and Ch. 3.

zero observations, but not all. Hence, the estimation is run with log of FDI+1, to also take account of this additional information and thereby avoid estimation biases. The same is done with the trade variables, as many register zero entries, especially in the years before a country obtained beneficiary status or this status was withdrawn.

Since 80% of US FDI stock mainly targets the mining sector and AGOA trade is also heavily skewed towards oil imports, two additional variables capturing the oil imports (*laxoil*) and apparel imports (*laxapparel)* under AGOA are also included. These further controls are considered to account for any sectoral determination which may be skewing results across the sample. Lastly, the same regression is run for a control group of the base estimation, consisting solely of countries which have been or currently are AGOA beneficiaries, this is to further control for a sample selection bias that may be determining results.

4.4 Results

4.4.1 Descriptive Statistics of the Panel

The panel contains bilateral investment measures (FDI stock) of the US as a source country with 53 African countries regressed over a set of explanatory variables for a 15-year period (2000–2014). This gives an estimated total of 795 observations in the specification. However, some country registries are inexistent, and some of the variables present are missing data entries for several years, so this considerably reduces the number to a total of 462 estimated observations, as shown in Table 6.2.

An important consideration when studying the datasets is multicollinearity, meaning that two or more independent variables are correlated.[13] Highly collinear variables may lead to an estimation bias, if not controlled for. In the present panel, some independent variables are correlated, as shown in Table 6.3. This is the case of some of the dummy variables such as *agoa*, *grule* and *srule*, as well as the AGOA trade variables *lax*, *laxoil* and *laxapparel*. However, this may not be a source of concern if it does not lead to a large variance of the estimators.

[13] Statistically, this means that the sample variation in the R^2 of an independent variable can be (partly) explained through other independent variables in a model. Wooldridge (2006), pp. 102–104.

Table 6.2 Summary statistics of the specification

Variable	*Obs*	*Mean*	*Std. Dev.*	*Min*	*Max*
host	795	26.71698	15.64287	1	53
year	795	2007	4.323214	2000	2014
lfdi	462	17.13114	4.723947	0	23.00338
ldis	795	8.970115	0.6749813	6.957659	9.630524
lgdpi	795	30.05443	0.6107323	27.78467	30.32542
lgdpic	795	10.68625	0.0394321	10.61982	10.74517
lgdpj	765	22.28359	1.742173	14.35283	26.51835
ltx	764	17.18965	3.89	0	27.53482
lax	764	6.923223	8.254788	0	23.59188
laxoil	764	2.452181	6.268715	0	23.59188
laxapparel	764	4.337846	7.575328	0	26.66333
agoa	795	0.7157233	0.4513532	0	1
grule	795	0.4264151	0.494867	0	1
srule	795	0.4100629	0.4921544	0	1
bit	795	0.1484277	0.3557472	0	1
tifa	795	0.5710692	0.495235	0	1
tidca	795	0.0440252	0.2052802	0	1

When running the model, none of the variables were dropped due to multicollinearity, which points to the unlikelihood of an endogeneity bias in the specification. Overall, all but five of the selected variables for the model have a statistically significant relationship with the dependent variable (*lfdi*), which suggests a good fit in terms of variable selection.

4.4.2 *Results of the Panel*

The results of the regression are presented in Table 6.4. First, column (1) portrays the results for the base regression. Subsequently, columns (2)–(6) show results after progressively dropping systematically insignificant variables, conducted as a robustness check to observe their impact on the base results once they are omitted.

As may be appreciated in Table 6.4, the r-squared reveals that 66.3% of the variations in US FDI to Africa are explained through the specification. This is considerable, taking into account the data limitations and numerous zeros. Further, the F-statistic shows that it is significant. The results in column (1), display the individual contribution of each specification variables to explaining FDI. Contrary to what was expected, none of the GDP variables portrayed a significant relationship with FDI in the base

Table 6.3 Correlation matrix of the specification variables

	lfdi	*ldis*	*lgdpi*	*lgdpic*	*lgdpj*	*ltx*	*lax*	*laxoil*	*laxapp~l*	*agoa*	*grule*	*srule*	*bit*	*tifa*	*tidca*
lfdi	1														
ldis	0.1014	1													
	(0.0293)														
lgdpi	0.0136	0.0000	1												
	(0.7702)	(1.0000)													
lgdpic	0.0206	0.0000	0.5419*	1											
	(0.6591)	(1.0000)	(0.0000)												
lgdpj	0.4081	0.0879	0.0584	0.1064	1										
	(0.0000)	(0.015)	(0.1067)	(0.0032)											
ltx	0.4035	0.1208	0.0394	0.0721	0.4001	1									
	(0.0000)	(0.0008)	(0.2771)	(0.0464)	(0.0000)										
lax	0.1433	0.2441	0.0692	0.1439	0.25	0.345	1								
	(0.002)	(0.0000)	(0.0559)	(0.0001)	(0.0000)	(0.0000)									
laxoil	0.2059	0.0772	0.0147	0.047	0.2514	0.3251	0.5715*	1							
	(0.0000)	(0.0329)	(0.6851)	(0.1944)	(0.0000)	(0.0000)	(0.0000)								
laxapp~l	0.1008	0.2504	0.0461	0.0701	0.1881	0.1171	0.5739*	-0.0714	1						
	(0.0303)	(0.0000	(0.2033)	(0.0529)	(0.0000)	(0.0012)	(0.0000)	(0.0486)							
agoa	-0.1981	-0.019	0.0498	0.0629	-0.1984	0.0104	0.5133*	0.2394	0.1986	1					
	(0.0000)	(0.5931)	(0.1611)	(0.0764)	(0.0000)	(0.7748)	(0.0000)	(0.0000)	(0.0000)						
grule	-0.0136	0.1316	0.1182	0.2099	0.1456	0.1221	0.6312*	0.0763	0.5071*	0.5434*	1				
	(0.7703)	(0.0002)	(0.0008)	(0.0000)	(0.0001)	(0.0007)	(0.0000)	(0.0349)	(0.0000)	(0.0000)					
srule	-0.0807	0.1056	0.1095	0.2024	0.0696	0.0676	0.5709*	0.0327	0.4492	0.5254*	0.9618*	1			
	(0.0833)	(0.0029)	(0.002)	(0.0000)	(0.0542)	(0.0619)	(0.0000)	(0.3673)	(0.0000)	(0.0000)	(0.0000)				
bit	0.1773	-0.1498	0.0159	0.0333	0.3168	0.1872	0.0133	0.1912	-0.2021	-0.1448	-0.081	-0.0675	1		
	(0.0001)	(0.0000)	(0.6542)	(0.3487)	(0.0000)	(0.0000)	(0.7136)	(0.0000)	(0.0000)	(0.0000)	(0.0224)	(0.057)			
tifa	0.0237	-0.0979	0.1289	0.2345	0.1541	-0.0297	-0.0433	-0.1595	0.0468	-0.0222	0.1768	0.2162	0.0187	1	
	(0.6109)	(0.0057)	(0.0003)	(0.0000)	(0.0000)	(0.4126)	(0.2322)	(0.0000)	(0.1959)	(0.5321)	(0.0000)	(0.0000)	(0.5988)		
tidca	0.0169	0.1559	0.0746	0.1254	0.0871	0.133	0.2385	-0.0295	0.2701	0.1352	0.2489	0.1701	-0.0896	-0.1609	1
	(0.7175)	(0.0000)	(0.0356)	(0.0004)	(0.0159)	(0.0002	(0.0000)	(0.4163)	(0.0000)	0.0001)	(0.0000)	(0.0000)	(0.0115)	(0.0000)	

Note: * indicates variables portraying significant relationships which may point to potential collinearity

Table 6.4 Specification Results for Effects of AGOA on US FDI stock for the Africa sample

	Column (1)	*Column (2)*	*Column (3)*	*Column (4)*	*Column (5)*	*Column (6)*
Lgdpi	0.020					
	(0.08)					
Lgdpci	-8.227	-8.0539*	-8.0259*	-7.9628*	-7.7264*	-7.0176*
	(-1.63)	(-1.79)	(-1.82)	-1.81	(-1.76)	(-1.78)
lgdpj	0.006	0.0061				
	(0.03)	(0.03)				
ldis	-3.346	-3.3559	-3.3473			
	(-0.48)	(-0.48)	(-0.48)			
ltx	0.229***	0.2285***	0.2285***	0.2303***	0.2320***	0.2128**
	(2.89)	(2.89)	(2.9)	(2.92)	(2.95)	(2.78)
lax	0.054	0.0534	0.0533	0.0561		
	(0.87)	(0.87)	(0.87)	(0.92)		
laxoil	0.055	0.0551	0.0551	0.0528	0.0919**	0.0867**
	(0.90)	(0.9)	(0.9)	(0.86)	(2.1)	(2.01)
laxapparel	0.094	0.0945	0.0945	0.0896	0.1239**	0.1215**
	(1.54)	(1.55)	(1.56)	(1.5)	(2.66)	(2.97)
agoa	-3.240***	-3.2384***	-3.2399***	-3.2737***	-3.1827***	-3.1232***
	(-4.42)	(-4.43)	(-4.44)	(-4.52)	(-4.43)	(-4.58)
grule	-4.575	-4.5894	-4.5903	-4.5401	-4.3839	
	(-1.41)	(-1.42)	(-1.42)	(-1.41)	(-1.36)	
srule	4.904	4.9166	4.9206	4.8957	4.8903	
	(1.53)	(1.54)	(1.54)	(1.54)	(1.53)	
bit	1.948	1.9505	1.9495	1.1236	1.1685	
	(0.99)	(0.99)	(0.99)	(1.17)	(1.22)	

(continued)

Table 6.4 (continued)

	Column (1)	*Column (2)*	*Column (3)*	*Column (4)*	*Column (5)*	*Column (6)*
tifa	-0.403	-0.4030	-0.4039	-0.3491	-0.3079	
	(-0.61)	(-0.61)	(-0.61)	(-0.54)	(-0.48)	
tidca	3.673***	3.6748**	3.6752***	3.6576***	3.7315***	3.5843***
	(4.18)	(4.19)	(4.19)	(4.18)	(4.28)	(4.19)
constant	131.131	129.9562	129.7192	99.0157**	96.4315**	89.3470**
	(1.61)	(1.63)	(1.64)	(2.12)	(2.07)	(2.14)
No. of obs.	462	462	462	462	462	462
F-stat	4.27	4.61	5.00	5.45	5.91	9.13
Prob>F	0.000	0.000	0.000	0.000	0.000	0.000
R-squared	0.6633	0.6633	0.6633	0.6631	0.6624	0.6589
Adj R-squared	0.6110	0.6120	0.6130	0.6137	0.6139	0.6136

Absolute values of t- stats are in brackets. ***, **, and * show significance of coefficients at 1%, 5%, and 10%, respectively regression. Only once the various robustness checks were undertaken in columns (2) to (6) did *lgdpci* portray a negative and significant relationship to FDI stock. In other words, as the US per capita GDP rose by 1%, US investment in Africa fell by 99%.[14] The relative market wealth of US investors has therefore a negative bearing on investment decisions in Africa, possibly due to an increase in risk averseness and subsequent migration to investment locations which are perceived as less risky by US investors.

As expected, the estimated effect of African exports (*ltx*) on US FDI is positive and very significant, as revealed by its t-stat, both in the base regression and throughout the robustness checks. This translates into an increase in FDI by 25.5%[15] given a 1% increase in exports from Africa to the US, and points to a relationship of complementarity between both. By contrast, the coefficient of the AGOA membership dummy is significant and negative, signalling an implicit decrease of FDI by 96% as countries gradually joined the AGOA.[16] It is important to highlight that though AGOA imports overall do not appear to have a meaningful relationship with FDI, the robustness checks in columns (5) and (6) reveal that when AGOA imports are disaggregated into oil and apparel, both these flows do portray a positive and significant relationship with investment.[17] Hence, when controlling for a possible aggregation bias of the variable *lax*, a 1% increase in apparel imports and oil imports under AGOA translates into an FDI increase of 13%, and 10%, respectively. These effects, however, are not sufficient to override the overall negative effect of the AGOA dummy variable which is of greater magnitude. Hence overall, when net effect of the AGOA effect on FDI is negative, pointing to a substitution of FDI for trade under this preference scheme.

Finally, from the various dummies denoting investment protection in the context of bilateral and regional endeavours in Africa, only the TIDCA signed with the SACU region has a very meaningful explanatory power which is consistently positive through the base regression and specification checks and translates into a 3.67% increase in FDI upon the signature of a TIDCA agreement. This suggests that US FDI in the SACU region is positively related to investment cooperation and protection these countries uphold with the US.

[14] Exp(−8.0539)-1=−0.9996

[15] Exp(0.229)-1=0.257

[16] Exp(−3.240)-1=0.960

[17] Exp(0.0919)-1=0.096 and Exp(0.1239)=0.131

To further validate the selection of variables for the model, the same estimation was also conducted for comparison with a control group, consisting only of the AGOA region countries. The results for this control group is presented in Table 6.5. Overall, the control group confirms the significance, magnitude and order of some variables as in the original estimation for the whole of Africa group, notably *ltx, laxapparel, agoa* and *tidca*. These results confirm the significance of the same set of explanatory variables and reduce the possibility of an estimation bias which may have been present in the base regression.

The base regression for the control group has a slightly lower R^2 of 64.5% when compared with the r-squared of the Africa group. Nonetheless, it is still highly significant in explaining the variation of US FDI in the AGOA region. When running the model, unlike the base regression where none of the variables were dropped due to multicollinearity, the control group appears to portray an endogeneity bias with the distance variable, hence it has been dropped from the specification. Given that the distance variable did not portray statistical significance (though the coefficient did portray the expected negative sign) in the base regression, it is assumed that the absence of significance stems for the limited variations portrayed in the data, as distance between the various African hosts and the US does not vary sufficiently, and as has been reported in gravity models considering AGOA trade (See, e.g., Didia et al., 2015).

Another notable difference in the AGOA sample is that two of the GDP variables are consistently significant throughout columns (1) to (5) and portray relatively large coefficients in Table 6.5. The first denotes relative market size (*lgdpi)* of the US, which has a negative effect on US FDI in the AGOA region. The second one denotes relative market size (*lgdpj*) of the AGOA hosts and is shown to positively affect US FDI in these countries, which overrides the negative effect of *lgdpi*. This suggests that FDI to AGOA countries is highly determined by the relative market size of the hosts.

Lastly, contrary to what was expected, the dummy variables portraying apparel-related benefits did not reveal any significance in explaining US FDI, nor did the investment agreement dummies other than the TIDCA.

Table 6.5 Specification results for effects of AGOA on US FDI stock for AGOA region control group

	Column (1)	*Column (2)*	*Column (3)*	*Column (4)*	*Column (5)*
lgdpi	-41.0726**	-25.3353***	-24.7022***	-24.6888***	-24.9572***
	(-2.58)	(-4.57)	(-4.48)	(-4.47)	(-4.68)
lgdpci	23.2972				
	(1.05)				
lgdpj	8.3306***	7.0281***	6.8536***	6.9705***	7.1624***
	(3.94)	(4.1)	(4.01)	(4.08)	(4.32)
ldis	(-)	(-)	(-)	(-)	(-)
ltx	0.4379	0.5157**	0.5445**	0.6146**	0.6242**
	(1.62)	(1.98)	(2.1)	(2.42)	(2.5)
lax	0.0778	0.0778			
	(1.18)	(1.18)			
laxoil	0.0114	0.0137	0.0670		
	(0.17)	(0.21)	(1.4)		
laxapparel	0.0992	0.1000	0.1468***	0.1451**	0.1338***
	(1.53)	(1.55)	(2.86)	(2.83)	(3.02)
agoa	-3.2055***	-3.1953***	-3.0710***	-2.9736***	-2.9699***
	(-4.04)	(-4.03)	(-3.9)	(-3.79)	(-4.04)
grule	-3.8056	-3.8675	-3.6678	-2.9586	
	(-1.09)	(-1.11)	(-1.05)	(-0.85)	
srule	3.4320	3.5934	3.6159	2.9647	
	(0.99)	(1.04)	(1.04)	(0.86)	
bit	0.6599	0.9088	1.1737	1.0454	
	(0.3)	(0.42)	(0.54)	(0.48)	
tifa	0.0472	-0.0423	0.0237	-0.0056	
	(0.06)	(-0.05)	(0.03)	(-0.01)	
tidca	4.3290***	3.9672***	4.0571***	3.9216***	3.7633***
	(4.15)	(4.02)	(4.12)	(4)	(3.94)
constant	812.2613***	614.0264***	598.3281***	594.1677***	597.8352***
	(3.49)	(4.47)	4.37	(4.34)	(4.59)
No. of obs.	365	365	365	365	365
F-stat	5.48	5.85	6.24	6.65	11.02
Prob>F	0.000	0.000	0.000	0.000	0.000
R-squared	0.6450	0.6437	0.6421	0.6399	0.6388
Adj R-squared	0.5832	0.5830	0.5825	0.5812	0.5852

Absolute values of t- stats are in brackets. ***, **, and * show significance of coefficients at 1%, 5%, and 10%, respectively

(-) indicates variable has been dropped due to collinearity with the dependent variable.

5 Conclusions

The present study assessed whether there is evidence of AGOA being instrumental in attracting US investment in Africa and whether both bilateral trade and investment between the US and Africa under this preferential trade agreement may be characterized as a mutually supportive endeavour. For this purpose a gravity model explaining changes of US bilateral FDI in Africa on the basis of a set of explanatory variables was constructed and tested with panel data for African countries during the reference period of 2000–2014, prior AGOA VI extension.

The gravity model found overall negative evidence of AGOA on US FDI. However, when disaggregated at sectoral level, AGOA apparel trade does consistently appear to have positively determined US FDI in the AGOA region. The effects are however small and overruled by the negative AGOA dummy effects once they are considered. This indeed corroborates the general findings of AGOA fostering a certain type of export specialization in the apparel sector in some African countries, determined through FDI. The overall effect, however, appears to be of substitution. In light of the heavy concentration of AGOA benefits in a few countries and product categories, this could be pointing to the need for improving the utilization rates of the AGOA, so that associated FDI benefits may be harnessed for the apparel sector but also for other product categories.

Improving AGOA utilization in the non-apparel sector still constitutes a major challenge for many AGOA beneficiaries. Indeed, if the goal is to contribute to promote Africa's trade and FDI concurrently, then AGOA will need to better support export diversification as a major endeavour to promote the crowding in of FDI. In order to achieve this, AGOA's existing rules of origin need to be relaxed, to promote vertical upgrading within existing niche markets which Africa may have (e.g. textiles and apparel) but also horizontally, to ensure that more non-apparel products are able to benefit from these preferences. Currently, preference-receiving countries cannot comply with the existing rules or can only do so at a prohibitive cost, as exemplified by the low AGOA utilization.

Another important finding relates to the positive impact regional integration has had on attracting FDI in the SACU region. The investment protection of this regional market under a TIDCA has been FDI creating. This brings an important consideration to the present analysis in terms of investment protection and regional integration not necessarily being mutually exclusive, provided that the benefits of regional integration can be harnessed.

But how to take advantage of investment under AGOA for the benefit of the whole of Africa? In the presence of the AfCFTA, which became operational in July 2019,[18] there are implications in terms of coexistence and compatibility of the unilateral trade preferences conferred under AGOA, and the obligations and commitments African State Parties have agreed to under the AfCFTA body of law.[19] Indeed, with the creation of a pan-African market of goods, services, capital and labour opportunities for the scaling up of investment through regional value chains abound, but it is necessary that the conditions of the AfCFTA are met, and the basis for this is non-discrimination. Under the present AGOA V regime, discrimination is at the heart of its preferences, since these are only conferred to a group of Sub-Saharan countries. This not only reduces the incentive structure for investors, who may be seeking to leverage the potential value chains *across* AGOA and non-AGOA beneficiaries, which abound in the textiles sector. It also automatically puts State Parties in a discriminatory (and hence non-compliant) position vis-à-vis their fellow AfCFTA members. This could potentially trigger disputes under the dispute settlement system of the AfCFTA.

Furthermore, regional industrial plans such as AIDA, cater for the setting up of African firms with a regional base and the Abuja Treaty envisions the establishment of African MNEs in the last phase toward the creation of the African Economic Community. In this context, the concept of regional cumulation of national inputs from Africa-based firms is relevant. AGOA VI could support this process if it relaxes its current rules of origin and allows for regional cumulation rather than national cumulation. Expanding the general rule across the whole of Africa would be a meaningful step in that direction, since the current regime artificially cuts Africa into Sub-Saharan and Northern Africa.

Encouragingly, the AGOA VI proposal seems to tackle some of the limitations of the previous AGOA I to V. It is however subject to bipartisan dynamics, which on several occasions have endangered this preferential scheme, only to be saved by a special dispensation known as the Trade Promotion Authority (TPA). The TPA gives special delegation of legislative powers to the US Executive to pass trade-related laws and also

[18] During an extraordinary Summit of AU Head of State and Government (HoSG), in Niamey Niger, it was declared that the AfCFTA entered its operational phase in July 2019. This phase has further reached its culmination with the formal start of trade on the 1st of January 2021. (AU, 2020)

[19] For a discussion on the issue of compatibility and coexistence, see Chapter 8.3 of this book.

negotiate trade agreements. Indeed, important changes during AGOA were possible under the Bush and Obama administrations using the TPA. There is a real danger for this opportunity to be missed if under the Biden administration the proposed bill is not passed. The TPA could be instrumental for the Biden administration, though it is indeed quite difficult to foresee what congressional dynamics may render in its current US Congress 118th session, which is deemed to run until January 2025, and is concurrent with the last 2 years of President Biden's first term in office.

The adoption of an AGOA VI as per the proposal being circulated at the US Congress, with the related flexibilities, including a 16- rather than a 10-year window, would give more certainties to investors vying to invest in a pan-African market. This in itself could be an additional contribution to attract investment from the US that is able to promote regional value chains to benefit from existing preferential trade arrangements, such as the AGOA. Such efforts may also crowd in further FDI, from within the continent and beyond.

Lastly, the AfCFTA could represent an opportunity to consolidate the various investment policies and regulations that exist at the regional level, as proposed in Páez (2017). Efforts to consolidate existing investment regulation have so far not been very successful in Africa, including the *AU Pan African Investment Code* which is a soft law instrument, preceding the AfCFTA Protocol on Investment and which was endorsed by the AU in 2017. With the AfCFTA Protocol on Investment, a binding instrument, there is a credible opportunity to harmonize the various investment regimes across the continent and provide a basis for common rules that level the playing field for domestic, intra-African and foreign investment, and that see the advent of a Common Investment Area, as was discussed earlier in Chapter 5 of this book. This would undoubtedly be a solid contribution towards one of the four freedoms of the AfCFTA, namely, the free movement of capital.

References

Literary References

AU (2020), Assembly decision on the start of trading under the African Continental Free Trade Area, {Assembly/AU/OSP/Dec.1 (06–20,II}, June 17, 2020.

AGOA Renewal Act of 2023, n.d. A draft bill for the 118TH CONGRESS 1ST SESSION by Congressman Coons.

Anderson, J. (1979). A Theoretical Foundation for the Gravity Model. *American Economic Review, 69*(1), 106–116.

AU Pan African Investment Code, 2017.

Belderbos, R., & Sleuwaegen, L. (1998). Tariff Jumping DFI and Export Substitution: Japanese Electronics Firms in Europe. *International Journal of Industrial Organization, 16*(5), 601–638.

Brainard, S. L. (1997). An Empirical Assessment of the Proximity Concentration Trade-off between Multinationals Sales and Trade. *American Economic Review, 8*, 520–544.

Brock, W. (2014). African Growth and Opportunity Act (AGOA): Background and Reauthorization. *Current Politics and Economics of Africa, 7*(3), 203–227.

Congressional Research Services (2022), "Trade Promotion Authority (TPA).", December. https://crsreports.congress.gov

De Sousa, J., & Lochard, J. (2011). Does the Single Currency Affect Foreign Direct Investment? *The Scandinavian Journal of Economics, 113*(3), 553–578.

Didia, D., Nica, M., & You, G. (2015). The gravity model, African Growth and Opportunity Act (AGOA) and US trade relations with sub-Saharan Africa. *The Journal of International Trade & Economic Development, 24*(7/8), 1130–1151.

EAC (2016), EAC African Growth Opportunity Act (AGOA) Strategy 2015–2025. "Harnessing the power of EA unity to transform doing business with U.S.A" EAC Secretariat, Arusha, May. http://repository.eac.int/handle/11671/24476

Eaton, J., & Kortum, S. (2002). Technology, Geography, and Trade. *Econometrica, 70*(5), 1741–1779.

Edwards, L., & Lawrence, R. Z. (2013). AGOA Rules: The Intended and Unintended Consequences of Special Fabric Provisions. Working Paper Series WP13-11, Peterson Institute for International Economics.

Gereffi, G. (1999). International Trade and Industrial Upgrading in the Apparel Commodity Chain. *Journal of International Economics, 48*(1), 37–70.

Gibbon, P. (2003). The African Growth and Opportunity Act and the Global Commodity Chain for Clothing. *World Development, 31*(11), 1809–1927.

Head, K. (2001). Overseas Investment and Firms Exports. *Review of International Economics, 9*(1), 108–122.

Head, K., & Ries, J. (2008). FDI as an Outcome of the Market for Corporate Control: Theory and Evidence. *Journal of International Economics, 74*(1), 2–20.

ICTSD (2015), "US, East African Community Ink Deal to Deepen Trade Ties", *Bridges Weekly*, Vol. 19 (8), 5 March.

Jones, Vivian (2010), "U.S. Trade and Investment Relationship with Sub-Saharan Africa: The African Growth and Opportunity Act", Congressional Research Service, 4 February, Washington D.C.

Karingi, S., L. Páez and D. Degefa (2011) "Survey of AGOA's Past, Present & Future Prospects: Experiences and Expectations of SSA", prepared for the AGOA Midterm Review, 11–12 May, http://programmes.comesa.int/attachments/article/235/AGOA%20Survey%20Report%208%20May%202011%20-%20formatted.pdf

Kelley, Kevin J. (2015), "AGOA forum to assess gains, losses of pact", *The East African,* 22 August http://www.theeastafrican.co.ke/news/Agoa-forum-to-assess-gains%2D%2Dlosses-of-pact-/-/2558/2842288/-/9cs3j7z/-/index.html

Lall, Sanjaya (2003), "FDI, AGOA And Manufactured Exports From A Land-Locked, Least-Developed African Economy: Lesotho", *QEH Working Paper Series*, 109, October.

Levy Y.E., E. Stein and C. Daude (2002). "Regional integration and the location of FDI", *Inter-American Development Bank*, mimeo.

Ligami, Christable (2015), "Region to export products under AGOA as a bloc", *The East African*, July 11, http://www.theeastafrican.co.ke/business/Region-to-export-products-under-Agoa-as-a-bloc/-/2560/2783922/-/12xy4i2z/-/index.html

Lipsey, R., & Weiss, M. (1984). Foreign Production and Exports of Individual Firms. *The Review of Economics and Statistics, 63*(4), 304–308.

Mckinsey (2015), "Sourcing in a volatile world: The East Africa opportunity.", April.

Morris, M., & Staritz, C. (2014). Industrialization Trajectories in Madagascar's Export Apparel Industry: Ownership, Embeddedness, Markets and Upgrading. *World Development, 56*, 243–257.

Njiraini, John (2014), "AGOA: The US-Africa Trade Dilemma", *AfricaRenewal,* December: 22-23.

Páez, L. (2017). Bilateral Investment Treaties and Africa's Regional Integration: Towards and African Continental Investment Area. *Journal of World Investment and Trade, 18*(2017), 1–35.

Páez, Laura (2011), *Liberalizing Financial Services and Foreign Direct Investment: Developing a Framework for Commercial Banking*, July, Palgrave Macmillan, Hampshire, UK. https://doi.org/10.1057/9780230316829

Páez, Laura, Stephen Karingi, Mwangi Kimenyi and Mekalia Paulos (2010a) "African U.S. Trade in the Spotlight: A Decade of AGOA", jointly with, African Trade Policy Centre (ATPC), *ATPC Policy Brief*, No. 16, November, https://hdl.handle.net/10855/22222

Páez, Laura, Stephen Karingi, Mwangi Kimenyi and Mekalia Paulos (2010b), "A Decade (2000–2010) of African-US Trade under the African Growth and Opportunity Act (AGOA)", *ATPC Work in Progress,* No. 81, https://hdl.handle.net/10855/29212

Páez, Laura (2008), "GATS Financial Services Liberalization: How Do OECD Members Schedules Impact Commercial Banking FDI?" Journal of World Trade 42, no. 6 (2008): 1065–1083.

Phelps, N., Stillwell, J., & Wanjiru, R. (2009). Broken Chain? AGOA and Foreign Direct Investment in the Kenyan Clothing Industry. *World Development, 37*(2), 314–325.

Rotunno, L., Vézina, P.-L., & Wang, Z. (2013). The rise and fall of (Chinese) African apparel exports. *Journal of Development Economics, 105*, 152–163.

Rueda Maurer, María Clara (2003), Regional Integration and Financial Foreign Direct Investment', SNB paper for the CGFS Working Group on Financial Foreign Direct Investment, 2003, September.

Svensson, R. (1997). Effects of Overseas Production on Home Country Exports: Evidence Based on Swedish Multinationals. *Weltwirtschaftliches Archiv, 132*, 304–329.

Swenson, D. (1997). Explaining Domestic Content: Evidence from U.S. and Japanese Auto Production in the U.S. NBER Working Paper, No.5495.

Tati, Gabriel (2014), "Reaping the benefits of preferential trade agreement : Asian FDI in the Lesotho and Swaziland garment industry", Autrepart 2014/1 (N° 69), p. 111–130.

The White House (2012), *U.S. Strategy Toward Sub-Saharan Africa*, June, Washington D.C.

Tinbergen, J. (1962). *Shaping the World Economy: Suggestions for an International Economic Policy*. Twentieth Century Fund.

UNDP. (2011). *Towards Human Resilience: Sustaining MDG Progress in an Age of Economic Uncertainty*. United Nations Development Programme.

US Congress (2015), *Trade Preferences Extension Act of 2015*, One hundred fourteenth Congress of the United States of America.

USAID. (2011). *U.S. Announces New African Trade Capacity Building Initiative at AGOA Forum*. USAID Press Office.

US GAO (2004), "Intensifying Free Trade Negotiating Agenda Calls for Better Allocation of Staff and Resources", Report to Congressional Requesters No. GAO-04-233, the United States General Accounting Service, Washington D.C., January, http://www.gao.gov/assets/250/240903.pdf

Vienna Convention on the Law of Treaties (1969), concluded in Vienna on 23 May 1969. United Nations, *Treaty Series*, vol. 1155, p. 331.

Williamson, O. E. (1975). *Markets and Hierarchies: Analysis and Antitrust Implications*. New York: Free Press.

Wright, Laura L. (2004), "Trade Promotion Authority: Fast Track for the Twenty-First Century", Volume 12 (18), 979–1006, Article 18, *Will & Mary Bill of Rights Journal*, https://scholarship.law.wm.edu/wmborj/vol12/iss3/18

Statistical Sources and Databases

Bureau of Economic Analysis (BEA), n.d. *National Economic Accounts Tables*. http://www.bea.gov/national/nipaweb/SelectTable.asp.

Mayer and Zignago (2011), Notes on CEPII's distances measures (GeoDist), CEPII Working Paper 2011-25. http://www.cepii.fr/anglaisgraph/bdd/distances.htm

Stata Corporation (2011), STATA Version 12, College Station Texas; Stata Corporation.

Wooldridge, Jeffrey M. (2006), Introductory Econometrics. A Modern Approach, Third Ed., Thomson South-Western.

World Bank (2013), *World Development Indicators Database*, http://databank.worldbank.org/data/databases.aspx

CHAPTER 7

Africa's LDC Trade: Harnessing the Variable Geometry of the AfCFTA and Beyond

1 Introduction

This chapter looks at the issue of African Least Developed Countries (LDCs) in the broader context of their international trade relations. As a starting point, it discusses these countries' international trade performance from a historical perspective and how, despite the special and differential treatment these countries have enjoyed, their trade performance has not necessarily translated into pro poor outcomes. The chapter subsequently focuses on the elements of variable geometry that accrue to African LDCs, comparing them at the multilateral and AfCFTA levels. Without missing out on the benefits of a "Single Undertaking" brought on by the launch of the AfCFTA, the chapter also discusses the role specific elements of preferential trade that have failed to deliver to LDCs through multilateral endeavors, and how these could be better harnessed within and projected via the AfCFTA, through strategic positioning and agenda setting in international fora.

This chapter was originally published by the author of this book as an article entitled "Africa's LDC trade: Harnessing the Variable Geometry of the AfCFTA and Beyond" in the *Journal of World Trade*, Vol. 58 (2024), no. 3. This material has been reprinted with all rights and permissions from © Kluwer Law International BV, with minimal edits.

L. Páez, *The African Continental Free Trade Area*,
https://doi.org/10.1007/978-3-031-66605-6_7

2 Differing Levels of Development: The Perennial Pressure Point of International Trade Negotiations

International trade, from a classical theoretical viewpoint, presupposes that the terms of trade are defined by comparative advantages of factor endowments (Ricardo, 1817), whilst assuming that trading partners are similar in size and consumers have similar tastes. But in the realpolitik of this world, trade models have often provided a nuanced representation of the stark differences across both developing and developed countries, through so-called stylized facts. The matter has been tackled over decades by economic research, much focusing on how to sophisticate oversimplified models, in order to reflect different sized economies, retrofeed differing tastes and overcome the limitation of a given set of factor endowments, in an effort to account for phenomena such as changing economic structures and intra-industry trade. This has been of great service to the economic paradigms of globalization (Nye & Donahue, 2000, and Dicken, 2003) and more specifically, global value chains (Gereffi et al., 2005).

And yet, the world finds itself at another juncture that the covid pandemic revealed and which was further exacerbated by the Ukraine-Russia war: the fact that such interdependence through trade was not only stoppable but also lopsided and questionable. This perspective may have arguably not only deepened the gap between the developed and developing world, but also accelerated the coming of age of an expected paradigm shift from outsourcing (Bhagwati et al., 2004) to reshoring and relocalized production (Reinsch, 2021) as the new normal. Global responses in the past 3 years to address the need for greater resilience and perhaps also less interdependence, have included traditional protectionist measures, such as export or import bans and various technical restrictions (International Trade Centre, 2020; World Trade Organization, 2022), as well as more innovative approaches, such as the local production and pooled procurement of goods which have ranged from vaccines, protective and medical equipment, to food, fuel and fertilizers.[1]

In retrospect, and whether we like it or not, we are in a world of considerable differences and differing capacities. The status quo of trade relations remains a "variable geometry", where these differences play out in the ability of countries to advance trade liberalization at differing speeds.

[1] For examples of pooled procurement in Africa in these sectors, see ECA (2021), Box 6.1, and also https://www.atex.africa/.

In practice, variable geometry presupposes that a country or group of countries can opt into an agreement devised by a larger (group of) countr(y)(ies) where unilateral trade preferences are conferred. The former can benefit from special and differential treatment (SDT), which can manifest itself through either classic market access type of benefits and/or other sets of conditions which are considered to be more beneficial that the standard conditions set by the agreement. A second cornerstone of such preferences is that they are not reciprocal, meaning that beneficiaries are not expected to afford preferential treatment to those who afford them such treatment. The downside of such preferences is that there can be no expectation of guarantees or continuity. They remain at the discretion of the issuer and can be withdrawn or suspended at any point in time, as has been witnessed historically.[2]

Agreements containing notions of variable geometry such as unilateral trade preferences are in essence very different from other agreements which have built in flexibilities to advance trade negotiations. So-called opt-in or critical mass agreements, which can be devised by a group of countries (Lloyd, 2009). Such as the efforts made by the WTO membership in the mid-1990s around negotiating agreements on the "Singapore Issues", and which recently only saw the culmination of the Investment Facilitation for Development Agreement (IFDA) this year.[3]

It is this realism that continues to define the terms in which countries trade, as well as the realpolitik of trade negotiations. In this setting, we still revisit the question of how much leniency is given to development considerations when working out the details of a preferential trade agreement and, as Bagwell et al. (2002) put it, the intentions may not always be transparent nor respond to pure altruism. In the wide spectrum of what can be offered to those that are less and *least* fortunate when full

[2] From the overall suspension of the Cotonou Agreement, which was superseded by regional EPAs, to specific withdrawal of GSP and AGOA preferences, numerous examples abound. For an illustration of the withdrawal of preferences and its impact under AGOA see (Páez et al., 2010a, 2010b; Karingi et al., 2012).

[3] The "Singapore issues" were four broad issues of interest (i.e. government procurement, investment, trade facilitation and competition) first introduced in the WTO trade agenda during the Singapore Ministerial Conference of 1996. Given the resistance from several member States, some of these issues were altogether dropped. Only investment facilitation remained relevant to some of the membership, which lead to the adoption of a plurilateral agreement at the WTO, which would be considered an opt-in agreement. For an explanation of the origins of the Singapore Issues see Páez (2011), p. 88.

reciprocity is not possible, the dangling carrot often comes in the form of unilateral trade preferences. But has this carrot been effective in terms of advancing poverty reduction in those countries that need it most? Has trade openness combined with SDT garnered the much-needed pro poor response to advance development? The present chapter looks into the issue of LDC trade performance in Africa and revisits the longstanding discourse on SDT with a focus of what may be needed to better support trade that has an impact on LDC's development through the AfCFTA.

3 Africa's LDC Trade Performance: An Overview

Africa is host to the largest group of LDCs, with a total of 33 out of the 46 countries which fall under this category.[4] Of these, 13 are also categorized as landlocked developing countries (LLDCs) out of a total of 32 LLDCs worldwide.[5]

The combined conditions of extreme poverty, vulnerability and dependency which constitute the LDC criteria,[6] have had a historical bearing on the continent's ability to meet development goals, let alone integrate deeper into the world economy through international trade. This has been particularly felt through the boom and bust cycles of recent international crises, and more recently through the covid-19 global pandemic. This

[4] Angola, Benin, Burkina Faso, Burundi, Central African Republic, Chad, Comoros, DRC; Djibouti, Eritrea, Ethiopia, The Gambia, Guinea, Guinea-Bissau, Lesotho, Liberia, Madagascar, Malawi, Mali, Mauritania, Mozambique, Niger, Rwanda, Sao Tome and Principe, Senegal, Sierra Leone, Somalia, South Sudan, Sudan, Togo, United Republic of Tanzania, Uganda and Zambia.

[5] There are 3 African LLDCs which do not fall under the category of LDCs, namely Botswana, Eswatini and Zimbabwe. Latin America accounts for 2 LLDCs, whilst Asia and the Middle East share the remaining 14 LLDCs.

[6] The LDC categorization of countries came to life through a UN General Assembly Decision in 1971. Countries are categorized as LDCs depending on the three defined criteria of low income, low human assets and the prevalence of economic and environmental vulnerabilities. Measurement of development against the said criteria relies on the meeting of given thresholds. See https://www.un.org/development/desa/dpad/least-developed-country-category/ldc-criteria.html.

dampens graduation prospects for African LDC and adds weight to the narrative of the "middle income trap".[7]

Despite the very positive post-pandemic rebound of Africa's trade, registering a record two-digit growth. As a point in case, LDC trade grew by 19%, from U$146 billion in 2021 to U$174 billion in 2022. This was above the growth witnessed globally and in other world regions.[8] Despite this spectacular growth, the narrative of the continent's poor participation in global trade has not changed. Africa's share of world trade has hovered under 3% over the last decade. Though stable, LDCs' share in global trade has remained minuscule, at just under 0.7%, as shown in Fig. 7.1.

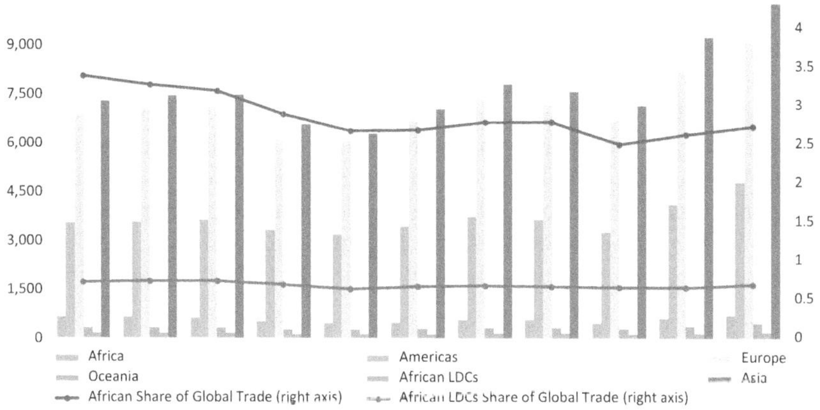

Fig. 7.1 Africa & LDC trade in global trade in US$ Billion and % Share (2012–2022). (Source: Based on data from UNCTADstat)

[7] Since the 90s, only 3 African countries have been able to graduate. Botswana, Cabo Verde and Equatorial Guinea graduated in 1994, 2007 and 2017, respectively. Angola and Sao Tome and Principe are expected to graduate in 2024. Other countries in the graduation pipeline are Comoros, Djibouti, Senegal, and Zambia, provided the threshold criteria are met in 3 consecutive years. Part of the discourse against graduation points to the empirical evidence in the developing world of the middle income trap (Griffith, 2011), as well as the risk of regression for countries that have graduated and yet continue to be exposed to high levels of vulnerability and inequality when exposed to shocks. This continues to a first line argument in the context of graduation experiences of the LDC group. See for instance (WTO, 2022).

[8] Annual growth calculations computed as averages of exports and imports UNCTADstat data.

Historically, neither the composition nor direction of African LDC trade has changed much. It remains trade of mainly raw commodities, either agriculture or minerals based, with little value added. Though there has been some diversification in the destination of trade over the past decades, increasingly with Asia (China, India and Japan) and also Africa, trade with traditional partners such as Europe and the US as single destinations is still substantial. As can be appreciated in Fig. 7.2a, b, on average, between 2016 and 2022, China led as both export and import destination with 30% and 20% shares, respectively, followed by Africa, the European Union and India.

Though the diversification in the direction of LDC trade over the last decade has been encouraging, when looking at the composition of such trade, data needs to be analyzed with caution. As shown in Fig. 7.3a, it appears that African LDC exports to the world are primarily be characterized as a trade in extractive commodities, namely fuels (37%) and ores and metals (24%), where there is little value addition. However, when considering LDC exports within the continent, there is more trade sophistication since there is more value addition in these products, with manufactures (32%) and processed food (24%) as leading sectors. Hence, LDC trade within the continent paints a more promising picture than trade with the

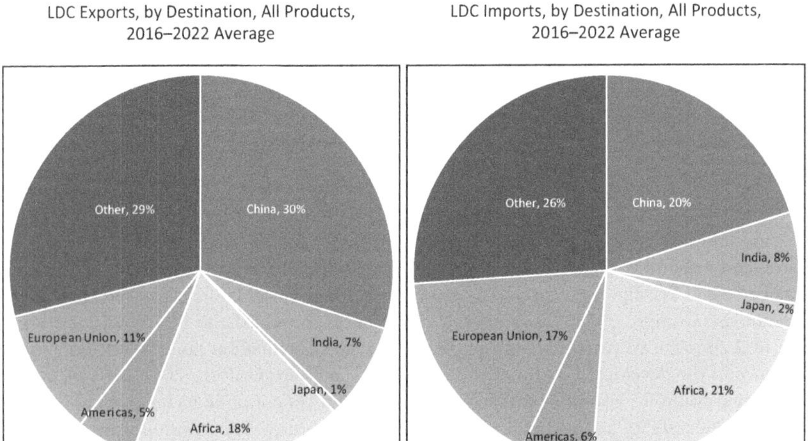

Fig. 7.2 Direction of LDC trade with the World (2016–2022). (Source: Based on data from UNCTADstat)

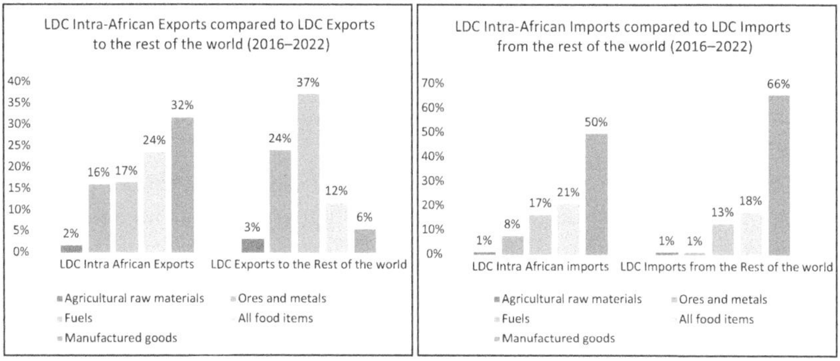

Fig. 7.3 Composition of LDC Intra-African and Global Trade in Shares (2016–2022). (Source: Based on data from UNCTADstat)

rest of the world. Even if in most cases this may be trade in light manufacturing, this provides scope for deeper industrialization where more value addition may be created from within Africa.

In turn, Fig. 7.3b shows import composition of LDCs as more aligned, with manufactures being the primary good LDCs imported both from Africa and the rest of the world (with a 50% and 66% share, respectively), followed by food (with a 21% and 18% share, respectively). This has a two-fold and two-staged explanation. Imports from the rest of the world respond to an interdependency pattern that has also been compounded by historical ties which shaped the development of African economies to respond to the needs of their colonial masters as a source for inputs, rather than a more organic development, where a traditional development pathway would imply that as economies mature, they would move from primary, to secondary and eventually tertiary activities. However, Africa's development trajectory has been haphazard, where currently we observe elements of primary and tertiary activities, with a weak or sometimes missing middle of manufacturing. Indeed, there has been evidence of deindustrialization over the past two decades (UNCTAD and UNIDO, 2011), in part also as a result of trade consumption patterns (Kaplinsky & Morris, 2008; Ighobor, 2013).

Such economic determination has also affected the import side of LDC trade and increased the dependency, in the sense that the region has had to import that which it cannot produce because of the structure of its economy. At a later historical stage, this dependency has been further compounded by the conditionalities associated with the unilateral trade preferences LDCs have received.[9] Over time, this has been a dampening factor on the ability of African LDCs to change the structure of their economy by industrializing through trade and also build resilience to global shocks.

LDC trade within the continent depicts a slightly different picture. Overall, intra-African trade has been gradually increasing, from a low base of around 10% in 2012 to 15% in 2021. LDC intra-African trade is in sync with the overall trend of intra-African trade trajectory, and has indeed surpassed it, as shown earlier in Fig. 7.2a, where LDC intra-continental exports stood at 18 percent and imports represented 21 percent of its global total. This LDC trade with Africa comprises more opportunities for value addition, as noted earlier, and also increasingly more trade of intermediary goods for further processing within the continent, which underscores that there are also significant opportunities for regional value chains and industrialization. Furthermore, the fact that trade in food ranks second when it comes to both intra-African exports and imports as shown in Fig. 7.3a, b, may also point to prospects for greater responsiveness from within the continent when there are food crises, especially since many LDC are net food importers grappling with food security, as is discussed down below (see Fig. 7.5).

By way of example, as illustrated in Fig. 7.4 down below, the agricultural sector is the main employer in LDCs, occupying nearly two thirds of the workforce. This sector is vital to the livelihood of the lower rungs of society, where subsistence agriculture is often the mainstay of the informal sector and hence its economic contribution is also likely to be underreported and underrepresented in the data. And yet, as shown earlier in Fig. 7.3, it is less of a tradable sector for LCDs.

In contrast, though minerals and fuels are top tradable sectors which constitute the mainstay of LDC exports to the world (as shown Fig. 7.3a), the sectoral employment data in Fig. 7.4 is rather low in the majority of the countries, with few exceptions. The sectoral share for LDCs stands on average at less than 2%, which implies that these are not job creating sectors. This is consistent with prior research that characterizes the extractive industries as enclave economies with little value addition and linkage

[9] From empirical evidence collected, much of trade lacks value addition because there are many technical barriers and non-tariff measures which deter potential exporters to access such markets (Páez et al., 2010b).

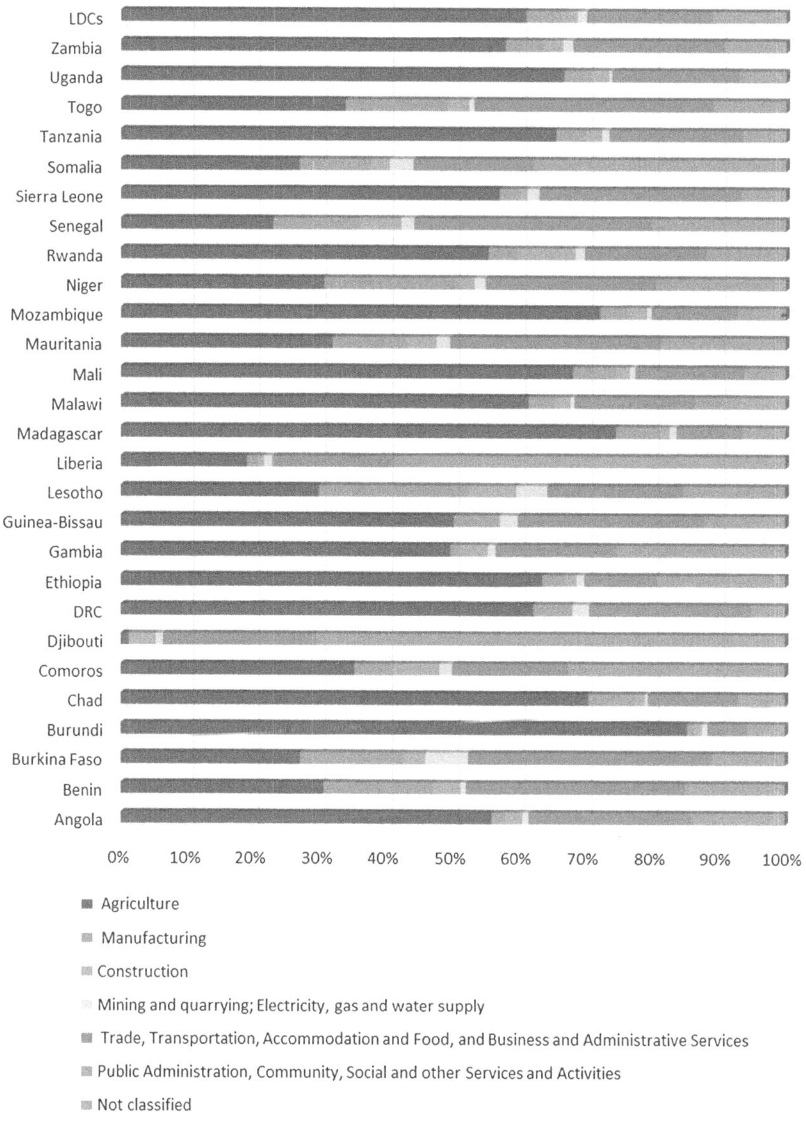

Fig. 7.4 Employment Shares by Economic Activity Sector in LDCs (2012–2022). Data was n.a. for Central African Republic, Eritrea, Guinea, South Sudan, Sudan, Sao Tome and Principe). (Source: Based on ILOSTAT Explorer. On the basis of latest available data)

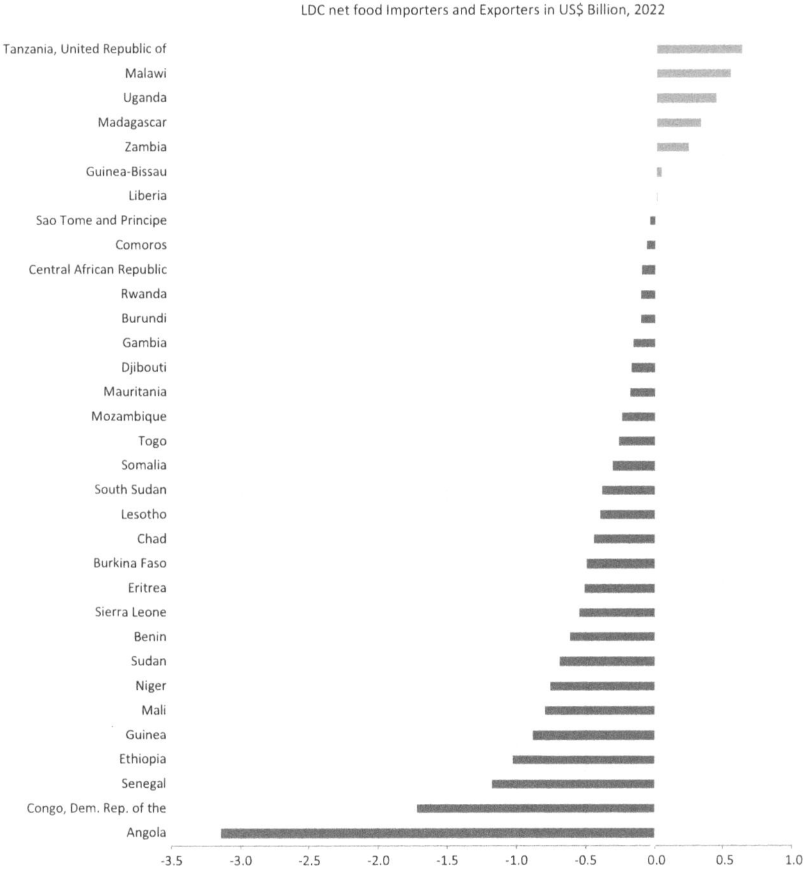

Fig. 7.5 LDC net food Importers and Exporters in US$ Billion (2022). (Source: Based on data from UNCTADStat)

creation within African economies. (ECA, 2013, 2016, 2019) More worryingly, this reality is a direct result of international investment and taxation laws under which the multinationals in the extractive industry operate, where trade and investment revenues are siphoned from Africa through transfer pricing activities which evade taxes. Such practices lead to illicit financial flows, which alone in the minerals sector have been estimated at US$ 73 billion a year between 2000 and 2015 (ECA, 2018, 2019).

The continent hosts 25 per cent of global population of 1.4 billion people and set to double by 2050. With a consumer market representing an estimated worth of U$1.4 trillion in 2015, and projected to grow to U$2.5 trillion by 2030 (Signé, 2018) and nearly two thirds of the world's arable land, Africa's share in global trade hardly does justice to the continent's agricultural resources. This is particularly alarming when we consider that agriculture concentrates the lion's share of Africa's workforce.

The picture becomes even more stark when the focus is narrowed down to food as a trading commodity. Though the African continent does boast some net food exporters, the majority of countries are net food importers, including 24 of the 33 LDCs, as shown in Fig. 7.5. Severe droughts and climate change, as well as conflict and war,[10] impact heavily on the ability of these countries to increase the local production of food, let alone withstand the price hikes that are associated with such phenomena. This points to greater propensity towards food crises a sustained vulnerability to external shocks.

Lastly, the geographical determination of *landlockness* for a subset of the LDCs combined with the fact that the continent spans over many relatively small and fragmented economies, has significantly marked Africa's ability to overcome the development challenge. This has been particularly felt when it comes to transportation, since landlocked countries rely on transit countries for their produce to reach their destination. Though a unit cost of production at the farm and factory gate in Africa are similar to those of other developing regions, it is once goods are moved that transport and trade facilitation cost become prohibitive and eliminate any competitiveness an African product may have in international markets. Indeed, it is estimated that for such countries, transport costs can range from 15 to 20 percent of import costs, which is double and even threefold of what most developed countries pay in terms of transport fees. Youssef (2019) notes that for LLDCs and LDCs, transport costs can be as high as 19 and 21 per cent of the price of a good, respectively, compared with the world average of 15 per cent.

Historically, with the expansion of trade, we have not necessarily witnessed poverty reduction in LDCs. This may at first seem counterintuitive,

[10]According to the Stockholm International Peace Research Institute (2022), of 18 countries in Sub-Saharan Africa experience conflicts in 2021, the following 15 were LDCs: Benin, Burkina Faso, Burundi, Central African Republic, Chad, DRC, Ethiopia, Madagascar, Mali, Mozambique, Niger, Somalia, South Sudan, Sudan and Uganda.

since the notion that trade can serve as a channel to promote growth has been widely accepted in economic growth theory and practice. As mentioned at the beginning of this chapter, it is argued that liberalizing trade will allow countries to specialize in goods and services where they hold a comparative advantage, leading to increased allocative efficiencies. If these efficiency gains translate into increase output and export revenue, then improved income will lead to greater consumption reporting growth. However, it is also cautioned that such trade-led growth needs to be translated into actual poverty reduction, as this is not an automatic outcome as is substantiated by a body of research.

Indeed, evidence in Africa has shown mixed results. International trade has increasingly played an important role in the economic performance of African economies, with exports growing rapidly, at 9% average yearly rate (2001–2021). In the case of African LDCs, export growth was even higher at an annual 12% for the last two decades. This trade expansion contributed to the high pace of economic growth in LDCs at an annual average of 17% during the same period, as shown in Fig. 7.6. Though LDCs outperformed other world regions, such trade has been very volatile in the face of recent economic crises. For example, African LDC exports registered a 29% leap from US$ 83 billion in 2009 to US$ 106 billion in 2010, following a slump 28% in the aftermath of the 2008 international financial

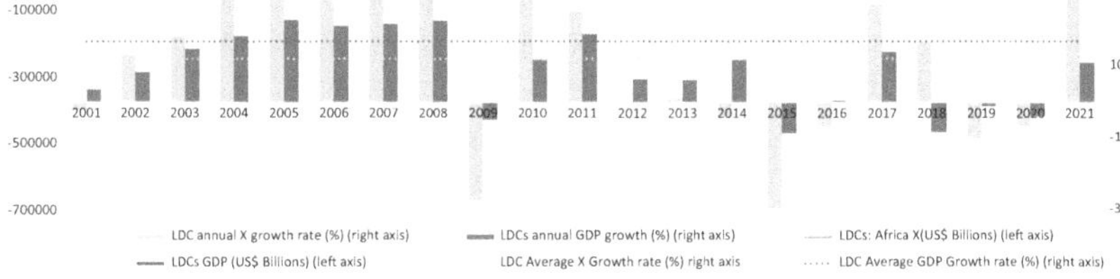

Fig. 7.6 Trade Expansion and Economic Growth in LDCs in US$ Billion and % Shares (2000–2022). (Source: ECA calculations using UNCTADStat)

crisis. As mentioned earlier, the same trend was observed with the pandemic, where overall LDC trade plummeted in 2020, to subsequently recover in 2021 and 2022.

Figure 7.7 down below seems to suggest that as much as LDCs did experience trade growth over the last two decades, this seems to have had less of a positive impact on poverty reduction. Though causality is not established, LDC export growth appears positively correlated with an *increase* in Fig. 7.7. As trade grew, measured as changes in export volume, so did the number of poor, defined as decreases in the poverty headcount, for LDCs as a whole. Despite the overall bleak picture, there are mixed results within the group, some of which are encouraging.

Countries which witnessed both trade expansion and poverty reduction were Djibouti, DRC, Senegal, Mali, Benin, Guinea, Guinea Bissau,

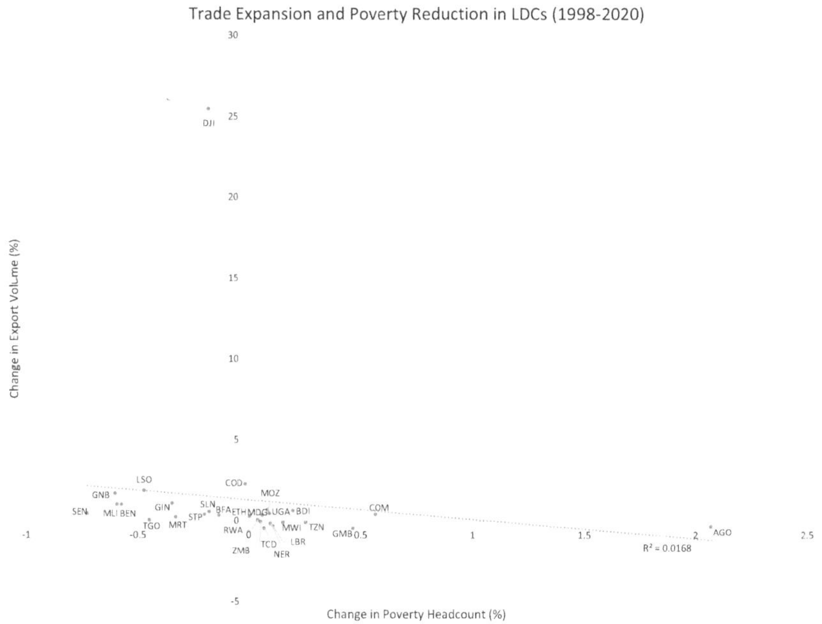

Fig. 7.7 Trade Expansion and Poverty Reduction in LDCs in % Change (2002–2020). Insufficient data for Central African Republic, Eritrea, Somalia, Sudan and South Sudan. (Source: Author's calculations using UNCTADStat and World Bank Datasets)

Mauritania, Burkina Faso, Sierra Leone, Lesotho and Sao Tome and Principe. Some countries experienced trade expansion whilst poverty increased, as shown in the upper right quadrant of Fig. 7.7 (Mozambique, Comoros, Ethiopia, Madagascar, Burundi, Rwanda and Uganda). Countries which experienced trade contraction whilst poverty increased are depicted in the lower right quadrant. They included Angola, The Gambia, Malawi, Tanzania, Liberia, Niger, Chad and Zambia. Finally, none of the LDCs experienced poverty reduction with trade contraction, underscoring causality of the relationship between trade and poverty.

This research therefore shows that whilst in theory, gains from trade are possible, they do not automatically translate into an improvement of people's lives. With many of the African LDCs participating in multilateral and well as regional and unilateral trade regimes with SDT, this seems to suggest that existing SDTs may not have done much to advance poverty reduction through trade expansion that may have come as a result of greater market access. Notwithstanding the empirical evidence that backs causality between greater trade and reduced poverty in Africa,[11] the data presented in this research seems to point to greater binding constraints that are increasing the development gap of LDCs. This may point to the need for deepened research to understand what policy calibration may be needed to allow LDCs to enjoy poverty reduction through greater trade integration.

In sum, the story of LDC trade performance has been a rocky one, as much as there is hope for greater trade within the continent. If this is to be considered as a pathway for development, a change is needed in the current state of global trade relations, as well as policies and regulations that govern trade.

4 Addressing Variable Geometry Through Special and Differential Treatment

Special and Differential Treatment (SDT) has a longstanding practice in the multilateral setting to account for the reality of variable geometries between nations. Historically, the focus has been on relaxing the main elements of reciprocity in a preferential trade agreement to the point where market access is provided through a most favored nation principle (MFN).

[11] An ample body of studies point to evidence on how trade has been detrimental to the poor. See for example Dollar and Kraay (2002) and Winters (2007).

MFN is instilled with life through the elimination of duties (tariffs), quotas or other restrictions on essentially all trade with some exceptions and is also often coined as duty free and quota free access (DFQF). This has been the basis of many SDT provisions in support of development, though arguably their results and impact have been very mixed and yet to be fully assessed.

Further to these, and more recently, in recognition that market access opportunities provided to LDCs in their traditional form may not have had the desired impact in the past, international community efforts have focused on ex post liberalization interventions to complement and bolster trade liberalization. (Saner & Páez, 2006; AfDB, ECA and WTO, 2011) These may comprise mechanisms to cover adjustment costs resulting from the loss in trade revenue as a result of liberalization; deferral or waiver of payments; longer transition periods or more time to operationalize aspects of the trade agreement or conduct performance reviews and evaluations. In a wider sense, special and differential treatment has also evolved to include technical assistance and capacity building in the form of Aid for Trade (AfT) or, to assist countries (and their private sector) in overcoming the structural barriers they encounter in a free trade setting.[12]

Table 7.1 summarizes some of the most salient aspects of SDT provisions that apply to LDCs in the multilateral WTO setting. As may be appreciated, the crux of SDT rests on market access provisions which provide MFN treatment without requiring reciprocity on the part of LDCs. Complementary to this cornerstone of SDT in goods and services trade, there are accompanying provisions in the GATT and GATS that stipulate longer transition periods for the operationalization of such reciprocal treatment.

For LDCs, several actionable flexibilities are also in place. As shown in Table 7.1, under the GATT, they provide for temporary suspension of trade based on BOP difficulties and the application of flexibilities in the tariff structures to protect an infant industry in the GATT (Art. XVIII). It further also allows for the carve of out liberalization for developing countries, including LDCs through an 'Enabling clause' (Art. XXIV). This

[12] This chapter considers the more traditional type of SDTs, as well as adjustment costs. It does not consider other types of international support measures, which may include financial or technical assistance through special programmes and/or budget allocations. For an array and description of these wider measures please visit: https://www.un.org/ldcportal/ https://www.un.org/ldcportal/content/preferential-market-access-goods-2.

Table 7.1 Illustration of Special and Differential Treatment (SDT) modalities in the WTO and AfCFTA compared

Elements of SDT	*WTO Agreement*	*GATT*	*GATS*	*TRIPS*
Principle	Preamble para 2. Recognizes the need of developing countries and especially LDCs to have partake in adequate share of global trade growth		Preamble recognizes asymmetries between members and takes in account the difficulties faced by LDCs services sector in view of their situation and needs	Preamble recognizes the need for maximum flexibility in the domestic implementation of IP rules to allow them to build their technological base
Scope	SDT is extended to developing countries and LDCs, irrespective of WTO membership[a]	Art. XVIII allows deviations from the agreement provided that an economy portrays low standards of living and is in the early stages of economic development	SDT is extended in differing levels to developing countries and LDCs	SDT is extended in differing levels to developing countries and LDCs
Market Access		GATT Part IV establishes that there is no reciprocity of tariff commitments or other barriers is expected by other parties from less developed contracting parties	Art. IV Specific commitments of Members should give priority to LDCs. Priority to be given to support LDCs services suppliers	

(*continued*)

Table 7.1 (continued)

Elements of SDT	*WTO Agreement*	*GATT*	*GATS*	*TRIPS*
Exceptions or deviations from an obligation		GATT Art. XVIII refers to flexibilities in tariff structures to protect an infant industry and apply quantitative restrictions to alleviate BOP difficulties. Temporary deviations from the GATT are permissible Art. XXIV and Enabling Clause allows for deviations for developing countries	Art. IV Special treatment modalities for services negotiations to be set up for LDCs in subsequent liberalization rounds Art. V(3) flexibility for developing countries entering economic integration agreements on the requirement of substantial sectoral coverage and elimination of discrimination	TRIPS 2005 Protocol which allows LDCs and developing countries that are part of regional trade agreements to be waived of complying with Art. 31(f). A pharmaceutical product produced or imported under a compulsory license in that Member can be exported to those other developing countries or LDCs in a regional trade agreement that share a common health problem
Transition Periods			Art III: 4 Longer time frame beyond 2 years for the setting up of enquiry points of developing countries	Art 65 & 66 Developing countries have a 5 year and LDCs and 11-year implementation period of TRIPS provisions, which can be extended, except for national treatment and MFN treatment

(*continued*)

Table 7.1 (continued)

Elements of SDT	*AfCFTA Treaty*	*Protocol on Trade in Goods*	*Protocol on Trade in Services*	*Protocol on IPR*
Principle	Art. 5 establishes variable geometry, and flexibility and special and differential treatment; as two of their governing principles of the AfCFTA	Preamble recognizes that there are different levels of development among the AfCFTA State Parties and the need to afford flexibilities, SDT and technical assistance for those with special needs	The Preamble acknowledges the serious difficulty, special economic situation and the development, trade and financial needs of LDCs, LLDCs, SIDs and vulnerable economies	Preambular language underscores the need for State Parties to make use of the flexibilities provided in the existing international IPR regimes
Market Access	Art. 18 says that though preferences are to be accorded on the basis of reciprocity, the levels of development of the State Parties shall be taken into account	Art. 4 State Parties shall afford opportunity to negotiate the preferences granted on a reciprocal basis, taking into account levels of development of State Parties	Flexibility is afforded to State Parties that have special trade needs, specificities and circumstances, within the scope of the market access negotiations and implementation of the agreement, such as exemptions	

(*continued*)

Table 7.1 (continued)

Elements of SDT	*AfCFTA Treaty*	*Protocol on Trade in Goods*	*Protocol on Trade in Services*	*Protocol on IPR*
Flexibilities or deviations from obligations		Art. 6 on SDT refers to the AfCFTA objective of ensuring comprehensive and mutually beneficial trade in goods as the basis for State Parties to provide flexibilities to other State Parties at different levels of economic development or with individual specificities. Among flexibilities are special consideration and additional transition period for implementation, case by case.	Art. 7 on SDT establishes to ensure increased and beneficial participation in services trade by all parties that be given (a) to the progressive liberalisation of service sectors commitments and supply modes in critical sectors of growth, social and sustainable economic development; and (c) to providing technical assistance and capacity-building through continental support programmes.	Art. 12 refers to existing deviation on the granting of licenses under the TRIPS Waiver to produce generic pharmaceuticals for public health purposes.

(*continued*)

Table 7.1 (continued)

Elements of SDT	*AfCFTA Treaty*	*Protocol on Trade in Goods*	*Protocol on Trade in Services*	*Protocol on IPR*
Transition Periods		Liberalization is targeted at 97% of the tariff lines. For 90% of the products, LDCs have 10 years to eliminate tariffs (compared to 5 years for more advanced African countries). For the remaining 7% of sensitive tariff lines LDCs have 13 years (more advanced countries have 10 years). LDCs can start liberalizing sensitive goods 5 years after the start of trading (1 January 2022), but have to complete liberalization by 1 January 2035.	Under Art. 7 (b), State parties should give due consideration to the challenges when implementing this Protocol and granting flexibilities such as transitional periods on a case by case basis, to accommodate special economic situations and various needs	Art. 35 (2) on the application of the Protocol establishes that LDCs have 3 years to implement the provisions of this Protocol within its entry into force. Para (3) further states that LDCs are not required to provide protection of pharmaceutical patents and pharmaceutical testing and other data for a period of time provided for in the relevant international treaties.

Source: Author's representation, on the basis of WTO and AfCFTA agreements and legal instruments

[a]Of the African LDCs, Eritrea, Ethiopia, Sao Tome and Principe, Somalia, South Sudan and Sudan are not members to the WTO. All of these, except Eritrea, are in the process of acceding the WTO

means countries which are members to an RTA do not need to extend more favorable treatment in the form of MFN and national treatment to the rest of the WTO membership, provided that such agreements are in the interest of their development and cover substantially all trade. A parallel provision in GATS mirrors the same type of flexibilities for regional integration agreements (Art. V(3)).

The TRIPS agreement also provides for several flexibilities in the form of longer time frames for implementation of the obligations in provisions in Art. 65 and 66, as shown in Table 7.1. In addition, there is a TRIPs

Waiver dating back to a Council Decision of 2003, which was later fully incorporated as an amendment to Article 31(f) through an Annex and Protocol. This allows for a deviation of producing or importing a pharmaceutical product under a compulsory licence in a Member State to be exported to the markets of those other developing or least developed country parties to the regional trade agreement that share a health problem. This waiver has been historically difficult to put into action (Hestermeyer, 2007), as was the case during the AIDS crisis some African countries encountered in the last decade. A more recently waiver to address the challenges developing countries were facing to access medicines and in response to the Covid-19 pandemic, was also bartered during the 12th WTO Ministerial Conference in June 2022 (WTO, 2022).[13] The adopted waiver was much criticized because it watered down the initial South-South proposal from India and South Africa, which would have given developing countries the needed backing.[14] At the time, the adopted waiver failed to provide a pragmatic solution to the health crisis the pandemic represented. It was difficult to set in motion, let alone afford developing countries with the necessary flexibilities to pool procurement for pharmaceuticals they cannot produce, but could easily source from other developing countries within their regions to overcome the prohibitive price structures they were facing at the aegis of the covid crisis for much needed covid related medications and vaccines.

Similarly, SDT also is reflected in the provisions of the Dispute Settlement Understanding (DSU) governing dispute settlement in the WTO. For example, particular attention should be given to the problems/ interest of developing countries during consultations (DSU, Art. 10(4)) and restraint is to be exercised when WTO members request for compensation retaliation, or other obligations from LDCs involved in a dispute (DSU, Art. 24 (1)). Lastly, the SG may be requested by developing country members to provide his/her good offices in solving a dispute or when consultations involving an LDC fail (DSU, Art. 3(12) and Art. 24(2), respectively).

[13] *Ministerial Decision on the TRIPS Agreement*, WTO Doc. WT/MIN(22)/30 (Jun. 22, 2022), available at: https://docs.wto.org/dol2fe/Pages/SS/directdoc.aspx?filename=q:/WT/MIN22/30.pdf&Open=True.

[14] See initial submission to the TRIPS Council, Communication to the TRIPS Council from India and South Africa, Waiver from Certain Provisions of the TRIPS Agreement for the Prevention, Containment and Treatment of COVID-19, Annex at 1, WTO Doc. IP/C/W/669 (October 2, 2020).

LDCs also count with more leniency in the form of longer cycles to conduct their trade policy reviews, a general monitoring and evaluation exercise all member countries are subject to the Trade Policy Review Mechanism (TPRM) audits of compliance with the WTO multilateral trade regime. Whilst developing countries have 6 years between each review, developed country members have to conduct such reviews every 2 years.

In the African regional setting, similar SDT has been put in place. Several regional economic communities (RECs) have catered for the special needs of countries in less advantageous positions. For example, the EAC clearly alludes to the principle of variable geometry in its constitutive Treaty to be "… the principle of flexibility which allows for progression in co-operation among a sub-group of members in a larger integration scheme…", in its Article 1 on interpretation.[15] It further enunciates that "…the principle of variable geometry which allows for progression in cooperation among groups within the Community for wider integration schemes in various fields and at different speeds…", listing it as one of its operational principles (Art.7(e)).

More recently, and as a point in case, the Tripartite Free Trade Area (TFTA) between COMESA, EAC and SADC and hence encompassing a membership of 26 countries, of which over two thirds are African LDCs. The TFTA Agreement clearly establishes the meaning of variable geometry as a "… principle of flexibility which allows for progression in cooperation amongst members in a larger integration scheme in a variety of areas and at different speeds;" (Art. 1 and Art 6 (b)). It further also includes flexibility and special and differential treatment as a subsequent principle (Art. 6 (c)).

In sum, efforts are being made in the African setting to cater for needs of less developed countries, and in particular, LDCs. With the aegis of the AfCFTA, which builds on the *acquis* of this emerging body of regional treaty law on SDT in Africa, a new standard on variable geometry is being shaped on the continent.

The Agreement Establishing the African Continental Free Trade Area (AU, 2018) (from now on the AfCFTA Agreement) provides for 2 principles that are to govern SDT in the AfCFTA space in its Art. 5. The first of these is the principle of *variable geometry*. The second principle refers

[15] Treaty for the Establishment of the East African Community entered into force on 7th July 2000 (EAC, 2000).

to *flexibility and special and differential treatment*. Nowhere in the agreement are these two principles defined. In an attempt to provide for an interpretation of their meaning, considering the *preservation of the acquis*, which is yet another negotiating principle of the AfCFTA Agreement (Art. 5(f)) of the legal body of law on variable geometry that is Africa centric, one could argue that the first principle is non-actionable, as it merely points to a situation faced or characteristic inherent to a part of the membership of the agreement, which is in fact, that members are in different stages of development and hence have different needs. One can further reason that the second principle is actionable and informed by the first, given the inherent heterogeneity in developamong the membership.

In addition, it could be further argued that these two principles are made actionable through the protocols that are subsequently derived from the AfCFTA Agreement. Indeed, the Protocols that supersede and are expressly stated to be integral part of the AfCFTA agreement (Art. 1, on definitions, and Art. 8 governing the status of derived instruments), do have provisions that offer more specificity on what SDT elements are being contemplated by the membership.

For example, as shown in Table 7.1, the Protocol on trade in goods contains both hortatory language in the preamble, as well as concrete obligations on SDT. There is the explicit recognition in the preamble of the Protocol on Trade in Goods which recognizes that Parties to the agreement are in different stages of development and thus may have different needs. This is followed by a dedicated Article 6 on SDT which caters for transition periods and flexibilities when liberalizing.

Equally so, the Protocol on Trade in Services contains similar preambular language, as well as a dedicated provision (Art. 7) on SDT. The nature of such treatment, however, is much more detailed and makes direct allusion to LDCs as compared with the Protocol on Trade in Goods, also providing for technical assistance and capacity building support through dedicated programmes (Art. 7(c)). This is further bolstered with clear concepts of what is meant by variable geometry, flexibility and special and differential treatment in the Negotiating Modalities of the Protocol (Annex V of the Protocol). Furthermore, the Negotiation Principles for Services (Annex X of the Protocol), which state that "... Based on the principles of variable geometry and reciprocity as set out in the agreed modalities, those Member States that wish to liberalise more sectors than the five priority sectors are free to do so", also operationalize the seemingly vague principles at higher (AfCFTA Treaty) level for services.

It is noteworthy to also mention that among the phase II protocols, neither the Investment nor the Competition Protocol mention SDT. One could argue that this has to do with the spirit under which these protocols were negotiated, namely, with the aim to develop common rules. In *strictu sensu*, these agreements were not intended to contain commitments or market access obligations that would affect investment, intellectual property or competition in the economic space of the AfCFTA.[16] Indeed, the Agreement clearly provides the basis for modalities of progressive tariff elimination and liberalization for trade in goods and services (Art, 4 (a) and (b)), whilst it merely points to cooperation modalities for investment, intellectual property and competition (Art. 4 (c)).

With this caveat in mind, it must also be noted that the IP Protocol enjoys a special status. It recognizes existing multilateral commitments made in the context of other international agreements in its preamble. As such, the protocol provides for longer implementation time frames for LDCs (Art. 35 (3)), and in particular refers to the timeframes already provided for in other international treaties with pharmaceutical patents protection. It further makes direct allusion to the TRIPS agreement, requesting AfCFTA State Parties which are WTO members to ratify the TRIPs Waiver within three years of the entre into force of the IP Protocol, and also directs non-members of the WTO which include 6 African LDCs (see footnote 14) to introduce procedures that are in accordance with the TRIPS Waiver (Art. 12 (b) and (c)) (TRIPS Council, 2020). This therefore only constitutes an additional burden for this subset of LDCs which may or may not already have such measures in place. It is not a waiver per se, as is the case of the WTO TRIPS waiver, which, as explained earlier, removes limitations on exports under compulsory license to countries that cannot manufacture the pharmaceuticals themselves in emergency situations, so that they may import such goods to overcome a given health crisis, such as the recent Covid-19 pandemic.

[16] This is unlike the phase I protocols on trade in goods and services, for which a single market is to be created and operationalized following the principle of progressive liberalization through successive negotiation rounds, as is provided for in the objectives of the AfCFTA agreement Art. 3(a) and (b).

5 Advancing in the AfCFTA at Differing Speeds

It is important from an outset to establish that reciprocity, as a principle whereby countries will confer MFN treatment to each other, is in natural conflict with the principle of special and differential treatment, which rids its beneficiaries from the obligation to reciprocate. The same applies to the concept of variable geometry, which recognizes that reciprocity may not be possible for all, but that it should not prevent those who wish to advance deeper integration or liberalization to do so, and it should most certainly not come at the expense of those that are not in a capacity to do so.

There are numerous examples in the multilateral setting, where the development of regulation has been necessary to overcome this perennial tension. Some of the regulation, such as the Enabling Clause, as well as the TRIPS waiver, have been discussed in this chapter and take account of such efforts. At times, WTO case law has had to dissipate conflicting views around the application and interpretation of the leniency that is afforded, which remains a second best in the form of remedial action.[17]

In the African context, there is little if no evidence of what is to be done when such tensions arise, perhaps justifiably so, since members to the various trade agreements discussed herewith are like-minded developing countries and stand only to benefit from the flexibilities the multilateral system has put in place. Nonetheless, the *Treaty Establishing the African Economic Community of 1991* (OAU, 1991) (from here on the Abuja Treaty) in its Art. 37(3) provides for some language on this conflict and what to do when incompatibilities arise. In essence, it defers any incompatibility in the MFN principle of the treaty with treaties of third parties.

However, the Abuja Treaty did not provide for or allude to an AfCFTA. Nonetheless, the AfCFTA does make explicit reference to and abides by the objectives and principles enunciated in the Abuja Treaty (AfCFTA Treaty and AfCFTA Goods Protocol preambles, respectively). It further builds on the rights and obligations emanating from that Treaty and self identifies the AfCFTA as a necessary foundation to the attainment of a Continental Customs Union (Goods Protocol, Art 3(d)), which is indeed one of the recognized steps envisioned in the Abuja Treaty, and

[17] See for instance WTO (2004).

which will lead to the ulterior achievement of an African Economic Community (Services Protocol, Art. 18(1)).[18]

The AfCFTA further caters for the possibility of differing speeds of integration. The Protocol on Trade in Goods states that: "Nothing in this Protocol shall prevent two or more State Parties from extending to one another preferences which aim at achieving the objectives of this Protocol among themselves, provided that such preferences are extended to the other State Parties on a reciprocal basis." (Art. 4(3)) and further establishes in the next paragraph of the same article that "… A State Party shall afford opportunity to the other State Parties to negotiate the preferences granted therein on a reciprocal basis, taking into account levels of development of State Parties." (Art. 4(4)). Similar language is also found in the Services Protocol.

This means that lesser developed State Parties such as LDCs could automatically benefit from deeper integration among non-LDC State parties through reciprocity principle, without needing to engage in progressive liberalization themselves during negotiations. In other words, variable geometry, in such an event would seem to supersede the principle of progressive liberalization.

Though the AfCFTA is at quite a young stage of operationalization, there seems to be some evidence that this principle of supersession is being put into practice. The initial Agreement on modalities for AfCFTA Trade in Goods Negotiations is a point in case. There has been agreement on an ambitious target of 97% for tariff liberalization. This caters for the overall objective of the AfCFTA Treaty of achieving an integrated continent and the requirement of covering substantially all trade under the WTO, as was discussed earlier in Sect. 3. At the same time, the adopted modalities provide sufficient flexibilities and length of time for some countries to adjust and implement the significant commitments they will be undertaking, as was portrayed in Table 7.1 of this chapter. The instrumentalization of this process has been the submission of tariff offers detailing the goods subject to duty free trade and also those that are sensitive or excluded and subject to more leniency when liberalized, as specified earlier in Table 7.1. All of these offers in the form of schedules are in the process of being consolidated into Annex 1 of the AfCFTA Treaty.[19]

[18] See also earlier discussion in Chap. 2, Sect. 2.3.

[19] The same process is expected for services negotiations, once the details are finalized.

Initially, 7 States Parties (Ethiopia, Djibouti, Madagascar, Malawi, Sudan, Zambia and Zimbabwe) requested for a variation from this requirement, based on their economic circumstances, upon which they underwent consultation with the then "Champion" of the AfCFTA, the former President of the Republic of Niger. Subsequent to this consultation, Djibouti withdrew its reservation, but the remaining six countries required and received special dispensation.

In services, whilst some countries such as Djibouti, needed additional time to be able to make their initial submission of offers, others have been very progressive in their approach, despite being LDCs. Malawi, for example, presented an initial offer which went beyond the 5 priority sectors, and included health, education social and recreational services. (Report of the 7th CTIS, 2022, para. 23–24) Other countries too have taken advantage of the variable geometry principle and have had ample consultations on their initial and revised offers, pointing to a very active negotiations arena.

It remains to be seen how the State Parties to the AfCFTA continue to instrumentalize the variable geometry and SDT principles in upcoming negotiation rounds, especially in the context of services trade in the new sectors, as the focus of negotiations has been on 5 priority sectors (Business, Communication, Financial, Tourism and Travel, and Transport services sectors), as initially outlined in the Guidelines for services negotiations. Equally so, given the existence of a dispute settlement mechanism, it also remains to be seen how in the wider context of application other State Parties give due consideration to the LDCs, as well as WTO members in the context of TRIPS or WTO related disputes which may arise in the future.

For the time being, it is encouraging to witness the innovative approaches and flexibilities with which the negotiations have unfolded when it comes to the design, as well as the application of variable geometry and SDT as negotiating principles. This is contributing to the deepening of the acquis of both existing approaches and references to approaches in the negotiation on trade agreements in Africa. It is also setting a new bar in supporting the empowerment of African LDCs in terms of using their home corner to widen their trading opportunities beyond their traditional partners.

6 Conclusions

The present chapter looked at the issue of variable geometry and special and differential treatment in its application to African LDCs, and more generally African developing countries, both in the multilateral and regional trade setting. From the research, it is clear that SDTs have been the mainstay of trade support to LDCs over the past decades. Nonetheless, the data presented in this chapter do not substantiate that greater trade flexibilities along with the witnessed increased trade performance in LDCs, has contributed to poverty reduction in these countries, as much as these may have received more leniency.

From this analysis and understanding that the AfCFTA is an agreement that is evolving in nature by virtue of the fact that State Parties are negotiating the rules, as well as the content and scope of their liberalization, the body of law that is emanating from it is not picture perfect. It will require articulation, application, interpretation and innovation. This analysis therefore comes at a time when LDCs are finalizing their liberalization offers in the context of the goods and services negotiations of the AfCFTA. At this critical juncture, they have been revving up their positions and strategies in the run up to two important international fora, where their fates when it comes to international trade relations in the multilateral area, could be sealed.

The first one is the run up to the 13th WTO Ministerial Conference (MC13), will take place in February 2024 in Abu Dhabi, United Arab Emirates. As we have experienced and highlighted in the past (Saner & Páez, 2005, 2006) with commitments and initiatives which could have been groundbreaking for LDCs, without an added impetus in this forum to prioritize the issues that are at the heart of LDC trade, it will be difficult to achieve a successful conclusion of a development oriented ministerial round, as was the initial intent with the Doha Development Round. The priorities for African LDCs in this context would continue to be agriculture, fisheries, WTO reforms. With the new IFDA, investment would also need to be considered as an area where LDCs should be given due consideration and afforded all the flexibilities to make the most of investment facilitation for impact investment. Lastly, the question of graduation and how it affects African LDCs who find themselves in the graduation pipeline must be revisited, to ensure there is a balance in terms of flexibilities and obligations so that these countries have a fair chance at a smooth transition and resilience, away from increased vulnerability.

The second such fora, which admittedly, goes beyond the scope of international trade relations is the Doha Programme of Action for Least Developed Countries (LDC V) adopted in 2022. With the sobering recognition that the Istanbul Programme of Action (2010–2020) fell short of its promise to LDCs, this new programme that presents itself with LDC V is an opportunity that cannot be missed.

In conclusion and going forward, this is going to be all the more important for an effective implementation of the AfCFTA, and joint pursuit of various objectives across global and regional initiatives, such as climate change, and peace and security, and which could help Africa optimize on the opportunities which the multilateral trading system avails to LDCs and African countries at large.

Against this backdrop, the AfCFTA, which epitomizes Africa's regional integration vision for the years to come, will need to test the waters in terms of coexistence and compatibility with the multilateral trading system, as well as other programmes and initiatives mentioned here. Support from within this integration reality called the AfCFTA is already being felt, in the way negotiations are advancing. International and regional partners will also need to come in to further invigorate this process when it comes to domestication and operationalization of the agreed liberalization, especially in the African LDCs for the fruits of these efforts to bare.

References

AfDB, ECA and WTO. (2011). African Case Stories: A Snapshot of Aid for Trade on the Ground in Africa. https://www.wto.org/english/tratop_e/devel_e/a4t_e/global_review11_e.htm

AU (2018). *Agreement Establishing the African Continental Free Trade Area.* https://au.int/sites/default/files/treaties/36437-treaty-consolidated_text_on_cfta_-_en.pdf

Bagwell, K., Mavroidis, P. C., & Staiger, R. W. (2002). It's a Question of Market Access. *The American Journal of International Law, 96*(1), 56–76.

Bhagwati, J., Panagariya, A., & Srinivasan, T. N. (2004). The Muddles over Outsourcing. *The Journal of Economic Perspectives, 18*(4), 93–114. https://www.jstor.org/stable/3216794

Dicken, P. (2003). *Global Shift: Reshaping the Global Economic Map in the 21st Century* (4th ed.). Sage.

Dollar, D., & Kraay, A. (2002). Growth is Good for the Poor. *Journal of Economics Growth (US), 7*(3), 195–225.

EAC (2000), Treaty for the Establishment of the East African Community. Entered into force on 7th July 2000.
ECA. (2016). *Investment Policies and Bilateral Investment Treaties in Africa: Implications for Regional Integration*. Economic Commission for Africa. https://repository.uneca.org/handle/10855/23035
ECA. (2019). *Linkages Between Double Taxation Treaties and Bilateral Investment Treaties*. Economic Commission for Africa. https://repository.uneca.org/handle/10855/43673
ECA. (2021). *Towards a Common Investment Area in the African Continental Free Trade Area: Levelling the Playing Field for Intra-African Investment*. Economic Commission for Africa. https://repository.uneca.org/handle/10855/46741
Economic Commission for Africa. (2013). *Economic Report on Africa: Making the Most of Africa's Commodities: Industrializing for Growth, Jobs and Economic Transformation*. Economic Commission for Africa.
Economic Commission for Africa. (2018). *Base Erosion and Profit Shifting in Africa: Reforms to Facilitate Improved Taxation of Multinational Enterprises*. Economic Commission for Africa.
Gereffi, G., Humphrey, J., & Sturgeon, T. (2005). The Governance of Global Value Chains. *Review of International Political Economy, 12*(1), 78–104. https://doi.org/10.1080/09692290500049805
Griffith, B. (2011). Middle Income Trap. In *Frontiers in Development Policy* (pp. 39–43). World Bank.
Hestermeyer, H. P. (2007). Canadian-made Drugs for Rwanda: The First Application of the WTO Waiver on Patents and Medicines. *ASIL Insights, 11*(28). https://www.asil.org/insights/volume/11/issue/28/canadian-made-drugs-rwanda-first-application-wto-waiver-patents-and
Ighobor, K. (2013). China in the Heart of Africa: Opportunities and Pitfalls in a Rapidly Expanding Relationship. *Africa Renewal, 26*(3), 6–8.
International Trade Centre. (2020). *Covid-19: The Great Lockdown and Its Impact on Small Business, SME Competitiveness Report*. ITC.
Kaplinsky, R., & Morris, M. (2008). Do the Asian Drivers Undermine Export-Oriented Industrialization in SSA? *World Development, 36*(2), 254–273.
Karingi, S. N., Páez, L., & Degefa, D. (2012). Survey of AGOA's Past, Present & Future Prospects: The Experiences and Expectations of Sub-Saharan Africa. *ATPC Work in Progress, 89*. https://repository.uneca.org/handle/10855/22210
Lloyd, P. (2009). The Variable Geometry Approach to International Economic Integration. *International Journal of Business and Development Studies, 1*(1), 51–66. https://doi.org/10.22111/ijbds.2009.1304
Nye, J., & Donahue, J. (2000). *Governance in a Globalizing World*. Brookings Institutions Press.

OAU (1991), Treaty Establishing the African Economic Community. (1991). https://au.int/en/treaties/treaty-establishing-african-economic-community

Páez, L. (2011). *Liberalizing Financial Services and Foreign Direct Investment: Developing a Framework for Commercial Banking*. Palgrave Macmillan. https://doi.org/10.1057/9780230316829

Páez, L., Karingi, S., Kimenyi, M., & Paulos, M. (2010a). African U.S. Trade in the Spotlight: A Decade of AGOA. Jointly with, African Trade Policy Centre (ATPC). *ATPC Policy Brief*, No. 16. https://hdl.handle.net/10855/22222

Páez, L., Karingi, S., Kimenyi, M., & Paulos, M. (2010b). A Decade (2000–2010) of African-US Trade Under the African Growth and Opportunity Act (AGOA). *ATPC Work in Progress*, No. 81. https://hdl.handle.net/10855/29212

Reinsch, W. (2021). The Manufacturer's Dilemma: Reshoring and Resiliency in a Pandemic World. *JSTOR*. Retrieved September 4, 2023, from http://www.jstor.org/stable/resrep36906

Ricardo, D. (1817). *On the Principles of Political Economy and Taxation*. John Murray.

Saner, R., & Páez, L. (2005). *Technical Assistance and Capacity Building for LDCs: Time to Reconsider*. CUTS International Briefing Paper No. 5/2005. http://www.csend.org/publications/development-int-rel/47-technical-assistance-and-capacity-building-for-ldcstime-to-reconsider

Saner, R., & Páez, L. (2006). Technical Assistance to Least-Developed Countries in the Context of the Doha Development Round: High Risk of Failure. *Journal of World Trade, 40*(3), 467–494. https://kluwerlawonline.com/journalarticle/Journal+of+World+Trade/40.3/TRAD2006027

Signé, L. (2018). *Africa's Consumer Market Potential: Trends, Drivers, Opportunities, and Strategies*. Africa Growth Initiative at Brookings, November.

Stockholm International Peace Research Institute. (2022). *SIPRI Yearbook 2002 Armaments, Disarmament and International Security*. Oxford University Press. https://www.sipri.org/yearbook/2022/06

TRIPS Council, (2020). *Communication to the TRIPS Council from India and South Africa, Waiver from Certain Provisions of the TRIPS Agreement for the Prevention, Containment and Treatment of COVID-19*. Annex at ¶ 1, WTO Doc. IP/C/W/669.

UNCTAD and UNIDO. (2011). *Economic Development in Africa Report 2011. Fostering Industrial Development in Africa in the New Global Environment*. United Nations Publication. Sales No. E.11.II.D.14. New York and Geneva.

Winters, A. (Ed.). (2007). *The WTO and Poverty and Inequality* (Critical Perspective on the Global Trading System and the WTO). Edward Elgar.

World Trade Organization. (2022). *Note by the Secretariat for the Twenty-Seventh Annual Review of the Implementation and Operation of the TBT Agreement* (Report No. G/ TBT/47). https://docs.wto.org/dol2fe/Pages/SS/directdoc.aspx?filename=q:/G/TBT/47.pdf&Open=True

WTO. (2004). *European Communities – Conditions for Granting of Tariff Preferences to Developing Countries.* Report of the Appellate Body, WT/DS246/AB/R, 7 April 2004.

WTO (2022), Ministerial Decision on the TRIPS Agreement. WTO Doc. WT/MIN(22)/30 (June 22, 2022). https://docs.wto.org/dol2fe/Pages/SS/directdoc.aspx?filename=q:/WT/MIN22/30.pdf&Open=True

Youssef, F. (2019). *Sustainable Transit and Transport Corridors in Support of LLDCs Trade and Regional Integration and Cooperation.* UNCTAD. https://unctad.org/system/files/non-official-document/cimem7p24_Frida%20Youssef_en.pdf

Databases and Sources

ILO. https://ilostat.ilo.org/topics/employment/#; https://ilostat.ilo.org/resources/concepts-and-definitions/description-labour-force-statistics/

UNCTADStat. https://unctadstat.unctad.org/wds/TableViewer/tableView.aspx?ReportId=17241

WDI. https://databank.worldbank.org/reports.aspx?source=world-development-indicators#

WTO Regional Trade Agreements Information System. http://rtais.wto.org/UI/PublicMaintainRTAHome.aspx

CHAPTER 8

The Political Economy of Preferential Trade in the Global Economy: Why Africa Needs to Refrain from Mega-regionals and Other FTAs with Third Parties

1 Introduction

Regional trade agreements are booming. With Covid-19 pandemic and the Ukraine–Russia conflict, which almost brought the multilateral trading system to a halt, many countries felt the urge and need to devise strategies that were more inward looking, or at least closer to home. Global value chains, which were in many respects seen as the solution to trade-led development, were quickly put under scrutiny. Investment which sought to follow the "supply on demand" models of global production was quickly dismantled and reshored or onshored (Reinsch, 2021).

After virtually two decades of seeing multilateral trade negotiations under the WTO operate on life support (Financial Times, 2015, 2022), how to advance free trade has become a prickly question. Among the various, and not-so-new responses, countries have resorted to free trade areas, big and small. Indeed, mega-regionals, which are FTAs spanning across countries and continents, seem to have taken the limelight in the global trade arena. Africa now has its own mega-regional, with the coming of age of the African Continental Free Trade Area (AfCFTA).

These developments not only beg the question whether the multilateral trading system has reached its limits, and bilateral and plurilateral settings are consolidating themselves as the new recipe for advancing global trade

L. Páez, *The African Continental Free Trade Area*,
https://doi.org/10.1007/978-3-031-66605-6_8

and investment agendas. They also point to important concerns about the remit of such agreements, their circle of influence and who they ultimately serve. The present chapter looks at some of the FTAs and mega-regional initiatives that affect African countries, against the backdrop of the AfCFTA, which is being operationalized.

2 Overview of Current Mega-regionals and FTA Initiatives Involving Africa

Given the longstanding stalemate of the multilateral trade negotiations under the Doha Round, many countries have preferred to advance trade integration through free trade agreements (FTAs). Not only have the numbers of FTAs in recent years mushroomed, but also the coverage and depth of such agreements has considerably expanded. Sometimes these agreements are also being referred to as "trade *and*" or "WTO+" agreements when their remit goes well beyond what may be considered standard trade liberalization (i.e. elimination of tariffs and dismantling of trade barriers). The former alludes to agreements where the scope of liberalization goes beyond trade in goods to include the liberalization of trade in services, investment, intellectual property, competition and, in some cases, even the seemingly far-reaching ambits of the environment, labor, health, digital economy, etc. The latter refers to agreements that require much deeper liberalization, than those which were pursued in the context of WTO negotiations. In some instances, this may involve regulatory reforms and giving up some elements of national sovereignty.

A parallel phenomenon which is equally worrisome is the geographical expansion of such agreements. When such agreements span over two or more regions and numerous countries, they are referred to as mega-regionals.

As a result of these fast-paced developments, most WTO members today are party to at least one of these FTAs with commitments that are WTO+. This has not only been the case of trade in goods, it has also been observed in services trade (Roy, 2011). Africa has not been oblivious to this trend. The number of such agreements within the continent and beyond has been quickly expanding, as is illustrated in Fig. 8.1.

One such mega-regional FTA that is currently being negotiated is the Trade in Services Agreement (TiSA). A total of 23 WTO members,

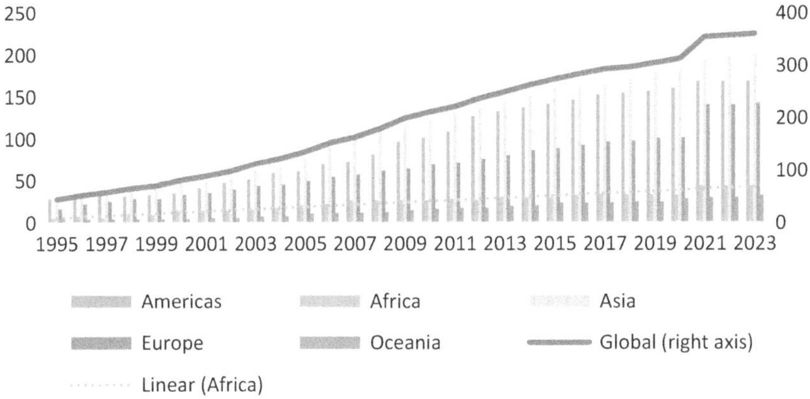

Fig. 8.1 Cumulative number of registered RTAs in force by region. Note: The numbers reflect only agreements that have been *notified* to the WTO. They include FTAs, customs unions and partial scope agreements. Agreements covering goods and/or services counted separately. They do not include agreements which are under negotiation, are inactive and/or are accessions of new signatories to existing RTAs. They may or may not include countries that are not WTO members. RTAs involving countries/territories in two (or more) regions are counted more than once. (Source: Author's representation based on WTO Regional Trade Agreements database)

including the EU as one of the 23, are participating in TiSA negotiations.[1] To date, Mauritius is the single African country involved in TiSA negotiations, and the agreement is open for others to join.

The sheer size and economic significance of the TiSA region is impressive. The region recorded almost two thirds of the global GDP and accounted for 1.7 billion people in 2022. During 2016–2021, the TiSA region alone registered just over 40% of global services trade, which closed at US$ 7 trillion in 2022 (see Fig. 8.2). It is therefore clear that if TiSA comes to life, its full implementation would dynamize services trade flows worldwide.

While currently the negotiations are pursued outside of the WTO, the future aim is to bring TiSA within the scope of the multilateral trading system. Given this aim, and how TiSA could potentially set the context for future services negotiations in the WTO, it is of critical importance for

[1] Countries participating in TiSA negotiations are Australia, Canada, Chile, Chinese Taipei, Colombia, Costa Rica, the EU, Hong Kong China, Iceland, Israel, Japan, Korea, Liechtenstein, Mauritius Mexico, New Zealand, Norway, Pakistan, Panama, Peru, Switzerland, Turkey and the US.

non-participating WTO members to follow this process closely. Thus, African member States today need to be aware of the risks and benefits of such an agreement, especially as it pertains to their own services liberalization process under the AfCFTA.[2]

Furthermore, there are other mega-regionals currently being negotiated that also have a bearing on Africa, as much as the continent is not part of these agreements. For instance, the Transatlantic Trade and Investment Partnership (T-TIP), the Regional Comprehensive Economic Partnership (RCEP) and the Comprehensive and Progressive Agreement for Trans-Pacific Partnership (CPTPP or TPP11) are trade (and investment in the case of T-TIP) agreements with considerable economic weight given their region's market, population and trade, as seen in Fig. 8.2.[3]

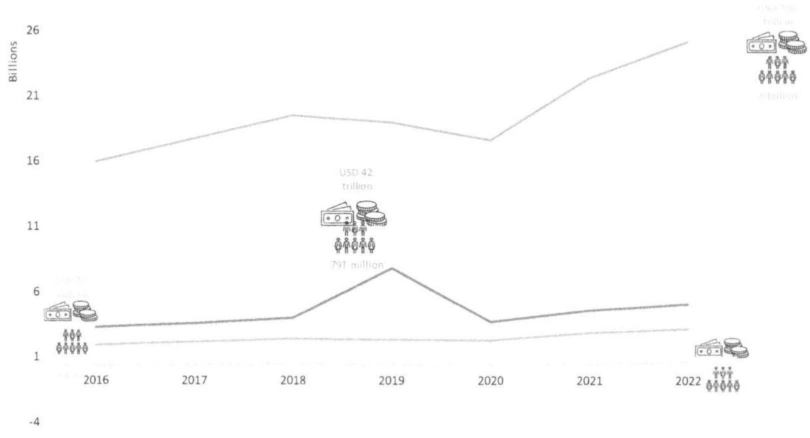

Fig. 8.2 Economic significance of selected mega-regionals (2016–2022). (Source: Author's representation based on UNCTADstat. Calculations include re-exports and re-imports)

[2] See Box 4.1 in Chap. 4 on specifics of TiSA.

[3] The T-TIP is a trade and investment agreement being negotiated between the EU and the US, and the (RCEP) constitutes an FTA between Australia, Brunei, Cambodia, China, Indonesia, Japan, South Korea, Laos, Malaysia, Myanmar, New Zealand, the Philippines, Singapore, Thailand and Vietnam. Currently, Bangladesh, Sri Lanka and Hong Kong are in the process of accession to the RCEP. Members of the CPTPP are Australia, Brunei, Canada, Chile, Japan, Malaysia, Mexico, New Zealand, Peru, Singapore and Vietnam. This is an evolved agreement from the former Trans-Pacific Partnership (TPP), which included US until it withdrew in 2017.

From a political economy point of view, mega-regionals have the potential to pull the center of gravity towards their sphere of influence and set the global trade agenda, with important implications for non-parties. Given the like-mindedness of the constituencies of some of these mega-regionals, the outcome of negotiations within such agreements are potentially expected to go well beyond the liberalization levels of the multilateral trading system (i.e. WTO+) and raise the bar of future trade negotiations, which calls for African countries to follow these developments closely.

Beyond FTA mega-regionals, a second phenomenon of recent years has been the pursuit of various trade and investment agreements on the part of big economies with partner countries and regions around the world, and especially since the stalling of multilateral discussions on investment and other issues (Páez, 2011, pp. 88–93), in the now defunct WTO Doha Round.[4] This too has impacted Africa, as shown in Table 8.1. For example, the US, through its Trade and Investment Framework Agreements (TIFAs), Trade, Investment, and Development Cooperative Agreements (TIDCAs) and Bilateral Investment Treaties (BITs) has an active agenda of work towards developing and deepening trade and investment relations with various African countries, as was discussed in Chap. 6 in this book. These agreements are also known to precede FTAs with the US, such as the bilateral FTA with Morocco.[5]

Another example in this regard is the EU with its Economic Partnership Agreements (EPAs), which were expected to substitute the prior unilateral preferential regime under the Cotonou Convention of the EU for the

[4] The multilateral trading system in the context of WTO trade negotiations does not formally include investment in its mandate, except for trade-related investment measures. Many countries at the time the Doha Round was launched had the expectation to advance on a set of issues brought forth during the Singapore Trade Ministerial of 1996. These issues were trade facilitation, competition, government procurement and notably investment. They were named the "Singapore Issues" and were included as part of a built-in agenda for during the launch of the Doha Round. Today, progress has been to advance investment facilitation, with the conclusion of the negotiations of an Investment Facilitation for Development Agreement (IFDA) in July 2023. The other issues were dropped under the Doha Round. See Páez (2011), pp. 88–93 for a discussion.

[5] TIFAs and TIDCAs exist bilaterally with several countries and RECs. The US and SACU had longstanding negotiations for an FTA which backtracked and were superseded by a TIDCA as a framework for discussions for a future FTA. Similar negotiations were conducted with Kenya for an FTA which also went cold, as is further explained in Sect. 3. For an updated list, see https://ustr.gov/trade-agreements.

Table 8.1 Overview of multiple memberships within Africa Regional Trade Agreements and beyond

	Algeria	*Angola*	*Benin*	*Botswana*	*Burkina Faso*	*Burundi*	*Cabo Verde*
Continental and inter-regional RTAs							
AfCFTA	✓	✓	✓ 1	✓	✓	✓	✓
TFTA (1)		✓		✓		✓	
Intra-regional RTAs							
CEMAC							
CU/MU							
COMESA						✓	
FTA/CU							
ECCAS		✓				✓	
FTA							
EAC						✓	
CU/CM							
ECOWAS			✓		✓		✓
FTA							
SACU				✓			
CU							
SADC		4		✓			
FTA							
WAEMU			✓		✓		
CU/MU							
RTAs with third parties							
Agadir Agreement							
Euro-Mediterranean Partnership (Euromed)	✓						

Economic Partnership Agreement (EPA)							
Interim EPA (iEPA)							
EU-SADC				✓			
EU–Eastern & Southern Africa (ESA)							
Full EPA							
Greater Arab Free Trade Area (GAFTA)	✓						
FTA w/							
China							
EFTA							
EU							
India							
MERCOSUR							
Pakistan							
Turkey							
UAE							
UK							
UK+Mauritius, Seychelles & Zimbabwe							
US							
SACU FTA w/							
EFTA				✓			
MERCOSUR				✓			
UK				✓			
US-EAC Trade & Investment Agreement						✓	

(continued)

Table 8.1 (continued)

	Cameroon	*Central African Rep.*	*Chad*	*Comoros*	*Congo*	*DRC*	*Côte d'Ivoire*
Continental and inter-regional RTAs							
AfCFTA	✓	✓	✓	✓	✓	✓	✓
TFTA (1)				✓1		✓1	
Intra-regional RTAs							
CEMAC	✓	✓	✓		✓		
CU/MU							
COMESA				✓		✓5	
FTA/CU							
ECCAS	✓	✓	✓		✓	✓	
FTA							
EAC						✓2	
CU/CM							
ECOWAS							✓
FTA							
SACU							
CU							
SADC				✓		4	
FTA							
WAEMU							✓
CU/MU							
RTAs with third parties							
Agadir Agreement							
Euro-Mediterranean Partnership (Euromed)							

Economic Partnership Agreement (EPA)			
Interim EPA (iEPA)	✓		✓
EU-SADC			
EU–Eastern & Southern Africa (ESA)		✓	
Full EPA			
Greater Arab Free Trade Area (GAFTA)			
FTA w/			
China			
EFTA			
EU			
India			
MERCOSUR			
Pakistan			
Turkey			
UAE			
UK	✓		✓
UK+Mauritius, Seychelles & Zimbabwe			
US			
SACU FTA w/			
EFTA			
MERCOSUR			
UK			
US-EAC Trade & Investment Agreement			

(*continued*)

Table 8.1 (continued)

	Djibouti	*Egypt*	*Equatorial Guinea*	*Eritrea*	*Eswatini*	*Ethiopia*	*Gabon*
Continental and inter-regional RTAs							
AfCFTA	✓	✓	✓		✓	✓	✓
TFTA (1)	✓1	✓			✓		
Intra-regional RTAs							
CEMAC			✓				✓
CU/MU							
COMESA	✓	✓		✓5	✓5	✓5	
FTA/CU							
ECCAS			✓				✓
FTA							
EAC							
CU/CM							
ECOWAS							
FTA							
SACU					✓		
CU							
SADC					✓		
FTA							
WAEMU							
CU/MU							
RTAs with third parties							
Agadir Agreement		✓					
Euro-Mediterranean Partnership (Euromed)		✓					

Economic Partnership Agreement (EPA)		
Interim EPA (iEPA)		
EU-SADC		✓
EU–Eastern & Southern Africa (ESA)		
Full EPA		
Greater Arab Free Trade Area (GAFTA)	✓	
FTA w/		
China		
EFTA	✓	
EU		
India		
MERCOSUR	✓	
Pakistan		
Turkey	✓	
UAE		
UK	✓	
UK+Mauritius, Seychelles & Zimbabwe		
US		
SACU FTA w/		
EFTA		✓
MERCOSUR		✓
UK		✓
US-EAC Trade & Investment Agreement		

(*continued*)

Table 8.1 (continued)

	Gambia	*Ghana*	*Guinea*	*Guinea Bissau*	*Kenya*	*Lesotho*	*Liberia*	*Libya*
Continental and inter-regional RTAs								
AfCFTA	✓	✓	✓	✓	✓	✓	✓1	✓1
TFTA (1)					✓	✓		✓1
Intra-regional RTAs								
CEMAC								
CU/MU								
COMESA					✓			✓
FTA/CU								
ECCAS								
FTA								
EAC					✓			
CU/CM								
ECOWAS	✓	✓	✓	✓			✓	
FTA								
SACU						✓		
CU								
SADC						✓		
FTA								
WAEMU				✓				
CU/MU								
RTAs with third parties								
Agadir Agreement								
Euro-Mediterranean Partnership (Euromed)								

Economic Partnership Agreement (EPA)				
Interim EPA (iEPA)	✓			
EU-SADC				
EU–Eastern & Southern Africa (ESA)			✓	
Full EPA		✓		
Greater Arab Free Trade Area (GAFTA)				✓
FTA w/				
China				
EFTA				
EU				
India				
MERCOSUR				
Pakistan				
Turkey				
UAE				
UK	✓	✓		
UK+Mauritius, Seychelles & Zimbabwe				
US				
SACU FTA w/				
EFTA			✓	
MERCOSUR			✓	
UK			✓	
US-EAC Trade & Investment Agreement		✓		

(*continued*)

Table 8.1 (continued)

	Madagascar	*Malawi*	*Mali*	*Mauritania*	*Mauritius*	*Morocco*	*Mozambique*
Continental and inter-regional RTAs							
AfCFTA	✓1	✓	✓	✓	✓	✓	✓
TFTA	✓1	✓			✓1		
Intra-regional RTAs							
CEMAC							
CU/MU							
COMESA	✓	✓			✓		
FTA/CU							
ECCAS							
FTA							
EAC							
CU/CM							
ECOWAS			✓				
FTA							
SACU							✓
CU							
SADC	✓	✓			✓		✓
FTA							
WAEMU			✓				
CU/MU							
RTAs with third parties							
Agadir Agreement						✓	
Euro-Mediterranean Partnership (Euromed)						✓	
Economic Partnership Agreement (EPA)							
Interim EPA (iEPA)							
EU-SADC							✓

EU–Eastern & Southern Africa (ESA) Full EPA	✓				✓		
Greater Arab Free Trade Area (GAFTA)						✓	
FTA w/							
China					✓		
EFTA						✓	
EU							
India					✓		
MERCOSUR							
Pakistan					✓		
Turkey					✓	✓	
UAE						✓	
UK						✓	
UK+Mauritius, Seychelles & Zimbabwe					✓		
US						✓	
SACU FTA w/							
EFTA							
MERCOSUR							
UK							✓
US-EAC Trade & Investment Agreement							

(*continued*)

Table 8.1 (continued)

	Namibia	*Niger*	*Nigeria*	*Rwanda*	*Sahrawi Republic*	*Sao Tome and Principe*	*Senegal*
Continental and inter-regional RTAs							
AfCFTA	✓	✓	✓	✓	✓	✓	✓
TFTA	✓			✓			
Intra-regional RTAs							
CEMAC							
CU/MU							
COMESA				✓			
FTA/CU							
ECCAS				✓		✓	
FTA							
EAC				✓			
CU/CM							
ECOWAS			✓				✓
FTA							
SACU	✓						
CU							
SADC	✓						
FTA							
WAEMU			✓				✓
CU/MU							
RTAs with third parties							
Agadir Agreement							
Euro-Mediterranean Partnership (Euromed)							

Economic Partnership Agreement (EPA)		
Interim EPA (iEPA)		✓
EU-SADC		
EU–Eastern & Southern Africa (ESA)		
Full EPA		
Greater Arab Free Trade Area (GAFTA)		
FTA w/		
China		
EFTA		
EU		
India		
MERCOSUR		
Pakistan		
Turkey		
UAE		
UK		
UK+Mauritius, Seychelles & Zimbabwe		
US		
SACU FTA w/		
EFTA	✓	
MERCOSUR	✓	
UK	✓	
US-EAC Trade & Investment Agreement		✓

(continued)

Table 8.1 (continued)

	Seychelles	*Sierra Leone*	*Somalia*	*South Africa*	*South Sudan*	*Sudan*	*Tanzania*
Continental and inter-regional RTAs							
AfCFTA	✓	✓	✓1	✓	✓1	✓1	✓
TFTA	✓1			✓		✓1	✓1
Intra-regional RTAs							
CEMAC							
CU/MU							
COMESA	✓		✓5			✓	
FTA/CU							
ECCAS							
FTA							
EAC			✓2		✓2		✓
CU/CM							
ECOWAS		✓					
FTA							
SACU				✓			
CU							
SADC	✓			✓			✓
FTA							
WAEMU							
CU/MU							
RTAs with third parties							
Agadir Agreement							
Euro-Mediterranean Partnership (Euromed)							

Economic Partnership Agreement (EPA)							
Interim EPA (iEPA)							
EU-SADC				✓			
EU–Eastern & Southern Africa (ESA)	✓						
Full EPA							
Greater Arab Free Trade Area (GAFTA)						✓	
FTA w/							
China							
EFTA							
EU				✓			
India							
MERCOSUR							
Pakistan							
Turkey							
UAE							
UK							
UK+Mauritius, Seychelles & Zimbabwe	✓						
US							
SACU FTA w/							
EFTA				✓			
MERCOSUR				✓			
UK				✓			
US-EAC Trade & Investment Agreement					✓		✓

(*continued*)

Table 8.1 (continued)

	Togo	*Tunisia*	*Uganda*	*Zambia*	*Zimbabwe*
Continental and inter-regional RTAs					
AfCFTA	✓	✓	✓	✓	✓
TFTA			✓	✓	✓
Intra-regional RTAs					
CEMAC					
CU/MU					
COMESA		✓	✓	✓	✓
FTA/CU					
ECCAS					
FTA					
EAC			✓		
CU/CM					
ECOWAS	✓				
FTA					
SACU					
CU					
SADC				✓	✓
FTA					
WAEMU	✓				
CU/MU					
RTAs with third parties					
Agadir Agreement		✓			
Euro-Mediterranean Partnership (Euromed)		✓			
Economic Partnership Agreement (EPA)					
Interim EPA (iEPA)					
EU-SADC					

EU–Eastern & Southern Africa (ESA) Full EPA				✓
Greater Arab Free Trade Area (GAFTA)	✓			
FTA w/				
China				
EFTA	✓			
EU				
India				
MERCOSUR				
Pakistan				
Turkey	✓			
UAE				
UK	✓			
UK+Mauritius, Seychelles & Zimbabwe				✓
US				
SACU FTA w/				
EFTA				
MERCOSUR				
UK				
US-EAC Trade & Investment Agreement		✓		

Does not include agreements under negotiation, not operational or with unilateral preferences granted

Source: Author's representation, based on WTO RIA Database. AfCFTA and RECs official cites and legal instruments

Key: Customs Union (CU), Free Trade Area (FTA), Monetary Union (MU), Common Market (CM); (1) signed, pending ratification, (2) joined the EAC, pending CU implementation, (3) under negotiation, (4) member of the SADC REC but not of the FTA, (5) in various stages of joining the FTA

ACP region.[6] Currently the EU has EPAs with some African subregions and countries. These comprise the Eastern and Southern Africa (ESA) region (Comoros, Madagascar, Mauritius, Seychelles and Zimbabwe) as well as with the SADC and SACU regions, as shown in Table 8.1. Furthermore, bilateral interim EPAs (iEPAs) with individual countries also abound, such as with Algeria, Cameroon, Cote d'Ivoire, Kenya,[7] Egypt, Ghana, Morocco, Rwanda, South Africa and Tunisia. This has been in part as a result of stalled EPAs negotiations with specific subregions in the aftermath of the Cotonou Convention. For least developed countries (LDCs), with or without an active EPA in place, their preferential access to EU is covered by the Everything but Arms Initiative (currently a total of 33 countries), which provides duty-free and quota-free (DFQF) access to virtually all trade from these countries to the EU, except for arms.[8] The expected gains and market access from signing EPAs for these countries is therefore relatively negligible.[9]

A final example footing the bill of worrisome bilateral FTAs which has also been increasing, is those of large developing countries or emerging economies and regions. African countries have also negotiated their fair share of FTAs with the likes of China, India, Turkey, Pakistan, as well as with regions such as MERCOSUR and GAFTA, among others. Some of the FTA negotiations preceding the signature of these agreements have been shrouded under the mantle of South-South cooperation, but the resulting FTAs represent a binding commitment on the part of the countries of reciprocal nature and have critical implications on the advancement of regional integration in Africa, as is further elaborated in Sect. 3 of this chapter.

[6] Prior to the Cotonou Convention, the EU governed unilateral trade preference schemes under the Yaoundé and Lomé conventions. See European Commission (2007) for the agreements and Gathii (2013) for an explanation.

[7] Kenya signed the full EPA with the EU on December 18, 2023.

[8] See https://trade.ec.europa.eu/access-to-markets/en/content/everything-arms-eba. Also see discussion on African LDC in the pipeline for graduation, which would affect this preferential access, in previous Chap. 7.

[9] See, for instance, Togo as an LDC example (ECA, 2018), but also Stack and Bliss (2020) for a comparison for the whole ACP region.

3 WTO Compatibility, Systemic Coherence and Future Trade Negotiations: What it Means for the AfCFTA

As FTAs multiply, so does the level of complexity of compliance with the new and prior obligations that bind the parties in FTAs (and the multilateral trading system). Countries can quickly lose oversight in terms of what may need to be done to remain compliant or bring the new set of conditions and preferences under an FTA into compliance with prior commitments. And this can naturally be challenged by the aggravated parties of prior agreements through dispute settlement, if such provisions exist.

But what does this mean for Africa's mega-regional, which is still in the making? AfCFTA Negotiations have been concluded in some of its integration pillars, but there is still earnest progress required for the implementation of the newly acquired obligations, which will ultimately be the litmus test for legal soundness of the AfCFTA agreement. Furthermore, negotiations are still unfolding in critical areas, such as the Protocols on Women and Youth and Digital Trade, respectively, which should complete another important segment of the AfCFTA puzzle. This clearly raises the bar in terms of expectations on negotiation outcomes of trade agreements such as the AfCFTA and poses the heightened risk of "forum shopping" for litigation in dispute settlement mechanisms, including those that are available in the WTO, prior to existing regional agreements[10] and in the AfCFTA itself through what has been provided in the Protocol on Rules and Procedures on the Settlement of Disputes, which forms an integral part of the AfCFTA Agreement.

There are several channels in which compatibility between the ever-growing myriad of trade agreements may be sought. In a way, the multilateral trading system (MTS) as we know it today was a major milestone in trying to bring predictability, transparency and accountability to the ever-rising trade disputes and wars which preceded the global economic order of today (Jackson, 2000). The operation of this rules-based system that we have witnessed for almost 3 decades since the coming into life of the WTO is perhaps the greatest attainment of the MTS, surpassing any of the progress made during the iterative ministerial trade negotiations rounds. Nonetheless, and given the fact that the "spaghetti bowl" of free trade

[10] Many examples of this motivation exist in the investment realm. See, for example, ECA (2019), Chap. 5, Sect. 2. Also see discussion in Chap. 5, Sect. 3.1.

agreements are outside the scope of the MTS, threatening to become a cauldron of disproportionate dimensions, different approaches must also be explored, beyond the multilateral setting.

Some of the approaches that can be suggested to achieve compliance and systemic application of trade rules which bring predictability and transparency to trade agreements are not new. Indeed, in many cases they are a reflection of the legal traditions and resonate with international treaty law and acquis, dating from the *Vienna Convention on the Law of Treaties* (1969) to best practices and experiences across the globe.

For example, an approach may be to seek compatibility upfront. This happens when newer trade agreements recognize existing commitments of parties derive from prior agreements with other parties. Many trade agreements do so in at least two ways. First, they include preambular language to recognize (at least) in spirit, the intention to comply with existing obligations acquired prior. Some even make direct allusion to specific commitments in hortatory language. Though non-binding, such language then sets the stage for actual obligations. Second, some agreements will have binding provisions that further elucidate how incompatibilities arising from the new agreement and existing obligations and commitments under old agreements and how these may be treated and resolved.

The AfCFTA agreement from the outset does both. For starters, it recognizes in its preamble the determination of its parties to build upon existing agreements such as the *Constitutive Act of the African Union of 2000*, the *Abuja Treaty* and, where applicable, the *Marrakesh Agreement Establishing the World Trade Organization*. Second, the agreement recognized the obligation to notify the agreement to the WTO on the part of its State Parties (Art. 26) and further refers to existing obligations and commitments on the part of State parties throughout its Protocols on Trade in Goods and Trade in Services. For example, the observance of existing antidumping and countervailing commitments, safeguard measures, balance of payments and quantitative restrictions obligations acquired under the GATT Art. 7, 9, 17, 18 and 28.[11] Equally, the Trade in Services Protocol mirrors adherence to obligations under the GATS in its Art. 3 and 4. Lastly, the Protocol on IP also recognizes WTO-related commitments on IP right which were discussed in the previous chapter in this book.

[11] For a discussion on the content of some of these measures, see Table 7.1 in Chap. 7.

In a third stance, the AfCFTA Agreement through its *Protocol on Rules and Procedures on the Settlement of Disputes*, recognizes the adherence to customary rules of treaty interpretation, such as those under the Vienna Convention (Art. 31). A provision within the Protocol further points to dispute resolution which can be activated, either when State Parties do not agree on the interpretation of the Agreement, or, when (a) part(y)(ies) is aggrieved as a result of (an)other part(y)(ies)' failure to comply with existing obligations under the AfCFTA Agreement (Art. 1(e)).

Furthermore, Art. 3(4) which speaks to the scope of application of the Protocol, attempts to pre-empt forum shopping by exercising judicial economy, in that "... A State Party which has invoked the rules and procedures of this Protocol with regards to a specific matter, shall not invoke another forum for dispute settlement on the same matter". In other words, if an AfCFTA State Party is aggrieved by an action from another State Party and both are members to the WTO or another agreement with DSM, they cannot seek legal redress in both forums concurrently. This serves as a pre-emptive provision to avoid forum shopping.

Lastly, the AfCFTA agreement also looks at the issue of precedence when a potential conflict or inconsistency with other regional agreements may arise. In its Art. 19(1) it states that "In the event of any conflict and inconsistency between this Agreement and any regional agreement, this Agreement shall prevail to the extent of the specific inconsistency, except as otherwise provided in this Agreement". It would therefore seem that the AfCFTA would take precedence over any existing REC FTA or CU, which would be a positive signal towards consolidation of the regional integration process towards a Continental Customs Union and ultimately the AEC. This would also eliminate any potential disputes arising from conflicting obligations resulting from the AfCFTA agreement and those which may exist in more dated regional trade agreements AfCFTA parties previously acquired, at least in principle.

Interestingly, the agreement also includes a proviso which complements that of variable geometry, discussed earlier in Chap. 7 of this book. In Art. 4 (2) of the Protocol on Trade in Goods, it is stated that nothing in the agreement will prevent States Parties from concluding or maintaining trade agreements with non-AfCFTA parties, *provided* (1) these arrangements do not impede or frustrate the objective of the Protocol and (2) the advantage or privilege is reciprocated to AfCFTA parties. Art. 4(2) of the Protocol on Trade in Services mirrors the proviso with almost identical language, but also includes that it should meet the requirements of Art. V of the GATS.

This completes the principle of variable geometry and special and differential treatment of the AfCFTA Agreement enshrined in the same Articles of the Protocols, as was discussed earlier in Chap. 7 of this book, and which catered for trade agreements between AfCFTA parties only. From a political economy point of view, this proviso speaks to the very sobering reality that countries may still have the incentive (or pressure) to deepen their trade integration with third parties, beyond the AfCFTA. It is the realpolitik of trade negotiations in years to come. Provisos such as this one may therefore anticipate (and hopefully also diffuse) the need for legal recourse from AfCFTA parties that are (potentially) discriminated with the signing of new trade agreements they are not members to. Nonetheless, it does not and cannot tackle the issue preference erosion, which responds to market signals as is explained in Sect. 3 of this chapter.

It is important to note that when such a body of agreements is well designed and their respective binding commitments are implemented without necessarily raising the alarm bells of litigation, or trade protectionism as a retaliatory measure in the absence of credible legal redress, it is possible to speak of regulatory coherence. If coexistence or cohabitation of these agreements is achieved in a lasting manner, one can speak of systemic coherence.[12]

Though from a public good perspective, systemic coherence of a body of law (such as FTAs that cohabitate harmoniously) may be desirable, in the present myriad of agreements it is highly unlikely. Nothing pre-empts countries from engaging in the negotiation of new FTAs. Indeed, most agreements, including the AfCFTA Agreement, provided certain conditions are met. So, what to do to achieve a certain degree of harmony at the backdrop of the spaghetti bowl of such agreements?

In today's set up, given the ever-growing number of FTAs highlighted at the beginning of this chapter, other approaches may be required to reign in their impact, achieve cohabitation and promote greater systemic coherence. An approach may be to consolidate existing treaties. Treaty consolidation may be done either through review, renegotiation and/or expiry of existing agreements, and also through treaty rationalization.

Some countries have also undertaken treaty review and/or termination, as well as expiry in the investment realm. Indeed, an emerging body of

[12] For a discussion on regulatory coherence, see Kuijper (2010) and Cai (2016).

practice that is Africa based and Africa driven is laying an interesting foundation. Countries such as Burkina Faso, Mauritius, Morocco, South Africa and Uganda have dared to review, amend, interpret or terminate some of their international investment treaties with third parties.[13] The trade realm can also borrow from the extensive model investment treaty experience that exists globally, regionally and bilaterally, and build in relevant provisions for reviews and/or termination and expiry of FTAs, Examples include the IISD Model International Agreement on Investment for Sustainable Development Negotiators Handbook (IISD, 2006), the Revised Investment Agreement for the COMESA Common Investment Area (2018), Africa Arbitration Academy Model Bilateral Investment Treaty for African States (2022), as well as the UNCTAD investment policy framework for sustainable development model (UNCTAD, 2015), and the SADC Model BIT Treaty Template (2012).

On another front, Africa has been avant-garde in advancing the option of treaty rationalization, as part of its efforts to deepen regional integration. The *AU Decision on the Moratorium on the Recognition of Regional Economic Communities* (AU, 2006) sets out a way in which such rationalization should happen, by identifying the eight recognized RECs and banning the creation of new RECs. It further builds on the Abuja Treaty (OAU, 1991), which established that there would be need for the coordination and harmonization of tariffs and non-tariff systems among RECs which have FTAs in place, and which would lead to a Continental Customs Union in a fourth stage of the regional integration process, culminating in the African Economic Community (Art. 6.2 (d)).[14]

As mentioned in the previous chapter, though the AfCFTA was not part of the vision of the Abuja treaty, in a way it has become a response to the "missing middle" of this fourth stage of integration. It does so in two ways. First, it offers the space to create the needed harmony of existing tariff and non-tariff systems across the constellation of RECs FTAs (and CUs) and further integrates those countries that are not part of the 8 recognized RECs mentioned earlier. Second, it allows for a more natural transition from these FTA regimes, by consolidating them into one through the AfCFTA, prior to moving on to a customs union. In its

[13] Some agreements may have expiration and/or review clauses, as is increasingly common in investment treaties. See ECA (2016, 2019), as well as the examples of treaty models in the footnote down below.

[14] Also see discussion in Chap. 3, Sect. 1.

Roadmap (AU, 2011),[15] the AfCFTA proposes ways in which RECs could be merged, as was discussed earlier in Chap. 2 of this book. This pathway has been given further impetus through the conclusion of TFTA negotiations, which, now that the agreement has kicked into place, will consolidate the subgroups of FTAs that exist in EAC, COMESA and SADC.

Lastly, a less popular way but perhaps more effective way to summon greater coherence, has been to activate dispute resolution clauses in such agreements. In the multilateral setting, requesting parties to bring trade measures into compliance with existing regulations and commitments has become a staple of the WTO jurisprudence. For Africa, no better example exists than the EU-ACP agreement[16] referred to earlier in Sect. 2. This agreement was found to be inconsistent with the Enabling Clause of the GATT,[17] on the grounds that it discriminated against other developing countries and did not provide for sufficient market access to ACP countries to cover substantially all trade (Gathii, 2013).

Learning from the EU-ACP example, compatibility with the multilateral regime will be critical to the success of the AfCFTA, in the roll out of implementation of the various protocols and as State Parties are able to increasingly trade with themselves under the AfCFTA rules. But this will not be sufficient on its own. Compatibility must also be sought with the overlapping and concurrent trade regimes that exist through the panoply of bilateral FTAs within the continent and beyond.

As mentioned in the previous chapter of this book, the issue of the *acquis* is an important benchmark for future interpretation of what is permissible in the AfCFTA, when a dispute may arise among State Parties with other FTAs in place. If we are to take the body of law, including jurisprudence emanating from the interpretation of existing obligations and commitments under RECs FTAs as the *acquis*, then utmost attention is necessary. The African trade and investment landscape is marred by sketchy legal redress and its enforcement that has emanated from weak regional tribunals.

For example, in *Mike Campbell (Pvt) Limited and others v Zimbabwe* (Campbell v Zimbabwe, 2007), the Southern African Development

[15] See prior discussion in Chap. 3, Sect. 2.

[16] See European Commission (2007).

[17] The Enabling Clause allows for a deviation from MFN principle under GATT Art. XXIV if substantially all trade is covered and supports development objectives of the countries in question. See earlier discussion in Chap. 7, Sect. 4 and also WTO (1979, 2004) for the regulation and filed dispute involving the EU-ACP agreement.

Community Tribunal (SADCT) in 2008, judged against the Government of Zimbabwe for a violation of human and property rights during a land redistribution programme and in favour of the aggrieved private person, Mike Campbell. In the wake of the case, regional governments circumscribed its jurisdiction, deferring the case to domestic courts, leading to a discredit and subsequent demise of the SADCT (ECA, 2016, 2019). The SADC Summit decided on establishing a new SADC Tribunal through a new Protocol which was adopted in 2014, which was signed by 9 of the SADC members but not ratified yet. The new Protocol is considered to provide for a tribunal which would be a watered-down version of the prior SADCT in terms of mandate and capacities and does not do away with the fact that there has been an unlawful act by the SADC Summit that violates the established rule of law as provided by the SADC foundational instruments (Erasmus, 2015). Furthermore, and because of this unlawfulness and weakened mandate, there is a movement against the new tribunal and in favour of the restitution of the former SADCT by the legal community and civil society at large (Shivamba, 2019; Shumba, 2023).

Unfortunately, this is not the first decision by a regional tribunal that has not been properly enforced. Another example relates to the COMESA Court of Justice (COMESACJ), received from Mauritius. In a nutshell, the *Mauritius vs Polytol Paints and Adhesives Manufacturers Co. Ltd* case (Mauritius v Polytol, 2012), was filed by a Mauritian company importing paints from Egypt, on the grounds that Mauritius had reimposed tariffs on paints imports from Egypt (another COMESA member) after the COMESA FTA came into force. As a result, the company had to pay customs duties to the tune of 40 percent on its paint imports. Polytol Paints initially filed the case in domestically, arguing the measure taken by Mauritius infringed Art. 46 of the COMESA Treaty and seeking compensation for the expenses incurred as a result of the levies it had to pay. The Mauritian Supreme Court ruled the obligations on the country derived from the COMESA Treaty could not be enforced domestically, upon which the complainant sought out the COMESACJ as an avenue for redress.

The ruling of Court was an important milestone in African regional jurisprudence, in that it recognized that private parties, and not only Parties to the agreement, had recourse to legal redress (i.e. enjoyed standing) when their rights are affected as a result of the obligations arising from a Treaty not being complied with. This case has been considered the only real trade case filed in any of the African regional courts with a trade remit until very recently and sets an important precedent in terms of legal interpretation of ruling remit of a regional court (Gathii, 2018).

Lack of effective enforcement through jurisprudence also points to the heightened risk of trade protectionism as retaliatory measure in the absence of credible legal redress, which was mentioned earlier. For example, the sugar wars between Kenya and Uganda,[18] and more recently the heightened dispute between Uganda and Kenya due Kenya's oil deal with Gulf countries for the import of oil (Kenya being the main entry point for oil for four of the landlocked EAC member countries Rwanda, Burundi, DRC and South Sudan), who have seen a substantial increase in taxes and levies imposed on petroleum through the Kenyan Finance Act 2023, in an effort by the Kenyan government to curb the free fall of the Kenyan Shilling and increase government revenue.[19] This is unfortunate and seems to be getting in the way of the EAC members in terms of being able to fully realize the benefits from the EAC. Evidence suggests that for these countries to maximize on the trade gains, there is need for them to prioritize implementation of the EAC Treaty, frameworks and protocols and also promote industrialization (Shinyekwa & Othieno, 2016).

Nonetheless, there is hope. Recent jurisprudence, such as the East African Court of Justice (EACJ) Decision (2022) on the right of Kenya to negotiate a bilateral FTA with the US set a precedent when assessing the impact of such a decision on the overall compliance with the ultimate objectives of the EAC. The court determined that though Kenya did announce its intent to negotiate an agreement with the US to the EAC, it did not adequately present the agreement for the membership's consideration and hence breached its obligation to consult.[20] It now rests to see what will happen with future FTA negotiations with the US, which as mentioned would require Kenya to not only inform its EAC partners of its

[18] There have been reports of trade wars on agricultural products between EAC members in the past. For example, Uganda has been reported to block Kenyan milk and Kenya Uganda's sugar, on the suspicion that it would be dumping of sugar from third countries. Even with the highest dignitaries intervening to remove obstacles, the matter has not been referred to adequate channels governing the EAC such as redress through the EACJ, in observance of the EAC Treaty and Protocols (Buyonge, 2018). Interestingly, the COMESA Council of Ministers has renewed Kenya's safeguard measures which protects its ailing sugar industry from competition since 2002 and applies tariff-based quotas on sugar imports from COMESA (COMESA, 2021).

[19] See the Kenyan Finance Act (2023) and KPMG (2023) for an analysis of economic impacts of the Act.

[20] See previous footnote in this chapter and also Khandwalla (2023).

intention to negotiate, but also afford them an opportunity to consider joint negotiations as a region with the US.

Under such circumstances, it is important to also lay out the options in terms of carving out a safe space for the AfCFTA to operate successfully and not whither under the weight of poor/inconclusive legal interpretation or lack of enforcement. One of these considerations necessarily has to be the institutional and governance structure of the AfCFTA dispute settlement, with credible enforcement mechanisms that all State Parties abide by.

4 Implications of the Prevalence of Mega-Regionals and FTAs for Countries Negotiating the AfCFTA

Given that African countries are members of deeper regional integration agreements under their RECs, bilateral FTAs with third parties create malaise within their RECs (Erasmus, 2021), to say the least. From a political economy perspective, the raison d'être of negotiating additional agreements may be justifiable in the short term. This was the case when Cameroon, Cote d'Ivoire, Egypt, Ghana, Kenya, Morocco, Tunisia, Eastern and Southern Africa States (Mauritius, Seychelles and Zimbabwe) and SACU countries (Botswana, Lesotho, Eswatini, Mozambique, Namibia, South Africa) engaged in FTA negotiations with the UK to retain their DFQF privileges after the UK exited the EU in 2020. However, from a strategic point of view this action dilutes the scope for these countries and regions to lobby and negotiate as a grouping vis-à-vis third parties in future trade negotiations and sets a timer for preference erosion, since the expected gains from future trade agreements would then be passed on to third parties.

Further to the issue of diffusing the gains future trade agreements may bring to parties through preference erosion (Hoekman et al., 2008), the negotiation of such agreements with third parties can also propel "a race to the bottom", as has been observed when there is competition in tax treaty-making. For example, countries within an existing agreement, in an effort to attract market-seeking FDI or access to new "trade *and*" markets from non-parties, may sign agreements unilaterally, leaving their regional setting behind. Ultimately, this can become a situation where member countries try to outcompete their offers by providing more advantageous conditions to third parties than they have within their regional market, at their and their region's detriment.[21]

It could be argued that the stalling of EPAs group negotiations by some of the RECs members has contributed to a situation where the other members prefer to advance on their own.[22] This has resulted in a "divide and conquer" strategy which has been played well by the EU. Currently, for the EAC and ECOWAS EPAs to kick in, Tanzania and Nigeria, respectively, would need to sign the existing agreements. In the interim, this has led to the other REC members to negotiate and sign interim EPAs (iEPAs) on their own, rather than within the group. The latest example has been the case of Kenya, which recently signed a full EPA in December 2023, as shown in Table 8.1 of this chapter. With Cameroon as the only Central African country having signed the iEPA, the EU-Central Africa EPA is also far from reaching a definitive stage, and such stalling could lead to further piecemeal negotiations of individual Central African countries with the EU.[23]

This level of fragmentation within the EPAs with Africa's main trading partner is worrisome and indeed counterintuitive to the fact that, after virtually 2 decades of stalled negotiations, official positions taken from within the AU on what needs to be prioritized (AU, 2008) to strike a balance between coherence within the continent, compatibility with the WTO and market access to the EU for African products have largely been ignored. The current constellation of concluded EU FTAs is considered a missed opportunity, in the sense that countries who negotiated EPAs unilaterally with the EU forewent the option to retain their bargaining power they initially had within their respective groupings (Krapohl & van Huut, 2020).

Furthermore, ignoring common positions on EPAs, such as the need to preserve the current processes for economic integration in Africa and ensuring adequate flexibility in the rules of origin across the various EPAs promote intra-African trade (AU, 2013a, 2013b), meant the continent

[21] Many examples of this motivation exist in investment and double taxation realm. See ECA (2020), Chap. 3, Sect. 2.

[22] Also see the discussion around this resistance from civil society as another reason for the stalling of EPAs in Chap. 3, Sect. 3.1.

[23] The other Central African countries that are part of this EPA are Gabon, Equatorial Guinea, Central African Republic, Congo, Democratic Republic of Congo, Sao Tome y Principe, Chad. All are LDCs, except Congo benefits from the preferential regime under the EBA.

gave way on the contentious issues which could have allowed for continental cumulation and aggregation of trade, an important prerequisite of deeper trade integration, developing regional value chains and advancing industrialization under the AfCFTA. To say the least, the continent appears to be worse off in the current setup, with all these fragmented and multiple agreements, which have also congested the negotiation capacity (Braude, 2008) and obstructed the consolidation of regional integration processes within Africa. This furthermore opens the door for EU's systematic strategy of advancing their agenda of non-trade policy objectives (NTPOs) beyond their internal market, with important extraterritorial effects on Africa's participation in value chains, as was discussed earlier in Chap. 4 on services.[24]

Lastly, it is noteworthy to also mention that various other agreements with individual countries or FTAs from beyond Africa also exist, as depicted earlier in Table 8.1. Here too, caution is of utmost importance to African countries. FTAs, especially with large trade partners go against the principles of variable geometry since they are based on reciprocity.[25] It is difficult to imagine trade of reciprocal nature to be desirable when trade imbalances are stark. This is the case of many African countries when trading with third parties from outside the continent. Similarly, as with EU, which is the largest trading partner for Africa, FTAs with other existing large trading partners such as India and China, only perpetuate and accentuate the imbalances over time, since African countries within such agreements continue to trade in primary commodities, with little value addition.

As a point in case, there are gaping trade imbalances between African countries and some of these large partners, which are masked by the average trade composition shares by destination in Fig. 8.3a. For example, in 2022, Africa's imports from China were US$ 130.2 billion, whereas its exports totalled US$ 100.5 billion, this becomes evident when the shares are disaggregated by imports and export in Fig. 8.3b, c. The resulting trade deficit between exports and imports was of a whooping US$ 29.7 billion. This gaping deficit has been continuously growing since 2012. Most of the imports from China were high in value added, as is the case of machinery and transport vehicles, whereas exports from Africa were mainly

[24] In particular, see Box 2 in Chap. 4, discussing the Extraterritoriality of EU Regulation on Africa's participation in global value chains.

[25] Please see Chap. 7 where the concepts of variable geometry and reciprocity were amply discussed.

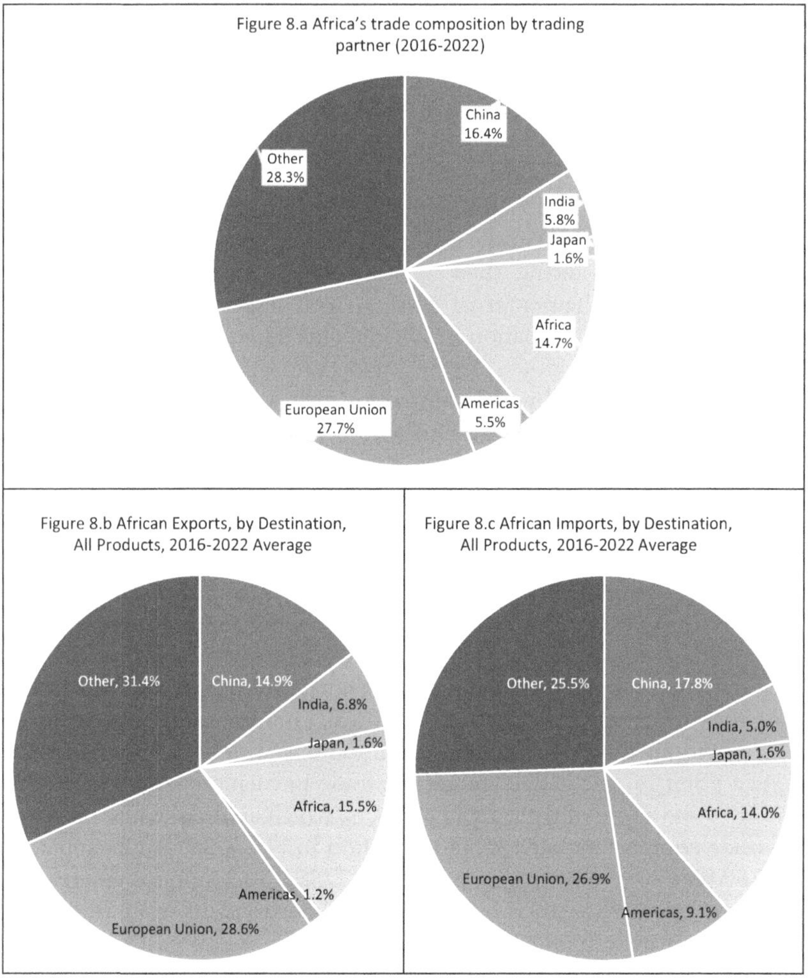

Fig. 8.3 Africa's trade composition by trading partner (2016–2022). Note: For a decomposed and deeper analysis of this figure, see also Páez (2023). (Source: Author's calculations based on data from UNCTADstat)

fuels and ores and metals.[26] Furthermore, such trade is at the mercy of the boom-and-bust cycles of commodity prices, which perpetuates the volatility of Africa's export revenue when trading in these traditional commodities and accentuates the associated vulnerabilities of Africa's economic trajectory.

In sum, the composition of this trade is unfavourable to Africa in that it perpetuates traditional trade patterns and is likely to only accentuate these imbalances through the bilateral FTAs. This is yet another very compelling reason for the continent to prioritize the implementation of the AfCFTA prior to signing new FTAs with external partners, and also revisit its South-South cooperation partnerships and modalities (Páez, 2023).

If we are also to gloss over the empirical evidence gravity models[27] provide on the benefits of trade (and investment) between large and small economies, these have a common corollary: the larger the partners, the greater the gains. Furthermore, such models also pinpoint to distance being a factor that is negatively related to trade, meaning the larger the distance, the costlier the trade.

In the African context, though empirical testing through gravity modelling is quite mixed, it is very telling when it comes to market size (measured as GDP per capita or income) and distance (geographical, economic, cultural, social, or otherwise). For example, when analysing the only FTA of the US and an African country (Morocco), Dadush and Saoudi (2019) find that trade with the US and large trade partners such as France and Spain as part of the EU under FTAs have revealed no significance in the country's export concentration. This has been unhealthy for Morocco's trade with external partners and has negatively impacted on its trade links with the rest of Africa. More recently, Stack and Bliss (2020) find that positive and significant trade-enhancing effects for EU membership and their FTAs, but negative and significant effects for regional EPAs between EU and the ACP region, which includes Africa.

The empirical testing of the gravity model on AGOA, presented in Chap. 6,[28] confirms the hypothesis that relative market wealth of US investors has a negative effect on US investment flows to AGOA beneficiaries when trading with the US, even though the AGOA is a preferential trade

[26] For a discussion on the composition of exports from African LDCs, which accentuate this pattern, also see previous discussion in Chap. 7.

[27] For a discussion on the evolution of gravity models, please see (Capoani, 2023).

[28] Also see the literature review in Sect. 3.3 of the AGOA in Chap. 6.

agreement and not an FTA. Furthermore, there is overall negative evidence of AGOA as an agreement on US FDI, with the exception of the apparel sector, which appears to have positively determined US FDI in the AGOA region. This corroborates the general findings of AGOA fostering a certain type of export specialization in the apparel sector in some African countries, determined through FDI. Therefore, these types of results may bolster the conclusion that when there are substantial asymmetries and distance between African countries and larger partners (such as those discussed in this section), the larger chunk of trade grains, as evidence suggests, goes to the larger partner.

In turn, when Africa trades with itself (where relative size and distance are closer between trading partners) and FTAs are taken account of, recent empirical literature tells a very compelling story. For example, Olayungbo and Iqbal (2021) use a gravity model to estimate trade effects between 1980 and 2018 in six African trade blocs and find that COMESA made the highest contribution to global exports, followed by EAC, ECOWAS and SADC and ECCAS and SACU having the lowest contribution. Admassu (2019), using a dataset of 148 countries during 1970–2010, finds robust evidence that African RECs do increase their intra-community trade, in varying degrees, and as much as 175% increase and 200% for exports and imports, respectively. They further determine that the broader and deeper trade blocs are, the stronger the intra-African trade.

In turn, Inançli and Mahamat Addi (2019) found trade creation between 2007 and 2016 in CEMAC, COMESA and EAC. Finally, Ngepah and Udeagha (2018) using panel data for (1995–2004) find that in the case of CEMAC, SADC, SACU and WAEMU, the gains from trade do not come at the expense of trade with non-members (i.e. there is no trade diversion, rather trade creation).

Mayer and Thoenig (2016) find large effects of trade creation in the EAC region, as high as 213% increase in bilateral trade, whilst in COMESA and SADC as much as 80% and 110%, respectively. In addition, they have found such agreements to have pacifying effects on inter-State relations. Finally, in earlier studies, Rojid (2006) determines that there is trade creation within the COMESA bloc, which did not come at the expense of trade with the rest of the world, whilst Musila (2005) found that ECOWAS and EAC trade blocs saw their members' exports increase by as much as 175 and 100%, respectively, whilst CENSAD and COMESA saw increases of 80 and 70%, respectively.

The recent Tripartite negotiations also showed that the actual result of the TFTA was binding existing commitments among the membership of COMESA, SADC and EAC. Unlike with what was expected from the level of ambition of the AfCFTA, there was little to no additionality from the TFTA, in the sense that negotiations virtually focused on making tariff concessions among member States of the Tripartite FTA that have no prior FTA or CU preferential arrangements between them. This was adopted as a Guiding Principle for those negotiations (Erasmus, 2021, 2022). Trade between the existing REC members that was already happening under the relevant REC FTA was not subject to additional or deepened liberalization.

Despite this important caveat, the trade creation estimates under the TFTA are nonetheless very encouraging. Mold and Mukwaya (2017) estimated a growth in intra-TFTA trade of 29% resulting from the tariff liberalization, and an aggregate welfare gain to the tune of US$ 2.4 billion. Other authors have estimated magnitude which resonate with the overall positive effects, though assumptions and shocks vary considerably.[29]

Though such estimations do allow the reader to have a sense of economy-wide impacts of the TFTA, they must be taken with a pinch of salt. CGE modelling have caveats due to their limitations. For example, they do not necessarily consider preference erosion.[30] Some of the expected trade creation now the TFTA has kicked is expected to be observed as member countries take measures to domesticate it. However, some of this trade creation could also potentially offset the preference erosion that is expected from the prevalence of FTAs that TFTA members already have in place (or continue to negotiate) with third parties. The gains from trade may therefore need to be looked at against the backdrop of possible dynamic and spin off effects, which may be positive or negative.

Furthermore, though negotiations were concluded in 2015, the agreement is going to operationalized now that the requisite 14 member States have introduced their instruments of ratification. Just recently, with the latest signature by Lesotho in October 2023, the TFTA agreement has

[29] See, for instance, Makochekanwa (2014).

[30] The underlying assumptions of the general equilibrium models can vary substantially. The CGE frameworks in these studies share these limitations in that they do not factor in the existing FTAs with third parties. Also see Fosu and Mold (2008) on preference erosion in Africa.

been signed by 23 of its 26 members, and had been short of 3 ratifications of the required representation for the agreement to kick in.

These are important lessons for Africa's newest mega-regional, which has advanced faster than the TFTA, with regards to operationalization of the agreement. If additionality is to have teeth in the AfCFTA, then efforts towards its full implementation need to be sustained. Indeed, the various modelling estimations on the impact of the AfCFTA point to important gains from trade, provided that certain conditions are met.[31] With the AfCFTA, traditional trade patterns as we know them will substantially change and result in significant trade creation. ECA (2023) estimates that by 2045, intra-African trade will grow by 34.2%, with sectors such as agri-food, services and industries increasing by 49.1%, 37.9% and 35.7%, respectively. The increase in energy and mining will be somewhat lower, at 19.4%, skewing trade composition away from these traditional sectors and towards the other sectors highlighted earlier. Furthermore, with the AfCFTA, the value of intra-African trade will increase by 577%, as opposed to a 405% increase in a non-AfCFTA scenario. This would result in trade creation to the amount of US$ 195 billion and would move the dial of intra-African trade from a share of 14.2% in 2020 to almost 25% share in total trade by 2045.[32]

Equally so, for these benefits to be accrued, trade in services and especially transport services have to be able to accommodate the expected growth in the demand for trade in goods.[33] From a supply side perspective, it is estimated that as a result of trade in the AfCFTA, Africa's demand of trucks would increase to 1.9 million by 2030. Intra-African trade in

[31] Several studies point to various scenarios with different assumptions in CGE modelling, such as Abrego et al. (2019), Fofack et al. (2021) and World Bank (2020). A caveat is that some of the assumptions in these studies are different from the status quo of negotiations, i.e. they do not necessarily reflect what State Parties have agreed to do and thus results may be under or overestimated. The footnote below, describes the assumption of the shocks which are currently closest to actual negotiations modalities, as at January 2024.

[32] Assumptions being made include the signing and ratification by all the AU membership (which are currently at 54 and 48 State Parties, respectively) and full liberalization of trade in goods as per the agreed modalities and 50% reduction of actionable non-tariff measures (NTMs). For services the assumption is that they are fully liberalized in the five services priority sectors along with education and health services, and also an observed 50 percent reduction of actionable restrictions to trade in those sectors.

[33] This has to do with the intrinsic intertwined nature of trade in goods and services, since many services today are embedded and embodied in goods trade. For an explanation and definitions see Chap. 4, Sect. 1.

transport services has the potential to increase by nearly 50%, whilst in absolute terms, over 25% of intra-African trade gains in services would go to transport alone; and nearly 40% of the increase in Africa's services production will be in transport. This means that investments to the tune of US$ 400 billion have to materialize for truck transport alone (ECA, 2022).

Beyond the clear impact liberalization will have on tourism and transport industries, and its direct effect on the movement of people through the implementation of the Protocol on Free Movement of Persons and the SAATM,[34] it will also have a dynamic effect on industrialization in other sectors, especially since transport services are the backbone of trade and industry and, if coupled with existing commitments in infrastructure and industrial development in Africa, the AfCFTA will unleash catalytic effects that promise to transform the African economy.

5 Conclusions

The present chapter looked at some of the FTA initiatives that are of concern to Africa and its regional integration trajectory. In particular, mega-regionals and bilateral FTAs with large third parties outside the continent, such as the EPAs, cause concern. As per the evidence that has been presented, they seem to come at the expense of the continent. FTAs of this nature would metaphorically equate to David carrying Goliath on his back across the desert and also paying for the service he rendered.

Although AU countries have clearly indicated that the eight recognized RECs are the pillars of African regional integration, and that no new REC should be further recognized until the moratorium is lifted (AU, 2006), there are many agreements in place and no indication of stopping. This naturally begs the question: What benefits actually accrue from these agreements? As long as these are not fully assessed, it is like pitching in the dark. Quantifiable costs come in the form of preference erosion and trade diversion as well as increased risk of litigation, negotiation fatigue and capacity overload, to name a few of the ailing troubles that have been discussed in this section.

[34] So far, 37 countries out of 54 AU members have subscribed to the SAATM. However, only 9 of these countries have been able to fully comply with the concrete SAATM measures and 17 have signed the MOI. The great majority are not compliant with the African Civil Aviation Commission (ACAC) standards. See https://www.afcac.org/saatm-dashboard/. See also discussion in Chap. 4, Sect. 5.

Lastly, there is a body of AU decisions and declarations that countries should be adhering to. This begs for a refreshed commitment. They require pronouncement on the part of current governments and resolve to be activated. Legal interpretation and the motion to ratify and domesticate existing decisions and declarations into national law and jurisprudence should be sought.

Moving forward, it is the transparency and predictability of a rules-based system that will ensure future trade negotiations are not frontloaded with additional legal burdens, nor endanger the adherence to agreements existing prior. This holds for African countries in the global trading system, be it in the multilateral, plurilateral and bilateral setting, as well as within the regional setting that today is advancing an African Continental Free Trade Area. It is of even greater systemic importance as the continent progresses towards the realization of an Africa Customs Union and, ultimately, the African Economic Community.

References

Abrego, L., Amado, M. A., Gursoy, T., Nicholls, G. P., & Perez-Saiz, H. (2019). The African Continental Free Trade Agreement: Welfare Gains Estimates from a General Equilibrium Model. *IMF Working Paper* WP/19/124.

Admassu, S. (2019). An empirical analysis of the trade-creation effect of African regional economic communities. *Empirical Economics Journal, 56*, 843–863. https://doi.org/10.1007/s00181-017-1382-7

Africa Arbitration Academy Model Bilateral Investment Treaty for African States. (2022).

AU. (2006). Decision on the Moratorium on the Recognition of Regional Economic Communities (RECs), DOC. EX.CL/278 (IX), Assembly/AU/Dec.112 (VII).

AU. (2008). Decision on the Report of Negotiations, DOC. EX.CL/422(XIII). http://archives.au.int/handle/123456789/1050

AU. (2011). The *Framework for the Continental Free Trade Area, Road Map, Architecture* (CFTA Framework).

AU. (2013a). AU Declaration on the Economic Partnership Agreements, AU/TI/TD/CAMoT-8/EPA.DECL/FINAL. 8th Ordinary Session of the Conference of AU Ministers of Trade 21st–25th October, Addis Ababa, Ethiopia.

AU. (2013b). Decision on the report on negotiations of economic Partnership agreements (EPAs), Doc. EX.CL/422(XIII).

Braude, W. (2008). *SADC, COMESA and the EAC: Conflicting Regional and Trade Agendas.* South Africa: Institute for Global Dialogue, Occasional Paper 57. https://igd.org.za/publication/igd-op-57/?wpdmdl=8237&refresh=654ddc3573b8a1699601461

Buyonge, C. (2018). Prospects for Africa's Tripartite Free Trade Agreement in the light of lessons learned from the East African Community. *WCO Magazine*, No. 78. https://mag.wcoomd.org/magazine/wco-news-78/

Cai, P. (2016). Regulatory Coherence and Standardization Mechanisms in the Trans-Pacific Partnership. *British Journal of American Legal Studies, 5*(2), 505–538. https://doi.org/10.1515/bjals-2016-0018

Cambell v Zimbabwe (2007), Mike Campbell (Pvt) Ltd and others v Republic of Zimbabwe. (2007). [2008] SADCT 2, [28 November 2008].

Capoani, L. (2023). Review of the gravity model: origins and critical analysis of its theoretical development, *SN Business and Economics Journal, 3*, 95. https://doi.org/10.1007/s43546-023-00461-0

COMESA. (2021). *Proposed Modalities for the Re-Allocation of Unutilized Brown Sugar Quotas under Kenya Sugar-Safeguard Measures*. Second Extra-Ordinary Meeting of Kenya Sugar Safeguard Sub-Committee, August CS/TCM/KSS/II/21/IV.

Dadush, U., & Saoudi, H. (2019). "Morocco's excessive geographic export concentration", Policy Center for the New South, Policy Brief PB 19/37.

ECA. (2016). *Investment Policies and Bilateral Investment Treaties in Africa: Implications for Regional Integration*. Economic Commission for Africa. https://repository.uneca.org/handle/10855/23035

ECA. (2018). *Economic Partnership Agreement and African Continental Free Trade Area: What is at Stake for Togo?* ATPC, ECA. https://hdl.handle.net/10855/24232

ECA. (2019). *Linkages Between Double Taxation Treaties and Bilateral Investment Treaties*. Economic Commission for Africa. https://repository.uneca.org/handle/10855/43673

ECA. (2020). *Drivers for Boosting Intra-African Investment Flows Towards Africa's Transformation*. Economic Commission for Africa. https://repository.uneca.org/handle/10855/43660

ECA. (2022). The African Continental Free Trade Area and Demand for Transport Infrastructure and Services. https://repository.uneca.org/handle/10855/47596

ECA. (2023). AfCFTA What You Need to Know: Frequently Asked Questions & Answers. https://repository.uneca.org/handle/10855/49411

Erasmus, G. (2015). *The New Protocol for the SADC Tribunal, Jurisdictional Changes and Implications for the SADC Community Law*. TRALAC Working Paper No. US15WP01/2015, January.

Erasmus, G. (2021). AfCFTA Parallelism and the Acquis. 10 February. https://www.tralac.org/blog/article/15085-afcfta-parallelism-and-the-acquis.html

Erasmus, G. (2022). *The Role of Negotiating Principles in the Design of the AfCFTA*. TRALAC Blog, September 5. https://www.tralac.org/blog/article/15746-the-role-of-negotiating-principles-in-the-design-of-the-afcfta.html#_ftn5

European Commission (2007), COUNCIL REGULATION (EC) No 1528/2007. (2007, 20 December). Applying the arrangements for products originating in certain states which are part of the African, Caribbean and Pacific (ACP) Group of States provided for in agreements establishing, or leading to the establishment of, Economic Partnership Agreements. https://eur-lex.europa.eu/eli/reg/2007/1528/2014-12-25

Financial Times. (2015). The Doha Round Finally Dies a Merciful Death. *Financial Times*, 21 December. Archived from the original on 11 December 2022.

Financial Times. (2022). The WTO is on Life Support—But the World Still Needs it. 19 June. https://www.ft.com/content/85ac7098-4d6d-4f93-9f5f-f12e373dd753

Fofack, H., Dzene, R., & Mohsen Hussein, O. A. (2021). Estimating the Effect of AfCFTA on Intra-African Trade Using Augmented GE-PPML. *Journal of African Trade, 8*(2), 62–76.

Fosu, A. K., & Mold, A. (2008). Gains from Trade: Implications for Labour Market Adjustment and Poverty Reduction in Africa. *African Development Review, 20*(1), 20–48.

Gathii, J. T. (2013). The Cotonou Agreement and Economic Partnership Agreements. In *Realizing the Right to Development* (pp. 259–273). United Nations. https://doi.org/10.18356/30b19eb6-en

Gathii, J. T. (2018). The COMESA Court of Justice. In R. Howse, H. Ruiz-Fabri, G. Ulfstein, & M. Zang (Eds.), *The Legitimacy of International Trade Courts and Tribunals*. Cambridge University Press. https://ssrn.com/abstract=3314213

Hoekman, B., Martins, W. J., & Primo Braga, C. A. (2008). *Quantifying the Value of Preferences and Potential Erosion Losses*. World Bank.

Inançli, S., & Mahamat Addi, H. (2019). Trade Creation and Trade Diversion Effects in the Economic Community of Central African States. *African Development Review, 31*, 307–317. https://doi.org/10.1111/1467-8268.12391

International Institute for Sustainable Development. (2006). *IISD Model International Agreement on Investment for Sustainable Development Negotiators Handbook* (April 2005 revised April 2006). https://www.iisd.org/system/files/publications/investment_model_int_handbook.pdf

Jackson, J. H. (2000). *The World Trading System. Law and Policy of International Economic Relations* (2nd ed.). The MIT Press.

Khandwalla, M. (2023, 26 April). *The East African Court of Justice Delivers a Landmark Judgement on Kenya's Bilateral Negotiation with the United States Without Involving EAC Partner States*. TRALAC Blog. https://www.tralac.org/blog/article/15989-the-east-african-court-of-justice-delivers-a-landmark-judgement-on-kenya-s-bilateral-negotiation-with-the-united-states-without-involving-eac-partner-states.html

KPMG. (2023). The Finance Act Analysis. Kenya, July. https://kpmg.com/ke/en/home/insights/2023/08/finance-act-2023-kpmg-analysis.html#:~:text=The%20Act%20introduces%20fundamental%20changes,the%20National%20Housing%20Development%20Fund

Krapohl, S., & van Huut, S. (2020). A Missed Opportunity for Regionalism: The Disparate Behaviour of African Countries in the EPA-Negotiations with the EU. *Journal of European Integration, 42*, 4.

Kuijper, P. J. (2010). Conflicting Rules and Clashing Courts: The Case of Multilateral Environmental Agreements, Free Trade Agreements and the WTO. *ICTSD Issues Paper*, No. 10, International Centre for Trade and Sustainable Development. http://ictsd.org/downloads/2011/12/conflicting-rules-and-clashing-courts.pdf

Makochekanwa, A. (2014). Welfare Implications of COMESA – EAC – SADC Tripartite Free Trade Area. *African Development Review, 26*(1), 186–202.

Mauritius v Polytol (2012), Republic of Mauritius v Polytol Paint and Adhesives Manufacturers Co. Ltd (2012) (Application 1 of 2012) [2012] COMESACJ 13 (6 December 2012). https://africanlii.org/judgments/COMESACJ/

Mayer, T., & Thoenig, M. (2016). *Regional Trade Agreements and the Pacification of Eastern Africa*. International Growth Center Working Paper.

Mold, A., & Mukwaya, R. (2017). Modelling the Economic Impact of the Tripartite Free Trade Area: Its Implications for the Economic Geography of Southern, Eastern and Northern Africa. *Journal of African Trade, 3*(1–2), 57–84.

Musila, J. W. (2005). The Intensity of Trade Creation and Trade Diversion in COMESA, ECCAS and ECOWAS: A Comparative Analysis. *Journal of African Economies, 14*(1), 117–141. https://doi.org/10.1093/jae/ejh039

Ngepah, N., & Udeagha, M. C. (2018). African Regional Trade Agreements and Intra-African Trade. *Journal of Economic Integration, 33*(1), 1176–1199. Retrieved November 23, 2023, from http://www.jstor.org/stable/26418780

OAU (1991), Treaty Establishing the African Economic Community of 1991.

Olayungbo, D., & Iqbal, B. A. (2021). An Empirical Analysis of African Trade Blocs Effects on the Global Economy: New Evidence from the Gravity Model. *Future Business Journal, 7*, 45. https://doi.org/10.1186/s43093-021-00089-2

Páez, L. (2011). *Liberalizing Financial Services and Foreign Direct Investment: Developing a Framework for Commercial Banking*. Palgrave Macmillan. https://doi.org/10.1057/9780230316829

Páez, L. (2023). *The African Continental Free Trade Area: Progress, Opportunities and Challenges*. FIW Spotlight Article, Research Centre International Economics (FIW), November. https://www.fiw.ac.at/en/2023/12/07/the-african-continental-free-trade-area-progress-opportunities-and-challenges-of-africas-mega-regional-initiative/

Páez, L., Karingi, S., Kimenyi, M., & Paulos, M. (2010). A Decade (2000–2010) of African-US Trade Under the African Growth and Opportunity Act (AGOA). *ATPC Work in Progress*, No. 81. https://hdl.handle.net/10855/29212

Reinsch, W. (2021). The Manufacturer's Dilemma: Reshoring and Resiliency in a Pandemic World. Center for Strategic and International Studies (CSIS). *JSTOR*. Retrieved September 4, 2023, from http://www.jstor.org/stable/resrep36906

Rojid, S. (2006). COMESA trade potential: a gravity approach. *Applied Economics Letters, 13*(14), 947–951. https://doi.org/10.1080/13504850500426061

Roy, M. (2011). Services Commitments in Preferential Trade Agreements: An Expanded Dataset. Available at SSRN: https://ssrn.com/abstract=1957564 or https://doi.org/10.2139/ssrn.1957564

SADC Model BIT Treaty Template. (2012).

Shinyekwa, I., & Othieno, L. (2016). Uganda's Intra-East Africa Community Customs Union Trade Performance in Comparison to Other Trading Blocs: A Gravity Model Analysis. *Journal of African Development, 18*(1), 99–111. https://doi.org/10.5325/jafrideve.18.1.0099

Shivamba, A. (2019). The Demise of a Legitimate Southern African Regional Court. Southern Africa Litigation Center, *SALC Policy Brief*, No. 6 of 2019.

Shumba, T. (2023). Rising from Its Ruins? The Southern African Development Community (SADC) Tribunal, Law. *Democracy and Development Journal, 26*(1).

Stack, M., & Bliss, M. (2020). EU Economic Integration Agreements, Brexit and Trade. *Review of the World Economy, 156*(3), 443–473. https://doi.org/10.1007/s10290-020-00379-x

The Finance Act. (2023). KENYA GAZETTE SUPPLEMENT ACTS, 2023 NAIROBI. 26 June. https://kra.go.ke/images/publications/The-Finance-Act%2D%2D2023.pdf

UNCTAD. (2015). *Investment Policy Framework.* United Nations Conference on Trade and Development, Geneva.

Vienna Convention on the Law of Treaties (1969), concluded in Vienna on 23 May 1969. United Nations, *Treaty Series*, vol. 1155, p. 331.

World Bank. (2020). *The African Continental Free Trade Area: Economic and Distributional Effects.* World Bank. https://doi.org/10.1596/978-1-4648-1559-1

WTO. (1979). Decision on Differential and More Favourable Treatment, Reciprocity and Fuller Participation of Developing Countries (L/4903).

WTO. (2004). *European Communities – Conditions for Granting of Tariff Preferences to Developing Countries.* Report of the Appellate Body, World Trade Organization (WTO), WT/DS246/AB/R, 7 April.

WTO Regional Trade Agreements Information System. http://rtais.wto.org/UI/PublicMaintainRTAHome.aspx

CHAPTER 9

Making the Most of Free Trade and Investment in Regional and Global Markets

Africa is realizing a major and imperative milestone in its regional integration story. With the AfCFTA, nothing will be the same. It is therefore timely to allow for the economic and social transformations it promises to cement themselves. The continent has the power to shift the narrative of its participation in the international trade and international investment arena through the AfCFTA. It can and should move away from a history of underrepresentation and the role of a "taker" of the global status quo to a future story of full participation and the role of a decision "maker", equal to other regions, which translates into a rebalanced and more equitable world economic order.

This book has delved into what is required from an institutional, policy, regulatory and political economy perspective to ensure the continent assumes its rightful role in global markets. It has also looked at the major pitfalls and what needs to be addressed in order for the AfCFTA to materialize its full promise to Africans and the world at large.

Much of the attention given to the AfCFTA as the latest effort under Africa's regional integration process assumes that there is no endgame. Indeed, as mentioned in Chap. 2, the AfCFTA has been part of a broader process of envisioned pan-Africanism rather than a product on its own. And this has been closely knit with Africa's development narrative. With a grim global outlook in the years to come, given the experiences of the pandemic, localized and global wars, the destiny of the continent greatly

L. Páez, *The African Continental Free Trade Area*,
https://doi.org/10.1007/978-3-031-66605-6_9

depends on its ability to materialize the vision it has articulated in Agenda 2063 and the associated imperatives of peace and stability for the continent. These are imperatives of a development roadmap that will define the future of Africa's participation in global trade and investment markets.

The ability of the AfCFTA State Parties to fully operationalize the continental market, its institutions and ensure the functioning of the four freedoms are part of a bigger canvas, that also needs to intertwine with the fabric of other existing regional initiatives and the African people at large. Stakeholders big and small must be part and parcel of this design. Recent experiences with multistakeholder consultations as part of trade policy-making and trade negotiations processes in Africa have been picking up and point to the inevitable and requisite need for inclusion as an axis for a future, broad-based uptake and success of the AfCFTA. In this sense, Chap. 3 made a case for a participatory framework for participation from the bottom-up approach rather than the traditional top-down approach through broad-based consultations. Providing the African people with a veritable platform to create and take part in the AfCFTA through a consultative process will also be necessary for a continent seeking to advocate for its views and needs in the global setting.

With a rising and youthful population, the ability of a pan-African market to make a difference not just for the few but really for the many will require going beyond what traditionally has been viewed as tradable. A mind shift from what was considered *trading in goods* to *trading in tasks* is part of the world economic order, as we know it today. Chapter 4 clearly outlined how services have stepped up to become a tradable sector that must figure more prominently in Africa's development agenda. This in itself is an opportunity for aligning both international and African efforts to harness services trade for the continent's development through the full operationalization of the AfCFTA. However, for services trade to become a conduit for broad-based, transformational growth and development, policies need to prioritize the sector. In particular, policies that directly target services, crowding in investment and promoting employment and human capital formation in sectors with trade potential are critical elements to unravel the full potential of services trade. And this is particularly the case for value chains, both within regional and global networks of global production. It is here where policy design and adjustment need to address the various policy disconnects that exist in Africa's current policy landscape. And this will require careful policy mapping, within and beyond national borders.

Particular attention will be needed when it comes to the extraterritorial effects, and potential liability of external regimes which have Africa under their influence. With the AfCFTA's critical mass, the continent has a turn to spin the tables and set policymaking right. If the continent is able to prioritize investment into services sectors where it is poised to upgrade and upskill its services base in GVCs, it can propel global trade and investment patterns that foster structural transformation of its economy.

As with services, the realization of the Investment Protocol under the AfCFTA represents an opportunity to unlock both domestic and intra-African investments, as well as those from beyond the continent, and these flows need to be adequately regulated. Chapter 5 looked at the international investment regulation involving Africa, ranging from BITs to regional investment agreements and other regimes that invariably clutter the investment landscape in Africa. The merit and viability of an African Continental Investment Area as an alternative to the existing investment regime, in favour of a more harmonized and developmental approach that builds on existing regional institutions and processes must not be understated. With the recently adopted Protocol on Investment there are elements for greater regional harmonization of investment regulation beyond the RECs, which to the date have been a fundamental building bloc to a unified continental space for investment under the aegis of an African Continental Investment Area. More importantly, this could bring on tectonic shifts in how Africa relates to external investors and rises to become a more attractive destination that provides transparency and certainty to investors in traditional sectors, but more interestingly in sectors such as services, and the knowledge, creative and digital economies, thanks to continental regulation being advanced through the AfCFTA, such as the Protocol on Competition, the Protocol on Intellectual Property and the upcoming Protocol on Digital Trade.

The ability of the AfCFTA to support Africa in making the most of free trade and investment in global markets currently also relies on the review and redesign of trade agreements, that have shaped trade and investment relations of the continent with external partners so far. The book has raised caution against the very deterministic and lopsided outcomes of some of these trade agreements both in Chaps. 6 and 7, but also cautioned against the grim outlook and possible impact of future mega-regionals and FTAs in Chap. 8. One such agreement which is preferential in its nature, and which has recently come under review, is the AGOA. Chapter 6 of this book assessed whether AGOA has been instrumental in attracting US investment in Africa and whether both bilateral trade and investment between the US and Africa may be characterized as a mutually supportive endeavour. The analysis presented found an overall negative relationship of AGOA on US FDI, and corroborated the general findings of prior studies which have revealed this preferential trade agreement as fostering a certain type of export specialization in the apparel sector in some African countries, determined through FDI. Beyond the apparel sector, the overall effect of AGOA, however, has been of substitution between trade and FDI with the US and improving AGOA utilization in the non-apparel sector still constitutes a major challenge for many beneficiaries. If AGOA is to support export diversification and crowd in FDI for Africa's structural transformation post AGOA 2025, the agreement will need to be revamped. As raised in this book, preference receiving countries cannot comply with the existing rules or can only do so at a prohibitive cost, as exemplified by the low AGOA utilization.

With the creation of a pan-African market of goods, services, capital and labour, opportunities for the scaling up of investments through regional value chains in the AfCFTA may abound, but a necessary condition for this is non-discrimination. Under the present AGOA V regime, discrimination is at the heart of its preferences, since these are only conferred to a group of Sub-Saharan countries. This not only reduces the incentive structure for investors, who may be seeking to leverage the potential value chains from sourcing inputs *across* AGOA and non-AGOA beneficiaries, which are manifold in the textiles sector. This automatically puts State Parties in a non-compliant position vis-à-vis their fellow AfCFTA members and could potentially trigger disputes within the AfCFTA, something that should be avoided at all cost, in what may be best described as a situation of importing discriminatory practices.

Encouragingly, the AGOA VI proposal seems to address the limitations of the previous AGOA I to V and proposes some interesting flexibilities, that could revamp the FDI storyline in Africa. Related flexibilities, including a 16- rather than a 10-year window, would give more certainties to investors vying to invest in a pan-African market. This in itself could be an additional contribution to attract investment from the US, that is able to promote regional value chains to benefit from existing preferential trade arrangements, such as the AGOA. Such efforts may also crowd in further FDI, from within the continent and beyond, if associated with more flexible sourcing within the suggested rules of origin of AGOA VI. This proposal is, however, subject to bipartisan dynamics, and there is a real danger for this opportunity to be missed if under the Biden administration the proposed bill is not passed.

Beyond this trade and investment-related preferential agreement, what really matters is that the AfCFTA could represent an opportunity to consolidate the various investment policies and regulations that exist at the regional level. Efforts to consolidate investment regulation have so far not been very successful in Africa, including the *AU Pan African Investment Code* which is a soft law instrument. With the AfCFTA Protocol on Investment which is a binding instrument, there is a credible opportunity to harmonize the various investment regimes across the continent and provide a basis for common rules that level the playing field for domestic, intra-African and foreign investment and that see the advent of a Common Investment Area, as was discussed earlier in Chap. 5. This would undoubtedly be a solid contribution towards one of the four freedoms of the AfCFTA, namely, the free movement of capital. And in a world where the free flow of goods is tightly intertwined with that of investment flows, the real gain of the AfCFTA would be to see investment scale-up concurrently with trade, and to the tune that does justice to the continent's real magnitude and potential.

But the major challenge in the way of this development pathway remains the level of inequality and divide that have been a scouring mark within Africa, and between the continent and the rest of the world. The continent is host to the largest number of LDCs and LLDs of this world. Chapter 7 unpacked the very issue of variable geometry and special and differential treatment in its application to African LDCs, both in the multilateral and regional trade setting. Though special and differential treatment has been the mainstay of trade support to LDCs over the past decades, the increased trade performance that African LDCs may have experienced does not appear to have contributed to poverty reduction in these countries. The real question is therefore how to reduce the inequality that divides Africa's society so that the real benefits that may accrue to the continent from trade and other associated gains from an AfCFTA are enjoyed by all and not just a few. An agreement that is fit for purpose must therefore invariably look at the articulation, application, interpretation and innovation of the rules that are part of the design of the AfCFTA. Beyond what can be done within the continent, a joint pursuit of various objectives across global initiatives, such as climate change, and peace and security, and which could help Africa optimize on the opportunities which the multilateral trading system avails to LDCs and African countries at large.

An associated concern of being fit for purpose is of course the issue of coexistence and compatibility with the multilateral trading system, as well as other legal regimes and existing programmes and initiatives mentioned in the book. Indeed, much of the focus of Chap. 8 was around elements of coexistence of multiple and sometimes conflicting rules and commitments in the context of mega-regional and FTAs with third parties, and those of existing RECs FTAs. But just as international and regional partners and players need to coalesce around the domestication and operationalization of the liberalization programme of the AfCFTA, for the fruits of these efforts to bare, so do the member States themselves. Failure to do so would come at dear costs, in the form of preference erosion and trade diversion as well as increased risk of litigation, negotiation fatigue and capacity overload, to name a few of the ailing troubles that have been discussed and seen with past trade agreements.

A final and associated clarion call is also deemed necessary when we look at the history of implementation of associated AU decisions and declarations that member States should be adhering to. This requires a refreshed commitment and activation on the part of current governments, especially those that could give the AfCFTA additional footing as a stronghold for development. Moving forward, it is the transparency and predictability of a rules-based system that will ensure the AfCFTA does not experience an early death, and gives adequate rite of passage to an Africa Customs Union and, ultimately, the African Economic Community. This is of systemic importance for Africa, in order to assume its role in global governance structures that beg for a change in the world economic order.

Pan-Africanism, as was initially conceived by visionaries of the likes of Nkrumah, Senghor and Nyerere, was bold and forward-looking. Africa needs this wonderful concept to shift from an elusive mirage to reality. It owes it to the 1.2 billion Africans that look up to the continent. The AfCFTA is therefore a palpable opportunity, at a hand's reach. Whilst others can afford to stroll down a chartered development path, Africa does not even have the luxury to walk. It has to run like Haile Gebrselassie and Tirunesh Dibaba have run for Olympic gold. And the continent can. It must therefore not miss a beat.

Index[1]

[1] Note: Page numbers followed by 'n' refer to notes.

L. Páez, *The African Continental Free Trade Area*,
https://doi.org/10.1007/978-3-031-66605-6

T

SPRINGER NATURE

GPSR Compliance

The European Union's (EU) General Product Safety Regulation (GPSR) is a set of rules that requires consumer products to be safe and our obligations to ensure this.

If you have any concerns about our products, you can contact us on ProductSafety@springernature.com

In case Publisher is established outside the EU, the EU authorized representative is:

Springer Nature Customer Service Center GmbH
Europaplatz 3
69115 Heidelberg, Germany

The manufacturer's authorised representative in the EU is Springer Nature Customer Service Centre GmbH. Europaplatz 3, 69115 Heidelberg, Germany. If you have any concerns regarding our products, please contact ProductSafety@springernature.com

Printed and bound by CPI Group (UK) Ltd, Croydon, CR0 4YY
01/10/2026
02225903-0011